First published in 2019 by Emma Davies

ISBN: 978-0-9956324-3-1

EmmaDaviesPhotography.com

CONTENTS

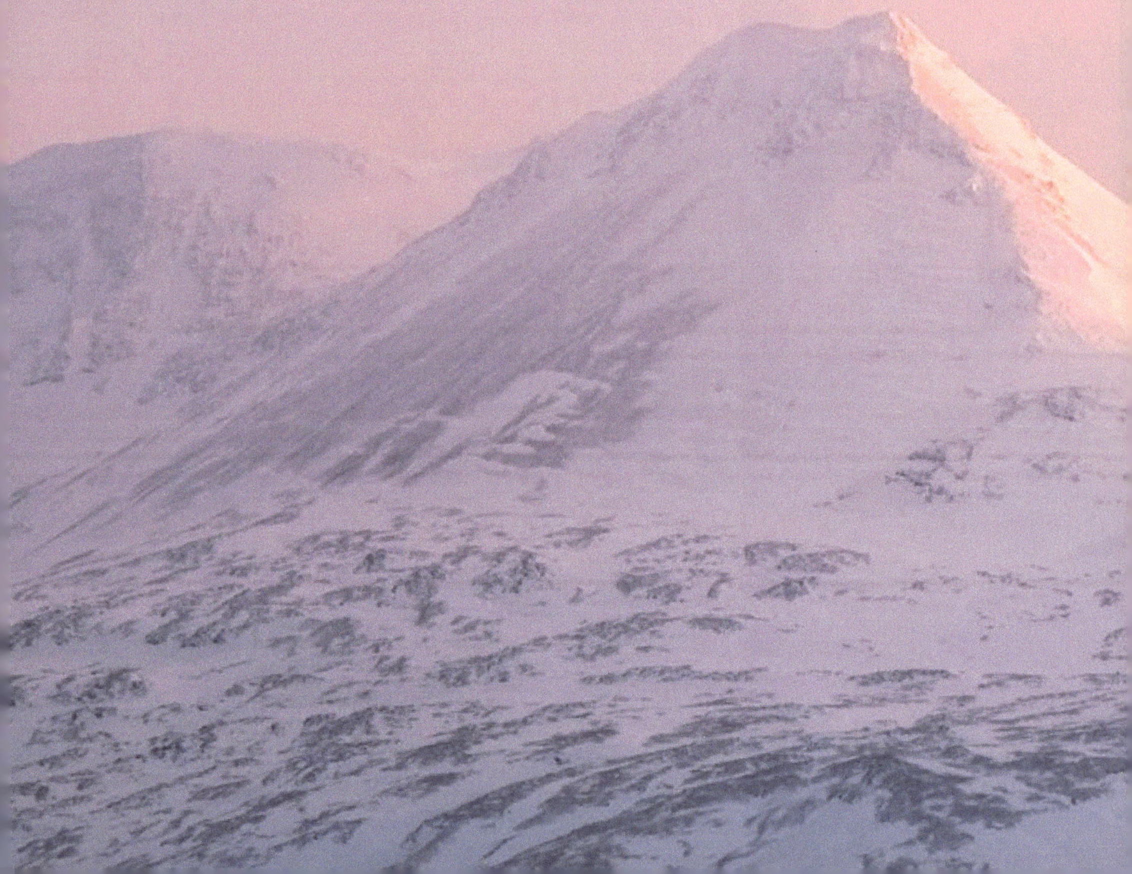

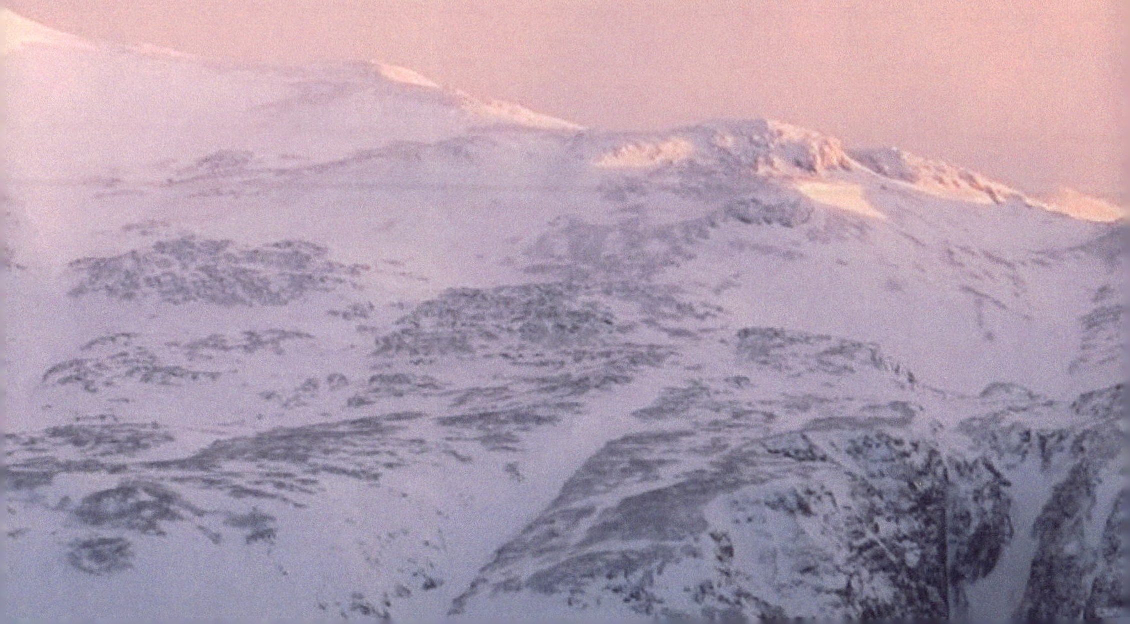

DO WHAT YOU CAN, WITH WHAT YOU HAVE, WHERE YOU ARE.

T ROOSEVELT

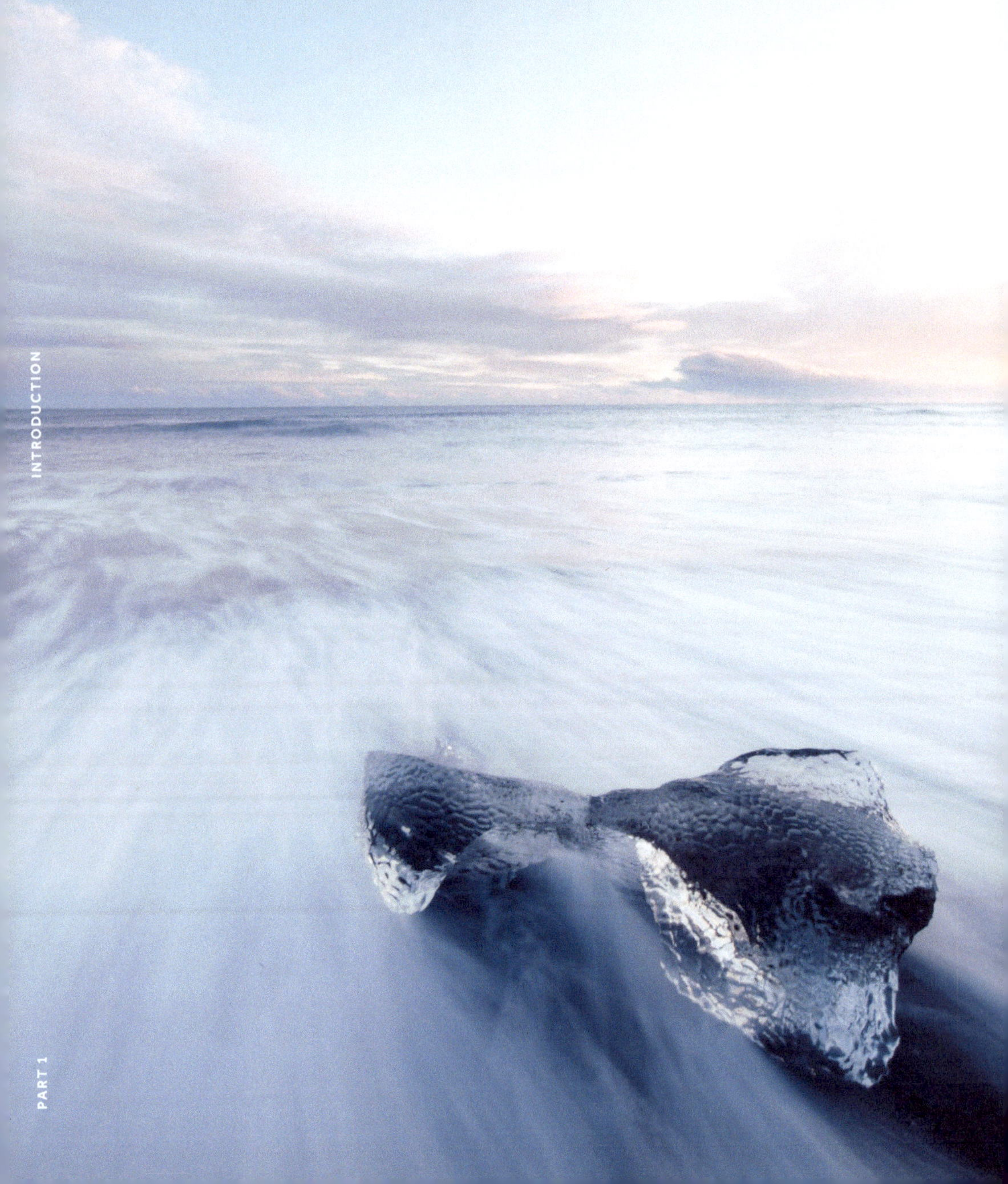

INTRODUCTION

Why is landscape photography so difficult? Why are your shots so disappointing? And how can you improve quickly and efficiently?

I spent most of my professional life as a studio photographer, shooting families and flowers. When I started shooting gardens my eyes were opened to the joys of outdoor photography. It took me a lot of trial and error, and months of pain to translate what I knew about tabletop-scale photography to a canvas that starts at your feet and doesn't stop until it reaches the horizon. I have condensed everything I learned and put it into this book.

The principles of good composition and working with light are the same whatever the genre of photography. It's just that with landscape photography everything is on an epic scale – and one over which you have no control. With indoor photography you can reach out and change the position of your subject when it is not quite right. But you can't reach out and move a mountain.

With studio photography you are in control of the light at all times – the strength, quality and direction can be tweaked at will. With the best will in the world you can't make the sun come up earlier or move a cloud out of the way when you are outdoors.

This is why landscape photography is the most frustrating and the most rewarding genre of photography. Frustrating, because everything you are working with is beyond your control pretty much the entire time. Rewarding, because when it all comes together it is worth it – you've put in more hours, had more failed shots and waited for the sun for longer than any studio photographer ever has to.

HOW TO USE THIS BOOK

Landscape photography is hard work. Really hard. This book takes the guesswork out of your journey. Part 1 covers the more technical and general aspects of landscape photography, and Part 2 goes into more detail about specific subjects within the genre. I will tell you the best settings to start with for a particular situation, how to find interesting light, and how to compose your image. But you will only make progress if you get out and try it.

So settle down and read through all the advice I have for you. Learn from my mistakes. Pick up my good ideas. And then pack up your camera, some spare socks, a spirit of adventure and head outside.

For more resources visit EmmaDaviesPhotography.com/landscape-links for links to recommended suppliers, a map marking the locations of all the shots in this book, free downloads and plenty of extra information that won't fit into the book.

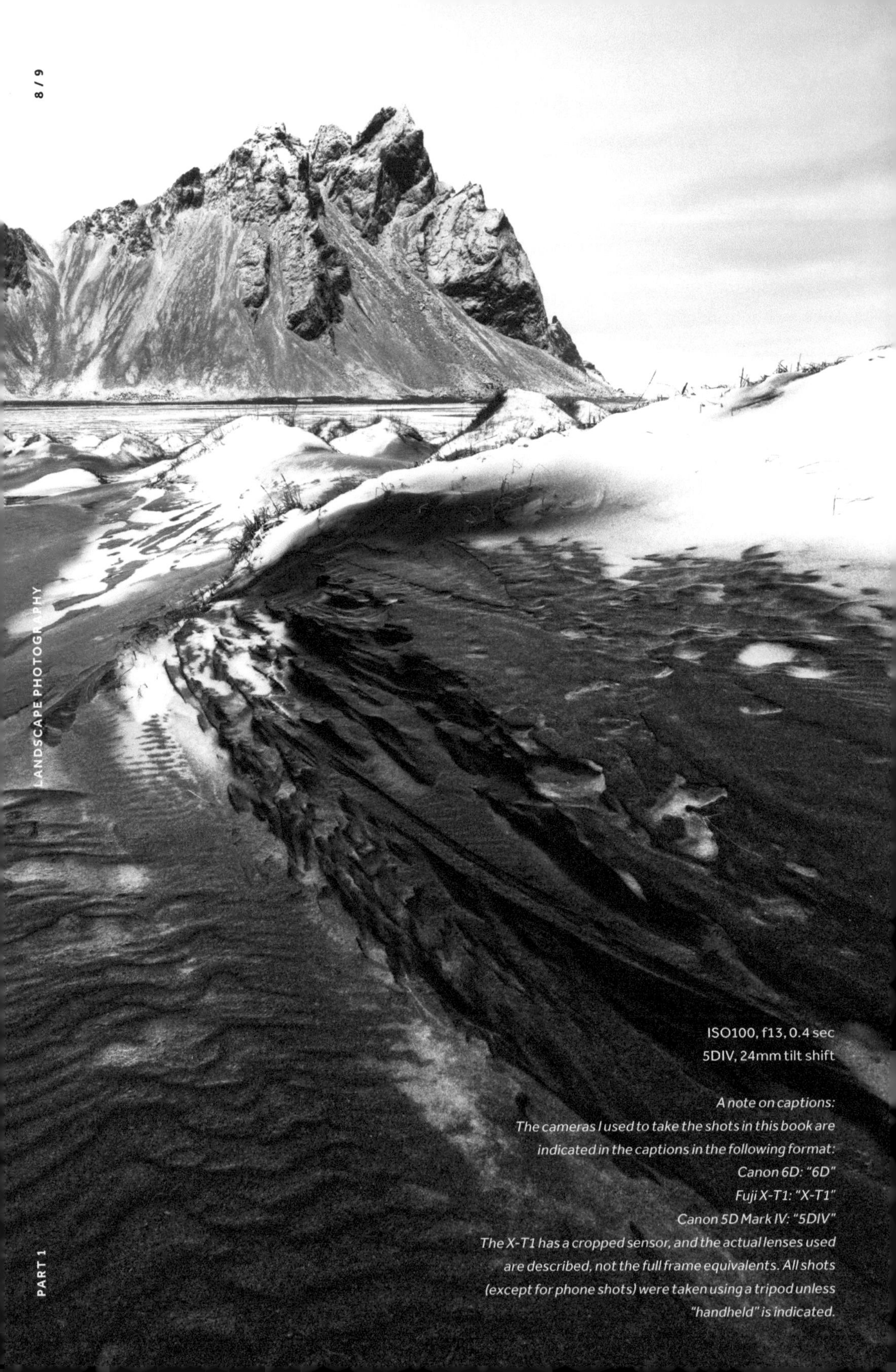

ISO100, f13, 0.4 sec
5DIV, 24mm tilt shift

A note on captions:
The cameras I used to take the shots in this book are indicated in the captions in the following format:
Canon 6D: "6D"
Fuji X-T1: "X-T1"
Canon 5D Mark IV: "5DIV"
The X-T1 has a cropped sensor, and the actual lenses used are described, not the full frame equivalents. All shots (except for phone shots) were taken using a tripod unless "handheld" is indicated.

PART 1

1 WHY IS LANDSCAPE PHOTOGRAPHY SUCH A CHALLENGE?

There is nowhere to hide with landscape photography. It is a genre that can make you feel strangely vulnerable: you are faced with a vista stretching from your feet to the horizon, and you have to pick the one place to stand out of an infinite number of choices that will give you the shot you want. Faced with this overwhelming choice, no wonder most people stay in the car and pop a quick shot out of the window.

If you've already had a go at shooting a view, you might have been very disappointed that the photo looked nothing like you hoped. Maybe the sky was blown out, or the distant mountains much smaller than you remembered. There might be a massive shadow that you hadn't noticed, or a field in the way that you can't crop out. Or possibly it was just a case that it was vaguely disappointing and you can't quite work out why.

This is the thing with landscape photography: you can't just turn up on day one and get a great shot. Not unless you are very, very lucky. You certainly won't be able to do it twice. You either need to research your location in advance, or you need to have a bank of experience behind you so you know what will make an epic shot in the moment.

Bottom left:
Blown-out sky
Bottom right:
Disappointingly small subject - far too much foreground and not enough mountain

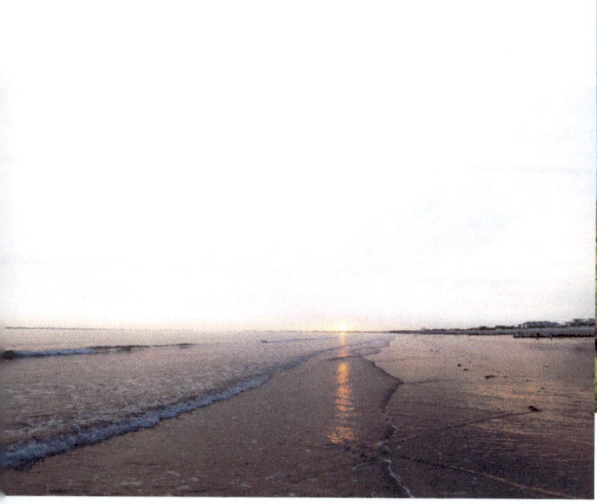

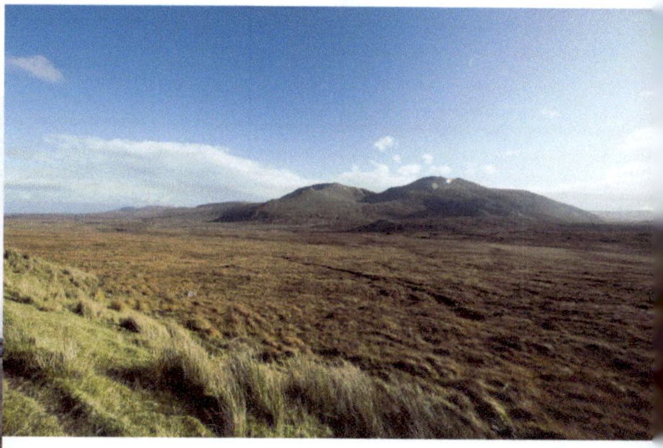

With landscape photography, it's not enough just to understand a bit about depth of field and know a few principles of composition. There are three areas you need complete mastery of:

1. **You need to know your kit inside out**

You will be working in challenging conditions. Shooting on a mild, sunny day, around lunchtime, close to a cafe and after a great night's sleep are rarely the conditions under which a legendary landscape is shot. It's more likely that you'll be battling a high wind with horizontal rain. If it's not actually pitch dark, the light will be changing fast. And if you've not left a vital piece of kit in the car, your hands will be freezing or your glasses will be misting up. Outdoor photography is not a walk in the park.

And what happens when the gods of landscape photography smile on you and give you that perfect break in the clouds, a momentary lifting of the rain or a wave about to break just where you want it? Will you be ready to shoot? Will you know which settings you need to change in the twenty second window you've got? Landscape photography is mostly planning, with the need for split-second decisions at the very last minute.

Your brain just won't want to start going back to basics in the field (or you simply won't have time). It's no good trying to remember which aperture gives a small depth of field just before you want to take your photo. Or what happens to shutter speed if you increase your ISO. There are certain things that need to become instinctive: you need to be able to change the controls on your camera without looking, you need to know how each of your lenses will reproduce the scene and you need to have an effortless understanding of aperture, shutter speed, ISO, and the way they interact.

2. **You need to understand how light behaves as if you've lived together for forty years**

Light is what makes or breaks a landscape photograph. Eighty percent of disappointing photographs are caused by dull midday light. I'm not saying you can only shoot in the hour before dawn, but I am saying you will probably only get your epic shots when the light is doing something magical. It might be glancing through a light shower of rain, it might be falling exactly on the side of hill in the distance, or it might indeed be bathing your whole scene in a pre-dawn glow.

3. You need to put your ego to one side and start composing from the ground up

I don't mean this in a critical way. I just mean that your ego, the bit of yourself that does all the talking, doesn't know as much as it thinks it does. To take great landscape photographs you will need to undo some things your ego thinks it knows. You will need to take a few photos that aren't as good as you know you can take, while you experiment with a couple of new ideas.

Be prepared to learn through your mistakes, to embrace disappointing images, and to try anything once. Composing a landscape shot is akin to spinning plates. If you take your eye off one part of the image to fix a different part, the first part starts to go wrong. You move slightly to get a couple of trees exactly where you want them only to find a parked car is now in the shot. You duck down a bit to screen the car behind a hedge and you lose the winding stream in the foreground. The only way to learn to compose outdoors is to try it. Try a shot. Look at it honestly – tell that ego to pipe down – and then try and take a better one. Fix one thing but keep an eye on what else changes. Very soon you'll find that your brain is more in touch with your eyes and you will start to anticipate what effect small changes will have on the whole image. You'll quickly learn to assess a scene and pick a better viewpoint right from the start.

The next few chapters will take you through these three topics in more detail. And then in Part 2, there are detailed descriptions of what settings you will need to remember when you are shooting particular landscape subjects.

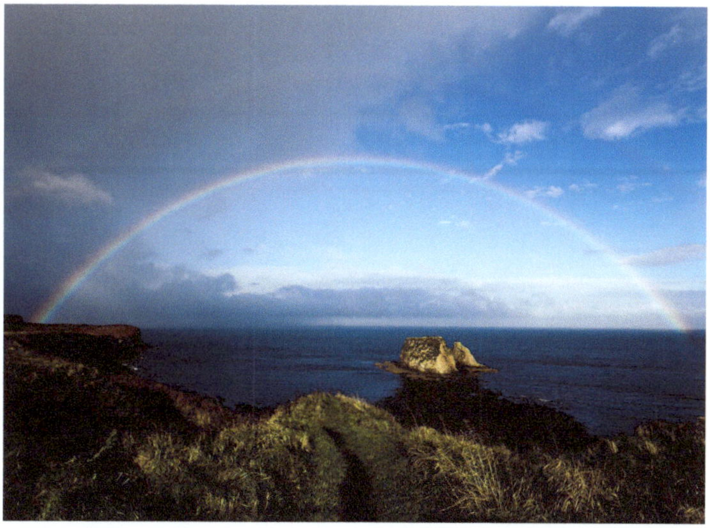

Left:
I had four minutes from when this rainbow appeared near Brough Bay in Scotland to when it vanished for good. I was on my way back to my car when I looked over my shoulder. Never have I been more grateful that I hadn't packed up my kit. I needed to decide aperture, shutter speed, ISO and focus point in a matter of seconds - it all had to be instinctive as there was no time to start thinking things through.
6D, 11-24mm at 18mm. ISO100, f8, 1/160th.

NOTES

Before you set off into the wilderness, consider these questions:

WHAT WILL YOUR IMPACT BE?

Will you disturb wildlife, local residents or other visitors? (If you send a drone up, the answer is probably, "Yes".) Have you parked considerately? Will you leave any trace?

WHY ARE YOU THERE?

There is no right or wrong reason to take landscape photos, but if you can address the question of why you want to take the photo you're about to take, it will be a more meaningful image.

ARE YOU COMPARING YOURSELF?

If you find yourself envious of another photographer's work, or becoming competitive in an unhelpful way, you may find your photography deteriorates. A negative mindset is not the most creative. Remind yourself it's your journey, not anyone else's.

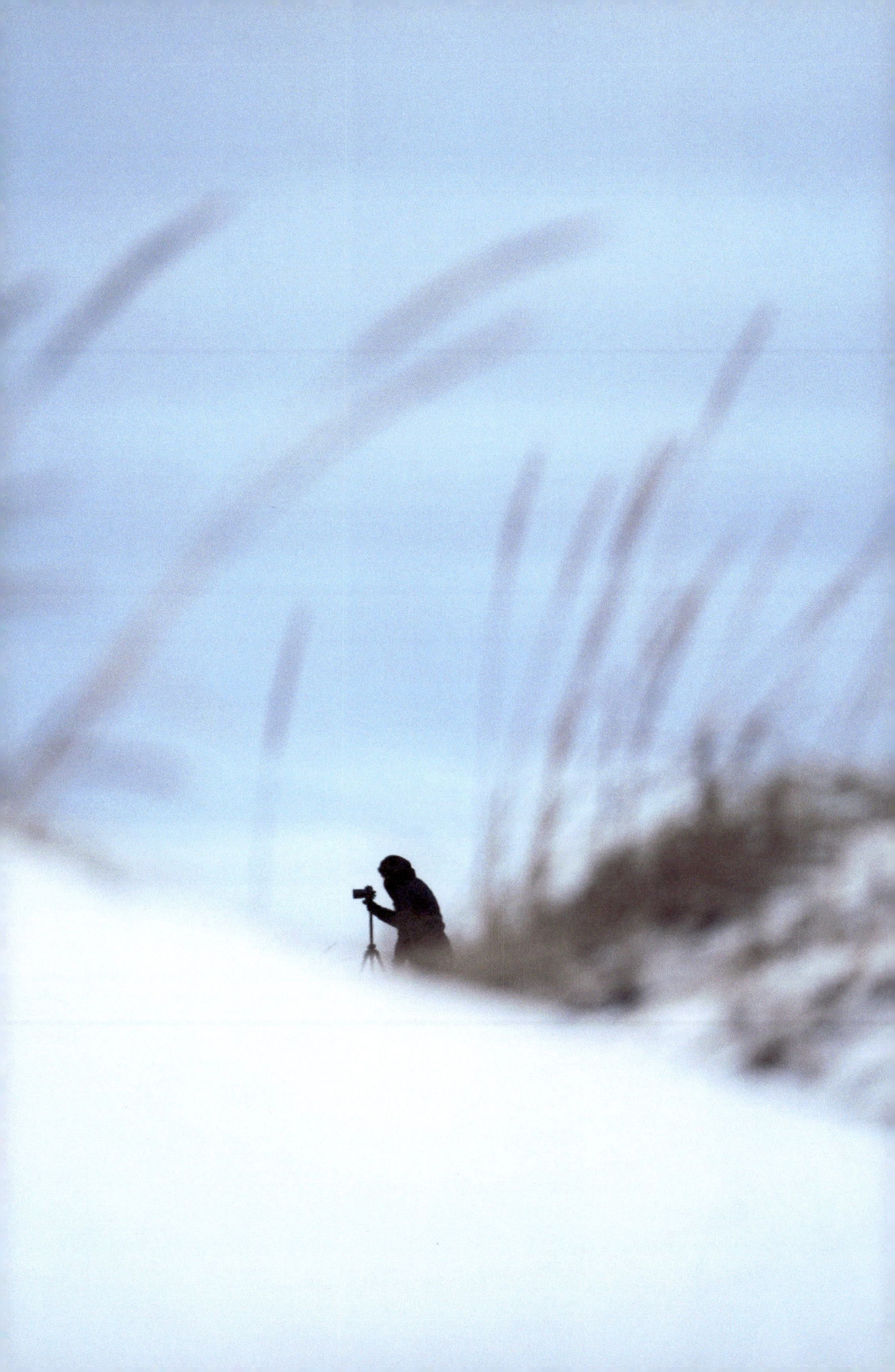

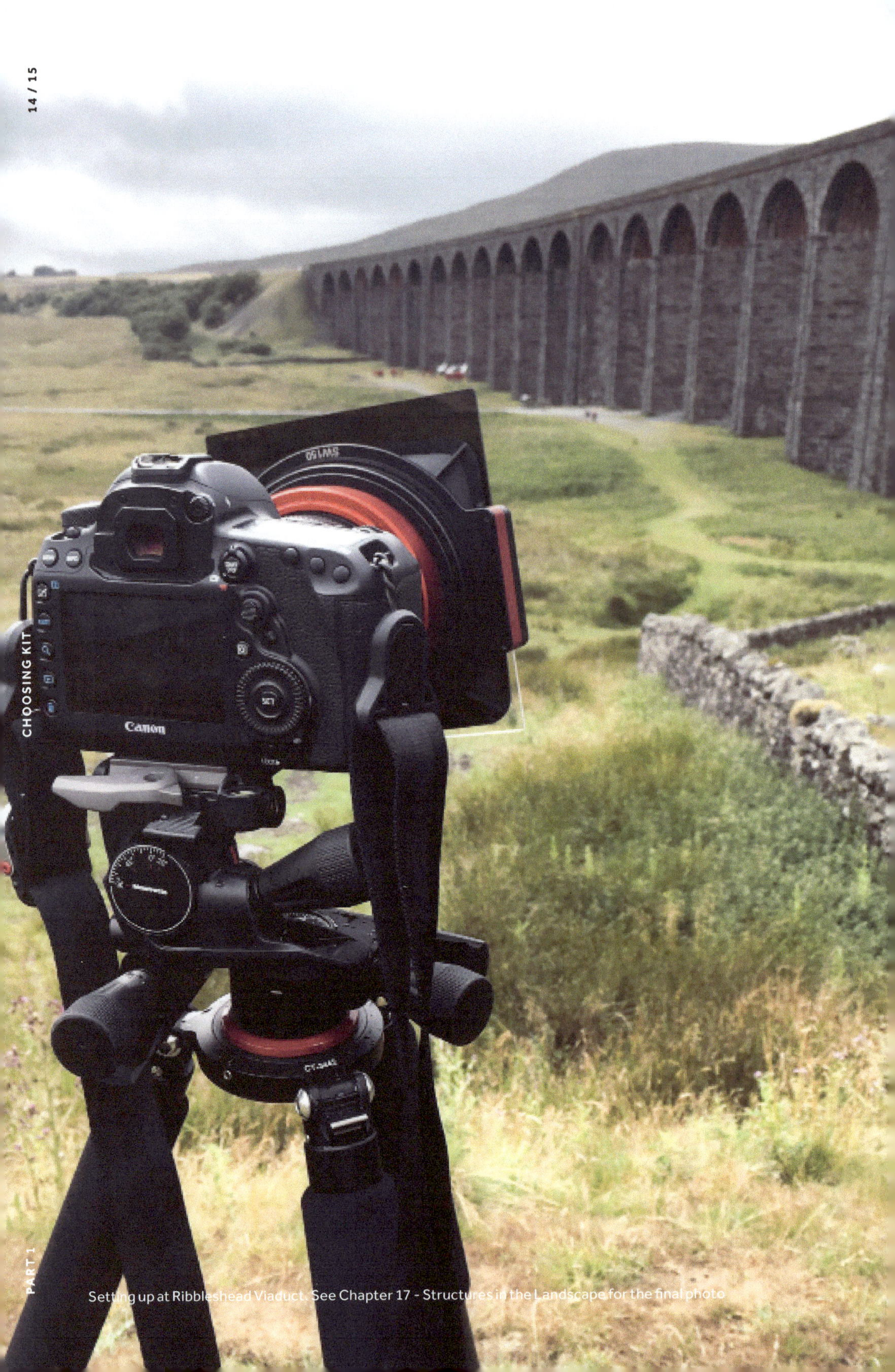

Setting up at Ribbleshead Viaduct. See Chapter 17 - Structures in the Landscape for the final photo

2

CHOOSING KIT

WHICH CAMERA?

When choosing a camera for landscape photography, I would suggest considering these things, and in this order:

1. How does it feel?
2. Sensor size and quality
3. Weatherproofing
4. Interchangeable lenses

How does it feel?

Please don't ever buy a camera without trying it first. Hold it, see if it fits your hands, see if you can change the dials. Have a go with the menus, and imagine your hands are frozen – can you get to the essential controls in two steps or less?

Mirrorless cameras (more below) are very popular because they are very light. But they can be *too* light, and can feel very unstable in your hands. I have long fingers, and find I can't grip some of the smaller mirrorless cameras properly. And the dials can be very small, making changing them difficult if you have anything other than very delicate fingers. Equally, before you buy a top-of-the-range professional camera, try carrying it. Feel the weight of the lenses you'll need to go with it. Are you up to carrying all that weight?

Sensor size and quality

Broadly speaking, a larger sensor will deliver a better quality photograph, but it's not always the case. My X-T1 has a smaller sensor than my Canon 6D, but in my opinion it takes sharper photos with better colour. Don't buy your camera based on sensor size alone: also take into consideration all the other things that will enable you to bring home great photos in difficult light – dynamic range, ISO performance, lens quality.

What are you going to do with your photos? If you want to blow them up to billboard size, you will want a big sensor that delivers huge file sizes. But if you only share on Instagram, all those extra pixels are wasted.

Full frame vs cropped frame sensors

A full frame sensor is one which is the same size as the old 35mm film negatives (24mm x 36mm). A cropped frame sensor is simply one which is smaller than that.

Full frame sensors have more pixels to record the available light and they necessarily produce much larger file sizes. Those files need more storage space and take longer to upload and download than the smaller files produced by a cropped sensor.

Cropped frame sensors only take information from the centre of the image, and discard the rest. Full frame sensors include everything. This has two important consequences. If you compare an image shot on a full frame sensor with one on a cropped frame, first, the same focal length lens on each camera will create a different image, and, secondly, the same aperture on each camera will give a different depth of field.

1. Focal length of lens

If you shoot with a 50mm lens (which is a standard lens, giving the best approximation to the human eye) on a full frame camera, your field of view (horizontally) will be approximately 40 degrees. On a cropped frame camera, it will be less, and in the region of 25 degrees.

This means that a 50mm lens on a cropped frame camera behaves as if it were a 75mm lens on a full frame camera. To get an equivalent 50mm field of view on a cropped frame, you would need to use a 35mm lens.

Examples of each are shown opposite: look carefully at the edges of each frame to see what is included and what is not. You will see that the full frame 50mm has the same field of view as the cropped frame 35mm. The cropped frame 50mm zooms in slightly closer to the scene.

2. Depth of field

Full frame cameras are claimed by their manufacturers to allow a shallower depth of field than a cropped frame. For our purposes this is broadly true, but the accuracy of the statement depends on whether you are comparing the same lens on each camera (e.g., a 50mm with a 50mm), or lenses which give an equivalent field of view (e.g., a 50mm with a 35mm).

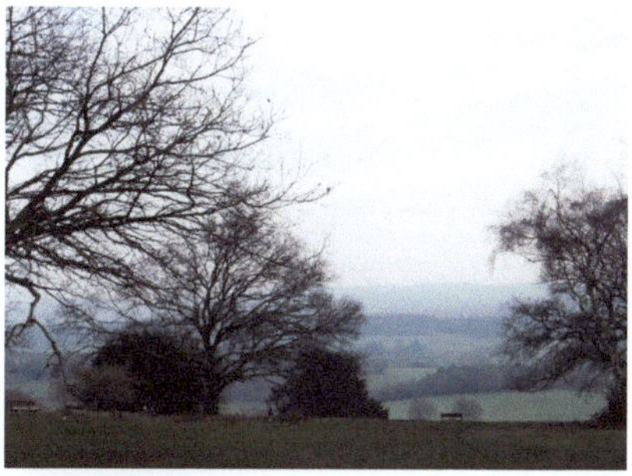

Full Frame 50mm

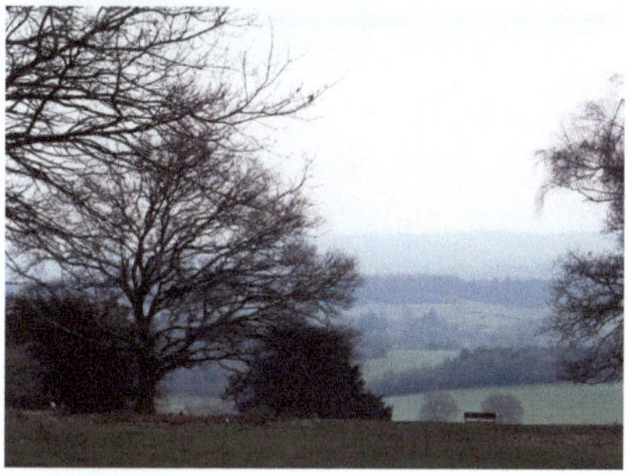

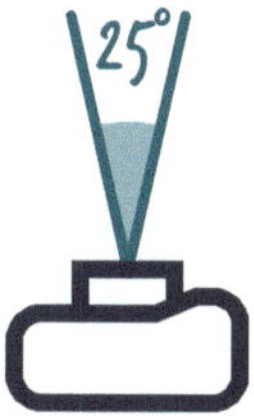

Cropped Frame 50mm

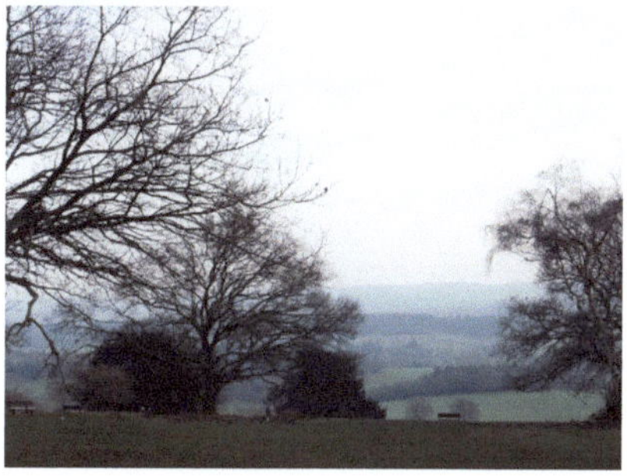

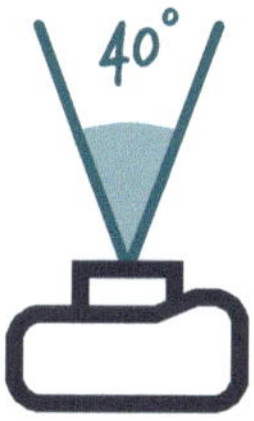

Cropped Frame 35mm

Weatherproofing

If you are going to do any amount of serious landscape photography, you will be out in the elements a lot. Cheaper cameras are not weatherproof. No cameras are waterproof (except ones designed to be used under water) – but the more expensive cameras will be "weatherproof", which will slow down the chances of the weather destroying your electronics.

Interchangeable lenses

Bridge cameras and point-and-shoots do not allow you to change lenses. You will find this a severe limitation if you enjoy landscape photography.

Which should you get – full frame or cropped sensor?

I shot some of the images in this book on my Canon 6D which is a full frame camera but not top-of-the-range. I shot many others with a Fuji X-T1 which has a cropped sensor. I upgraded recently to a 5D Mark IV which is both full frame and professional. Can I tell the difference between the 5DIV and the X-T1? Only in these areas:

- The 5DIV has noticeably less noise in low light.
- The 5DIV has more detail available in the RAW file.
- The 5DIV has 2 memory card slots, meaning I always have a back up in camera.
- The 5DIV allows me wider angle shots – my widest Fuji lens is a 14mm which is only a 22mm equivalent on a full frame.

If you can afford it, can carry it and all other things are equal, a full frame sensor will give you higher quality images. But if your budget doesn't stretch or the kit is too heavy, you can get fantastic shots whatever your camera. Most of the work is done in finding the light and composing the shot (of which more later in the book).

WHICH LENS?

Focal length

The focal length of a lens is the number followed by "mm" and refers to the distance between the lens and the sensor when the subject is in focus.

The focal length affects the field of view (what is included in the frame) and is sometimes referred to as "angle of view". A 50mm lens on a full frame camera has what's called a "standard" field of view, one that is approximately that of a human eye. A wide angle lens (e.g., 24mm) has a wider field of view and can "fit more in" to the shot. A telephoto lens (e.g., 100mm) has a narrower field of view and seems to bring distant things closer.

Telephoto lenses are often incorrectly called zoom lenses because they do let you zoom in on things in the distance, but to be a zoom lens it needs to have more than one focal length. Zoom lenses are capable of changing focal lengths (usually by twisting the barrel) and are referred to by the minimum and maximum focal lengths, e.g., 50-140mm.

A fixed focal length lens (one that isn't a zoom) is called a prime lens. Prime lenses usually produce higher quality images than zoom lenses, because there is less glass for the light to pass through, therefore less diffraction (which degrades the final shot).

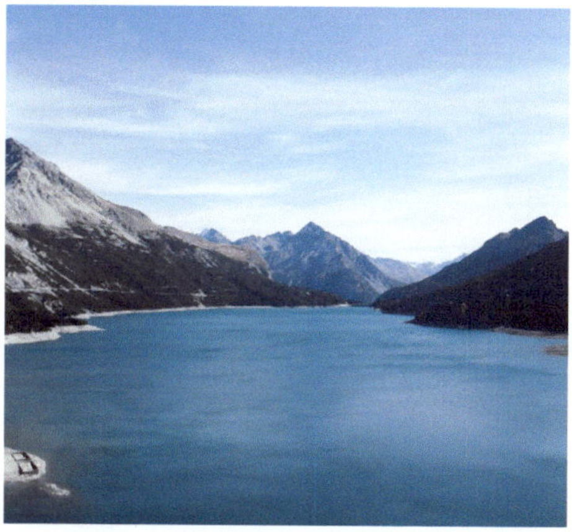

18mm (X-T1) – wide angle

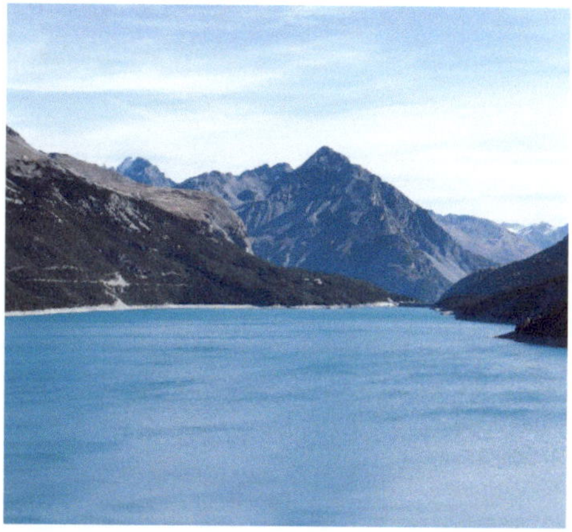

35mm (X-T1) – less wide/standard

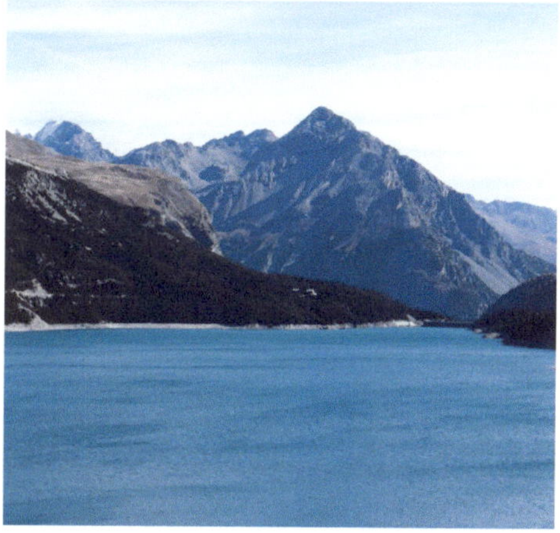

50mm (X-T1) – standard/shorter telephoto

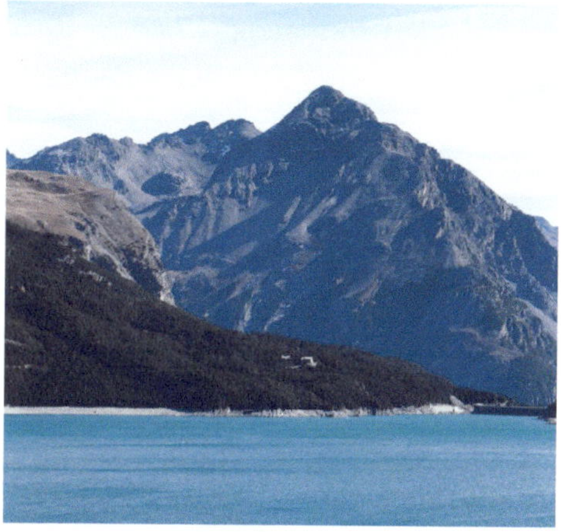

70mm (X-T1) – short telephoto

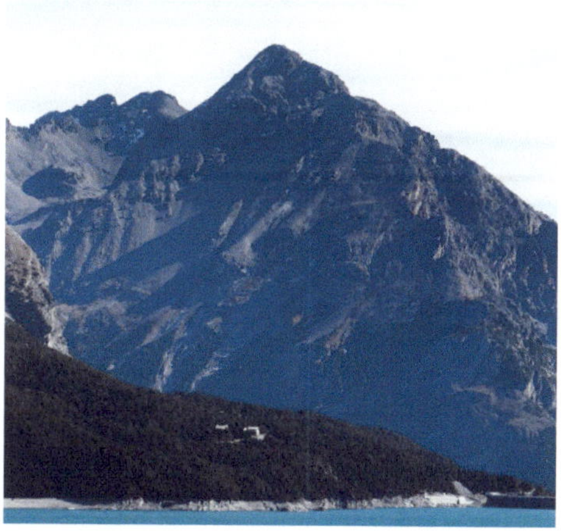

100mm (X-T1) – telephoto

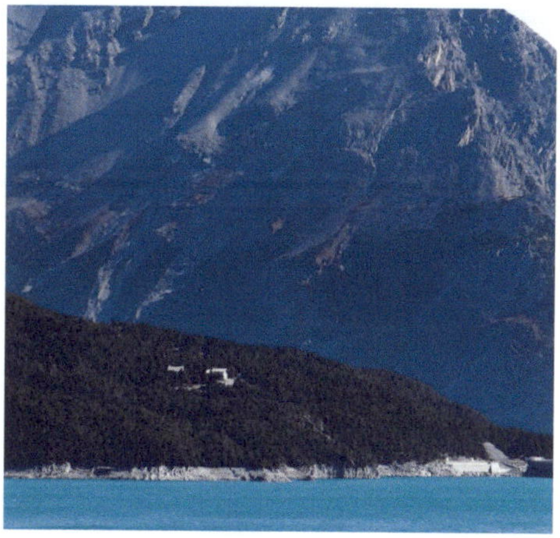

135mm (X-T1) – telephoto

Landscape photographers traditionally work with wider angle lenses (at least 24mm if not wider, on a full frame camera), so that would be your first lens purchase for this genre. But don't dismiss a 50mm and a telephoto lens. A longer lens can produce some attractive compressed perspective (where the depth of the image seems to be squashed together) and a 50mm is perfect for shooting intimate landscapes.

Maximum aperture

Before you buy a new lens, check what its widest maximum aperture is (the largest size aperture is denoted by the smallest number, e.g., f4 or f2.8). Cheaper lenses will have a relatively small largest aperture, e.g., f5.6. And cheaper zoom lenses will have a maximum aperture that reduces in size as you zoom, so it might be f3.5 at the wider end of the zoom, but only f8 at the telephoto end of the zoom.

Tilt-shift lenses

A tilt-shift lens is one where the glass elements can be tilted in relation to the sensor (in a normal lens they stay parallel). They are used in landscape photography for two main reasons: to extend the available depth of field by tilting the plane of focus; and to create panoramas.

How to do a full frame/cropped frame conversion

To work out the equivalent focal length for your cropped frame camera, first look online and find out what its crop factor is. For example, if I search, "What is the crop factor for an X-T1?", I find out it is 1.53. (The crop factor is calculated by dividing the diagonal of a full frame sensor by the diagonal of your cropped sensor.) Then multiply the focal length of the full frame lens to find out the equivalent focal length on your sensor: eg. 50mm x 1.53 = 80mm. So something called a 50mm lens when used on my X-T1 will behave like an 80mm lens would on a full frame camera.

How to change a lens

Every time you take a lens off your camera you risk dust getting on your sensor. You can lessen the risk by always switching the camera off before you change a lens (this reduces the static charge on the sensor which attracts dust), having everything ready so you can be quick and holding the body upside down while the lens is off. Never, ever change a lens in a dusty environment.

WHICH TRIPOD?

Your tripod has to keep your camera rock-steady, otherwise there's no point in having it. In the studio, tripods are used to enable the photographer to work hands-free, or to ensure perfect replication between a series of images. But in the field your tripod has one function only: to keep your camera perfectly still during a shot.

There are two things that will conspire to stop this happening: the wind and the weight of your camera itself. You can employ some countermeasures, but often you have to accept defeat and use a fast enough shutter speed to cope with the potential camera movements (making necessary compromises to ISO or aperture as needed).

The wind

No matter how sturdy your tripod, in a gale, it will not stop the camera moving.

In anything less than a gale, you can help it out by weighting it down. Hook your camera bag underneath the tripod head, if there is a handy hook there ready to receive it. Otherwise just use the shoulder straps to attach your bag and help gravity keep the tripod firmly anchored to the ground. You can also spread the legs of the tripod wider, to have a firmer base.

In lighter winds you can simply use yourself as a windbreak. Cheaper tripods really aren't fit for purpose for outdoor photography. A flimsy tripod will wobble in the slightest breeze. Also, avoid raising the central column if your tripod has one. You then effectively have a monopod balanced on top of a tripod, and you lose the benefit of having the stable three-point base.

The weight of your kit

The distortion of the image to the left is caused by lens droop. This was because the tripod plate (the bit you attach to your camera which then clips into the tripod) was not tight enough. During the long exposure, the heavy lens caused the whole camera to slowly droop downwards.

To avoid lens droop you need to be able to tighten two things up so that nothing moves: the tripod plate and the point at which the tripod head joins the tripod. But you also need to be able to undo it all again – it's a bit of a balancing act. Just make sure you review your images at 100 percent whilst you are still shooting, to make sure you aren't getting any unintended droop. If your camera and lens are on the heavy side, you may want to invest in an L-plate (or L-bracket). This is a plate that wraps around two sides of your camera and secures it to the tripod much more firmly than a simple square plate.

You might be tempted to switch your lens stabilisation/anti vibration setting on, to help cope with small camera movements. Don't do it. The camera will be searching for movement to stabilise, and when it can't find any (because the camera is steady on a tripod), it will actually add movement instead, as it constantly hunts for vibrations.

Use the self timer or a cable release to avoid nudging the camera as you press the shutter. This is critical if you are using longer exposures (anything over about 1/60th).

Buying a tripod

You've decided to get a sturdy tripod, now you have some more decisions to make.

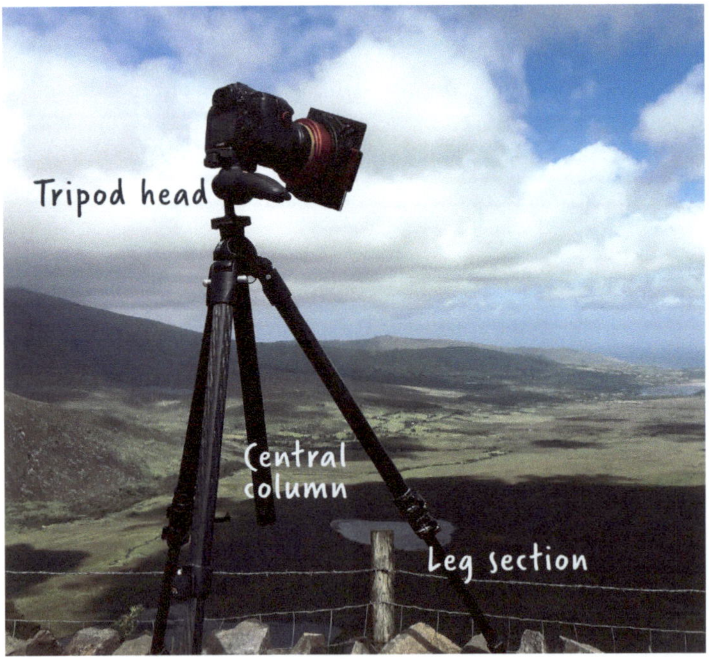

1. What is it made of?

The lightest tripods are made of carbon fibre. They are also the most expensive. Metal tripods are less expensive, but heavier.

2. Should it have a central column?

If you also intend to use your tripod indoors or for studio photography, a central column can be useful to easily change the angle of your camera. But as previously noted, in the field, it becomes a liability, lessening the overall stability of the whole tripod.

3. What kind of head?

If your tripod comes with an integral head, it is too basic for landscape photography in any kind of weather. You need to buy your tripod and tripod head separately. You don't have to buy them from the same manufacturer (I now use a Feisol tripod with a Really Right Stuff head).

There are two main types of head: a ball head and a three-way head. A ball head is like a ball and socket joint – it allows the camera to rotate smoothly around a ball in any direction. A three-way head requires you to adjust each of the three axes separately – tilting forwards/backwards, tilting side to side and swivelling. Ball heads are quicker to use, but can be less accurate.

4. How many leg sections?

I swore by a three-section tripod for a long time. I found it was quicker to put up and take down. But since I started travelling a bit more, I prefer my four-section tripod because it folds down much smaller, is easier to carry and doesn't actually take that much longer to set up.

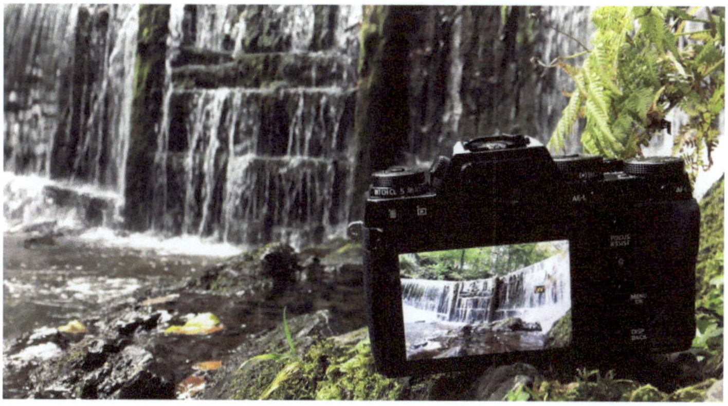

No tripod? No problem.
Caught without a tripod, here I balanced my X-T1 on some rocks, and wedged some pebbles under one side to get it as level as possible. With a two-second delay on the self timer, the camera was perfectly still when the shutter fired. The final image needed straightening in Lightroom.

FILTERS

If you are new to filters, there are a bewildering array to choose from. You don't need to use filters for landscape photography, but three in particular may be useful: a neutral density ("ND") filter, a graduated ND filter and a polarising filter. But first a word on UV (ultra-violet) filters:

Do you need a UV filter?

In the days of film, an ultra-violet filter stopped UV rays adding a blue tint to your images in situations with too much UV light. But digital sensors have their own ways of coping with this interference. So no, you don't need a UV filter simply to filter out UV light.

But many people like to use a UV filter (which is effectively just a clear piece of glass) to protect their lens against dust, scratches and damage. Yes, it will do this. But you are putting a (relatively) cheap piece of glass in front of an expensive lens. Your lens is now only as good as the cheap piece of glass.

Neutral density filter

A neutral density filter (sometimes known as an "ND" filter) simply reduces the amount of light hitting the sensor. It's just a big piece of dark, neutrally coloured, expensive glass. You would use one to reduce the amount of light hitting the sensor, but without introducing a colour cast.

ND filters are used in landscape photography for two main reasons: first, to enable shooting during bright sunlight at larger apertures, or secondly, when you wish to use very long shutter speeds for a creative effect (see Chapter 19 – Long exposure). ND filters are calibrated by the amount of light reduction they produce - usually three, six or ten stops.

Graduated neutral density filter

This is a filter that is split into two halves. The top half of the filter is an ND filter, and the bottom half clear. The join between the two is the"graduated" part. There are two kinds of graduated filters: "soft" and "hard". A soft graduation has a gentler join than a hard graduation. Hard graduated filters are used when you have a clean horizon with no trees or buildings jutting up into the sky.

These filters are used to balance the contrast between sky and land: you line the join up with the horizon, and the ND part of the filter stops the sky blowing out while the clear part of the filter doesn't affect the bottom half of the shot at all.

Polarising filter

A polarising filter makes the colours in your image more vibrant, and can be used to get rid of reflections on glass and water. They are most often used to increase the saturation of a blue sky.

Things to remember

- Anything you put in front of your lens will reduce the quality of the final image, which is why filters are so expensive.
- It's not worth buying a cheap filter – you're better off not using anything.
- If you use square filters, you'll need to carry the slot-in holder plus an adaptor for every lens size you have.
- If you use screw-on filters you'll need a new filter for every lens size, unless you buy the largest size and then use adaptors to size them down. (Your lens filter size can be found on the front of the lens – it's just the diameter of the lens and will be something like 52mm or 77mm.)

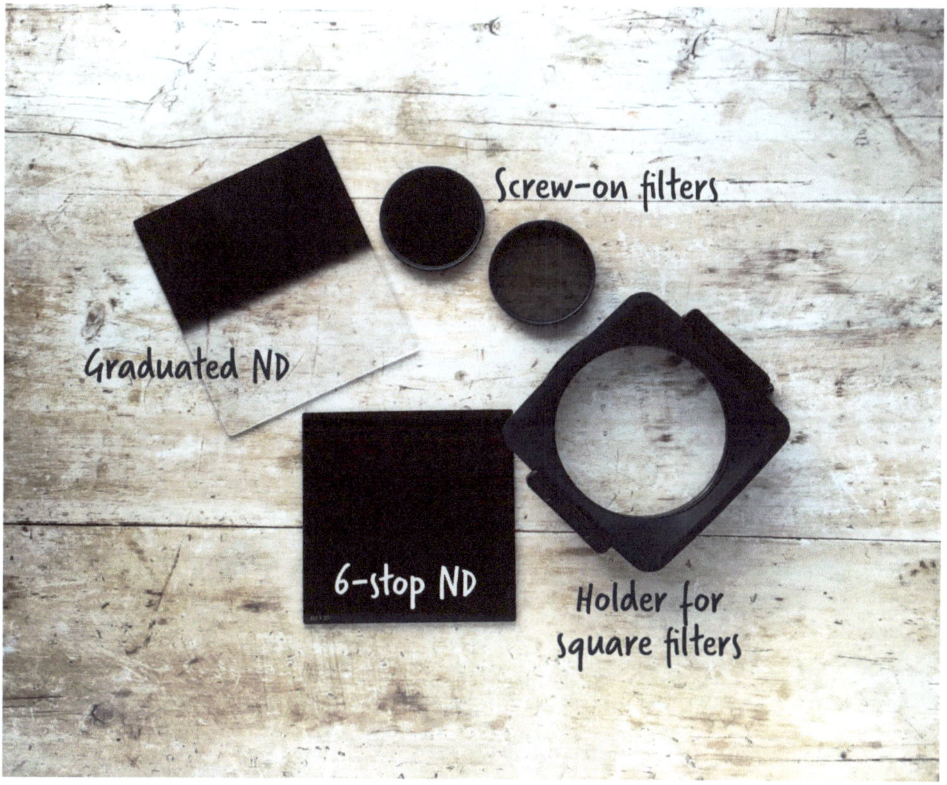

These essentials are always in my camera bag. If I'm going on a longer trip I'll add a few extras: see Chapter 9 – Road trip tips.

Lens wipes

You can never have too many. Check your lens multiple times during the day, and between every shot if it's raining or you're shooting near sea spray.

Spare batteries

Batteries wear out quickly if you are using Live View, and if you're working in the cold. Keep spares next to your skin so they are not cold when you switch them out.

Spare memory cards

Have a system for full ones and empty ones. Back up full ones as soon as possible. Once they are backed up in two places, clear them for reuse by formatting them in the camera you will use them in – don't just use the "delete images" option in your software or on your camera.

Screwdrivers

Bring with you whatever you need to be able to tighten everything on your tripod.

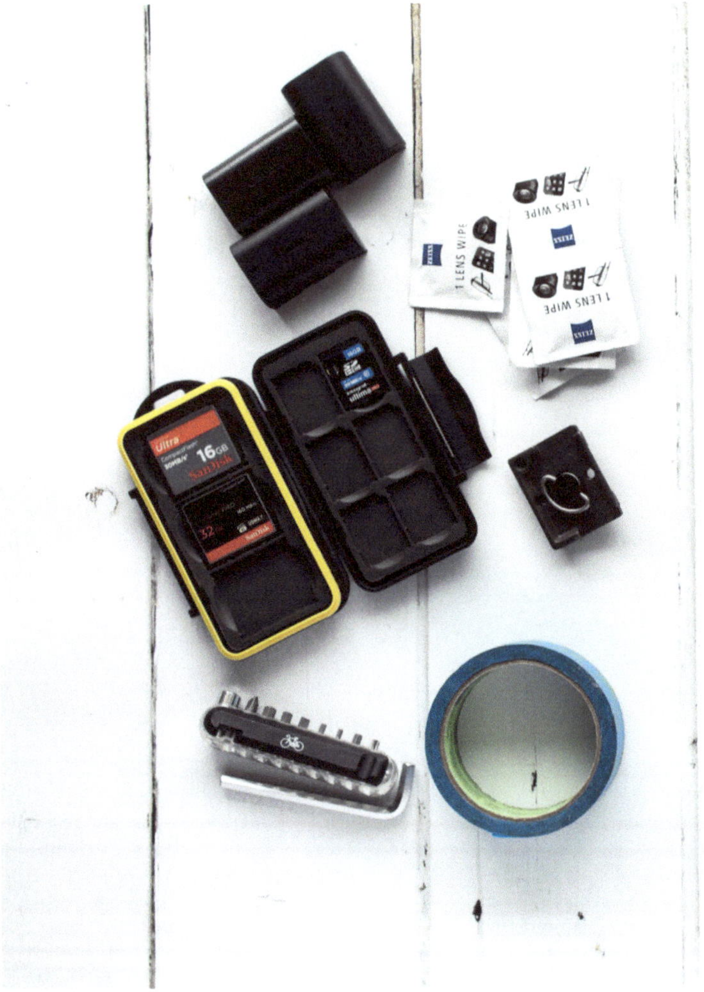

Strong tape (I use painter's tape)

The most useful bit of kit in the bag. You can use it to repair things for long enough to keep shooting, hold things out of the way, and to cover the viewfinder for long exposures (see Chapter 19 – Long exposure).

Spare tripod plate

If you've got a spare, bring it with you – you can't shoot without one and they are so easy to forget, and to lose.

Cable release

You can use the self timer if you can't find yours, but they come into their own if you are doing ultra-long exposures (more than 30 seconds) because you can use bulb mode and lock the shutter open (see Chapter 19 – Long exposure).

Sunscreen

Always have it with you, even if the day looks cloudy

Spare socks

The second most important thing after the tape. Being able to have warm dry feet again will mean you will feel like keeping shooting, where you might otherwise have called it a day.

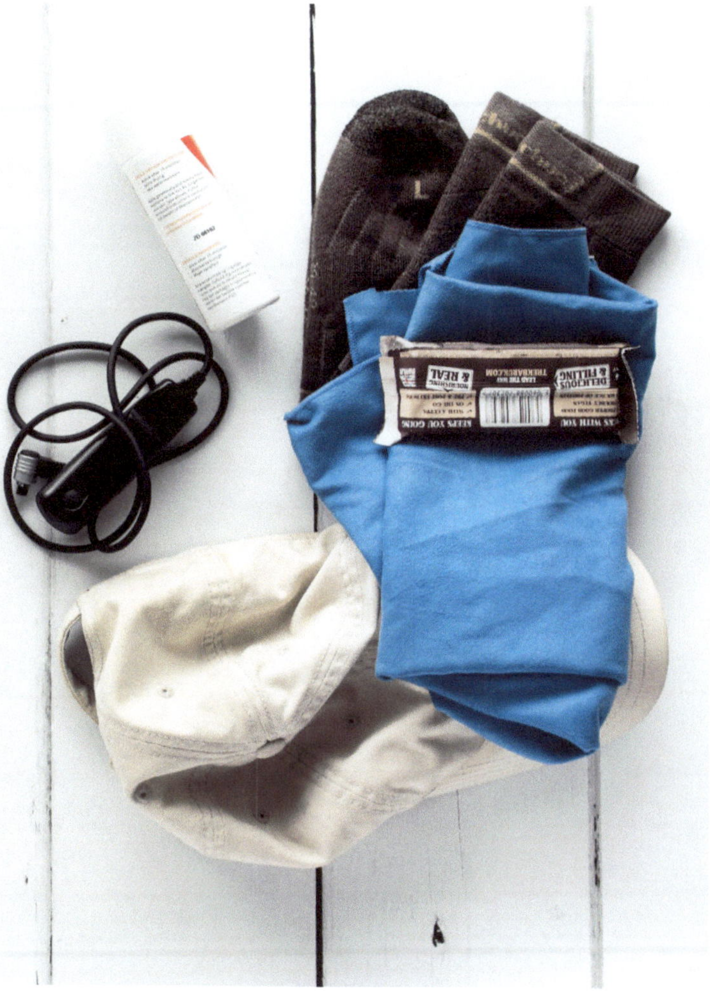

Microfibre cloth

Not to clean your lens with, but to drape over your whole camera to keep a light rain off it. And to wipe a heavier rain off your kit from time to time. If you don't mind what you look like, an umbrella held over your kit works better at keeping it dry.

Snacks

Much the same as spare socks – their function is to keep you shooting as long as possible.

Hat

Keeps the sun off your face, or your head warm, depending on the season. Can also be used as an impromptu lens hood to stop sun flare, and to cover the viewfinder if you forget your tape.

You'll also need a bag or backpack to put everything in. For landscape photography you'll want a backpack rather than a bag, for ease of carrying whilst walking. Make sure it can hold your tripod tight on the outside – you don't want a tripod weighing you down from behind. You may be working in extreme weather conditions so it pays to invest in a good, waterproof backpack too.

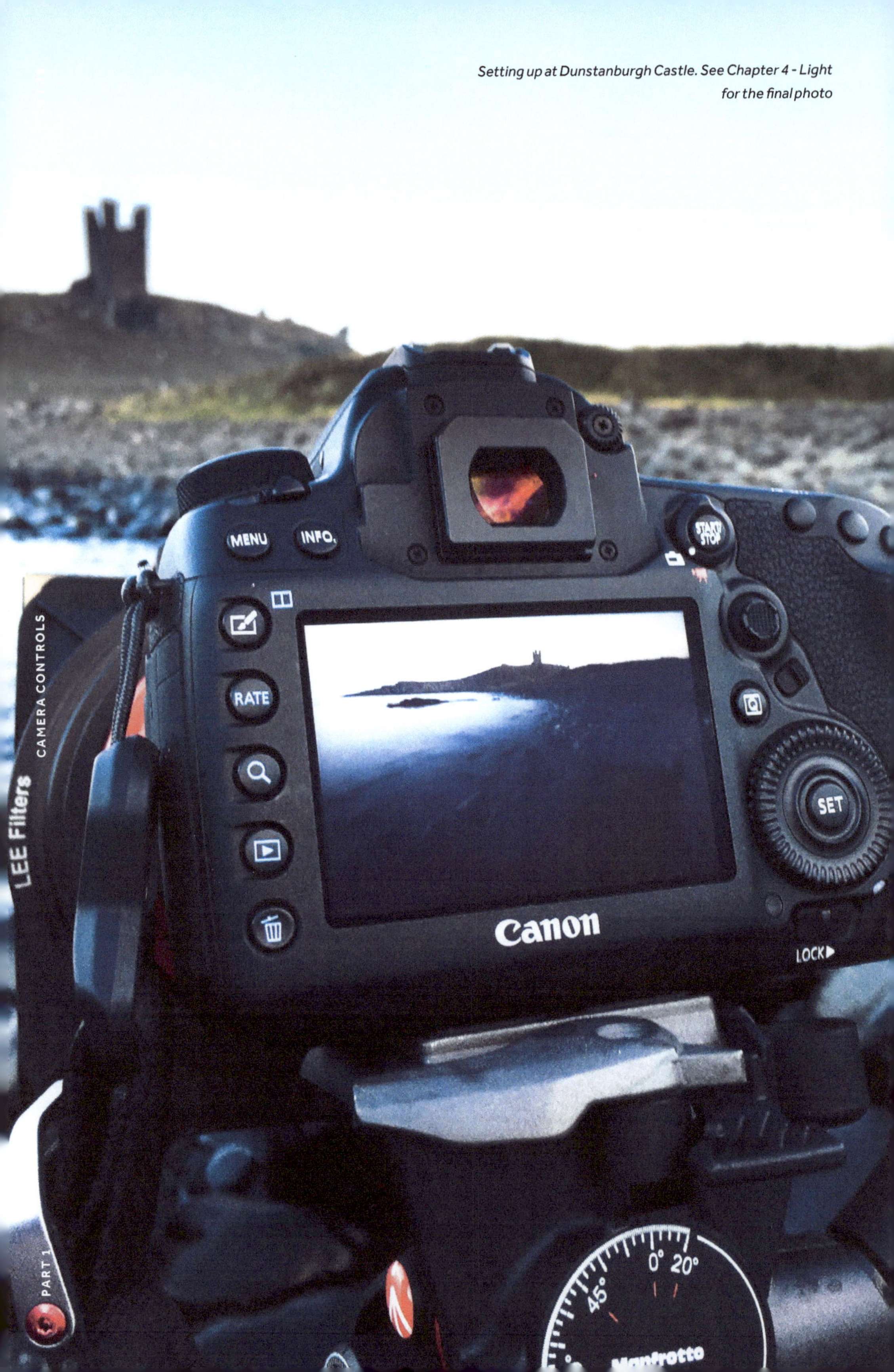

Setting up at Dunstanburgh Castle. See Chapter 4 - Light for the final photo

3

CAMERA CONTROLS

Landscape photography is a constant compromise. Changing light, rising winds, high contrast and a vast canvas all conspire to push your camera and your patience to their limits. It is a very, very rare day when you can use exactly the settings that you want to. Usually you have to trade a shorter shutter speed for a lower ISO, or sacrifice some depth of field to stop the trees moving in the wind.

You can't shoot epic landscape shots on auto modes. If you still shoot on fully auto, now is the time to take the plunge and get off auto. (I don't include aperture or shutter priority modes as fully auto – you can make a good start with landscape photography on aperture priority mode).

BACK TO BASICS

This is a list of the concepts you need to understand for landscape photography. You can use your camera manual to find out how each one works on your particular camera. If the concepts are completely new to you, the first six lessons of my beginner's photography course, A Year With My Camera, will get you to the place you need to be, step by step, with a series of very easy to understand exercises.

Visit EmmaDaviesPhotography.com/landscape-links to download a free pdf with the first six lessons from the A Year With My Camera course – everything you need to get off auto.

Aperture

The aperture is an adjustable hole in your lens that controls how much light reaches the sensor. A large hole (e.g., f4) also creates a small depth of field. A small hole (e.g., f16) creates a large depth of field.

Depth of field

There is an area of your image that appears acceptably sharp and this is known as the depth of field. It starts from the point you focus on and extends backwards towards the horizon, and forwards towards the camera.

Shutter speed

Measured in fractions of a second, shutter speed is the speed at which the shutter (like a tiny curtain inside the camera) opens and closes in front of the sensor. A very short shutter speed (e.g., 1/500th of a second) lets in very little light and is used in bright conditions. A longer shutter speed (e.g., 1/30th of a second) lets in more light and is used in darker conditions. If anything in your shot is moving faster than the shutter speed it will show on your image as a blur.

ISO

A measure of the sensitivity of your sensor, ISO stands for "International Standards Organisation". A low ISO (e.g., ISO 100) is not very sensitive and would be used in bright light conditions. A high ISO (e.g., ISO 1600) is more sensitive and would be used in lower light conditions. The disadvantage of using a high ISO is that digital noise is introduced to the image, reducing the quality.

Exposure

The amount of light that hits the sensor is known as the exposure. It is measured in "stops" (see below) and is created by a combination of the aperture, shutter speed and ISO used (sometimes referred to as "the exposure triangle").

Exposure modes

Your camera will have a dial on the top where you can select whether to shoot on fully auto exposure, fully manual mode, or something in between (e.g. aperture priority mode). Other than shooting fully manual mode, the most useful modes for landscape photography are aperture priority and shutter priority modes. With these modes, you choose either the aperture or the shutter speed, and then the camera picks the other two settings needed to get the exposure.

Your camera may have some other auto modes indicated by a symbol depicting, for example, a person (portrait mode) or a flower (macro mode). These are auto exposure modes, but you are telling the camera what you are taking a photo of – so for a portrait the camera will try and blur the background to prioritise the person, and in macro mode the camera will force a very close focus. The "landscape" mode isn't too helpful if you want to take anything more than snapshots. It will just assume you want a front-to-back depth of field, and force a narrower aperture.

But there's a lot more to landscape photography than that, so I wouldn't advise you use this mode.

Stop

A stop is simply a unit of light, as an inch is a unit of length and a kilogram is a unit of weight. If you increase the aperture, shutter speed or ISO by one full measure, you are increasing it by one full stop. This makes it easier to balance changes in one camera control by making an opposite change to another. For example, if you *increase* the size of your aperture from f11 to f8 (one full stop larger in size), to keep the same exposure, you would also need to *reduce* your shutter speed or your ISO by one full stop. So, if your shutter speed had been 1/500th, you could reduce it to 1/1000th. Or if your ISO had been 400, you could reduce it to 200. There is a chart with all the stops on the following page, and this is covered in detail in the free pdf mentioned above.

Auto exposure

If you leave the camera on any auto exposure mode (i.e., anything except fully manual mode), it will assume the scene before it is made up of a mid-grey tone that is sometimes referred to as 18 percent grey. This is why if you take a shot of anything *not* 18 percent grey (or the colour equivalent), the exposure will be wrong – your shot will be too light or too dark. And a landscape shot is almost never a mid-grey tone, which is why you need to be able to override the camera's auto exposure, either by shooting on fully manual mode, or by using your exposure compensation dial.

Try it now, if you haven't already done A Year With My Camera (this is the very first lesson from the course, and is available in the free pdf download above). Put your camera on fully auto mode and take a photograph of something white – a piece of paper or a wall. It shouldn't have any shadows on it, it needs to be fairly well lit but not in direct sunlight, and it needs to fill the viewfinder. If your camera has trouble focussing because there is no detail, just pop it onto manual focus for the shot (but don't forget to put it back again). Then do the same with something black. You should find that both shots come out grey, neither white nor black. This is your camera turning everything to that 18 percent grey tone.

Metering

When your camera assesses how much light there is falling on a scene it is called "metering". "Metering modes" are the different ways it can do this. Your camera probably has three metering modes (check the manual to be sure): a general one where it meters from the whole frame; a more specific one where it prioritises what's in the middle of the frame; and a very specific one where you pick exactly which spot in the frame to meter from. Using the default "whole frame" mode is fine to get started with landscape photography but as you become more experienced you might prefer to use spot metering for more control.

Exposure compensation

Your camera almost certainly has a dial for exposure compensation. This is a very useful feature if you don't want to shoot on fully manual mode. If you shoot on the semi-auto modes (aperture priority or shutter priority) and the camera gets the exposure wrong (because you aren't shooting something that is a mid-grey tone), you can simply dial in more or less exposure to brighten or darken the image. And you don't need to switch to manual mode to do it. Do remember to put the dial back to zero once you've taken your shot.

Focus

There will be a switch on your lens that lets you move from auto focus to manual focus (on some cameras it is buried in a menu or may be activated by touching your LCD – check your manual if you can't find it). On auto focus, the camera decides where to focus, based on what's closest to the camera and what's biggest in the frame. If it gets it wrong, you can either switch to manual focusing and turn the lens barrel to focus, or use the touch screen if you have it, or you can take control of the auto focus points. If you do the latter, you can choose exactly which spot in the viewfinder the camera should focus on.

White balance

All light has a colour temperature – think of an orange sunset or a blue-tinged snow scene. The auto white balance ("AWB") in the camera attempts to make sure that temperature is neutral. If the AWB gets it wrong, you can end up with an unexpected colour cast on your photo. For example, if you were expecting to see a beautiful orange sunset but the camera corrects it to a neutral bluer tone, you might be disappointed. You can take control of your white balance using manual white balance, or by correcting it easily in editing afterwards.

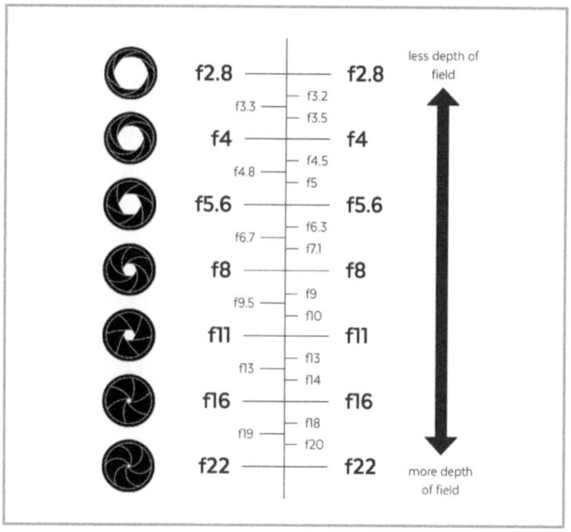

Apertures

This chart shows the most common apertures, from largest size at the top, to smallest size at the bottom. The full f-stops are shown in bold (f2.8, f4, f5.6 and so on). Most cameras will also show either half-stops or third-stops as well as the full stop settings. These are shown on the left side of the scale (half-stops, eg f3.3) and on the right side of the scale (third-stops, eg f3.2 and f3.5).

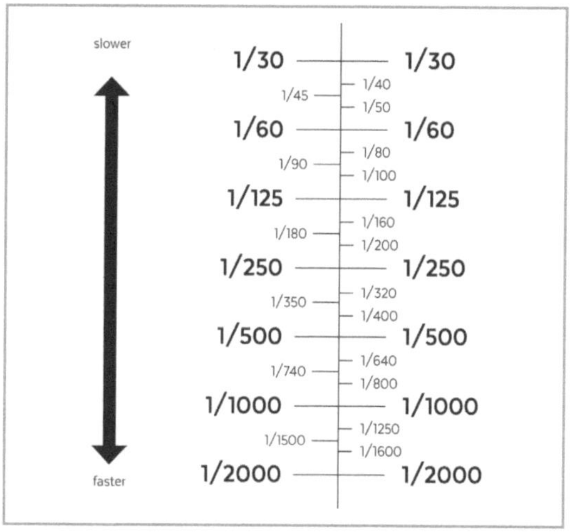

Shutter speed

This chart shows the most common shutter speeds, from the slowest at the top, to the fastest at the bottom. The full, half and third-stops are shown as for the apertures.

Note: if you want to use a shutter speed longer than 1/30th of a second (or whatever the slowest shutter speed is for your camera), you will need to use "bulb" mode. This is usually indicated by a "B" on the top dial, and allows the shutter to stay open for as long as you press the shutter button. It is usually used together with a cable release which allows you to lock the shutter open without having to hold the button down.

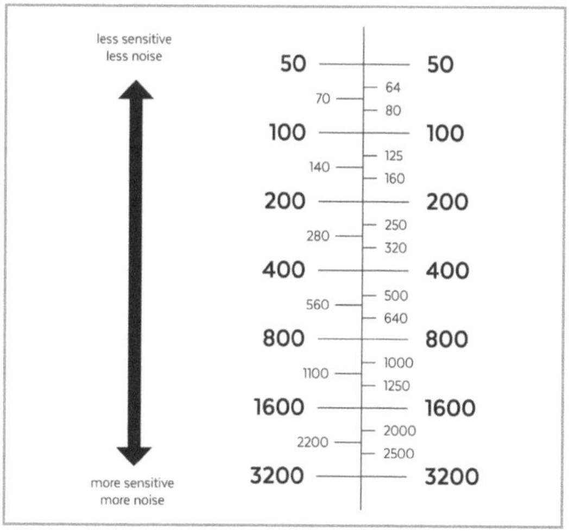

ISO

This chart shows the most common ISO settings, from the least sensitive at the top, to the most sensitive at the bottom. The full, half and third-stops are shown as for the apertures and shutter speeds. The image quality degrades as the ISO setting increases, so always aim to keep your ISO as low as possible.

Note that some cameras have an artificial low and high ISO option. For example, the lowest native ISO on my X-T1 is 200, but there is the option to extend that to 100 or 50. However, the camera is simply using native ISO of 200 and then over exposing it by one stop and creating an edited JPEG file - it's not available to export as a RAW file.

WHERE DO YOU START, WITH SETTINGS?

It can be overwhelming when you suddenly take control of all the settings on your camera, if you've been used to letting the camera make most of the decisions. With landscape photography however it's very easy to make a start. You only need to make two choices: one, what is the creative effect you want?; and two, what compromises will you need to make to get it?

The creative effects come from the aperture and the shutter speed. With aperture, you control the depth of field of the image (the part that appears acceptably sharp). With shutter speed, you control the motion blur (that is, whether moving things show as blurred or frozen).

The compromises arise when you need to use an extreme setting to achieve your desired creative effect as explained further below.

For a large depth of field

If you want front-to-back sharpness in your shot, you will need to select a small sized aperture (e.g., f11).

Now look at the compromises you have to make. If it is a gloomy day, it might be that ISO needs to climb to 1600 or higher, to preserve a shutter speed that you can hand-hold. To keep ISO down to 100 or 200, you will need to change the shutter speed to a longer one, which will, in turn, allow motion blur to start appearing where anything is moving. You might not mind the motion blur but if you want a large depth of field with no motion blur, you will have no choice but to wait for a brighter day, or to let the ISO increase.

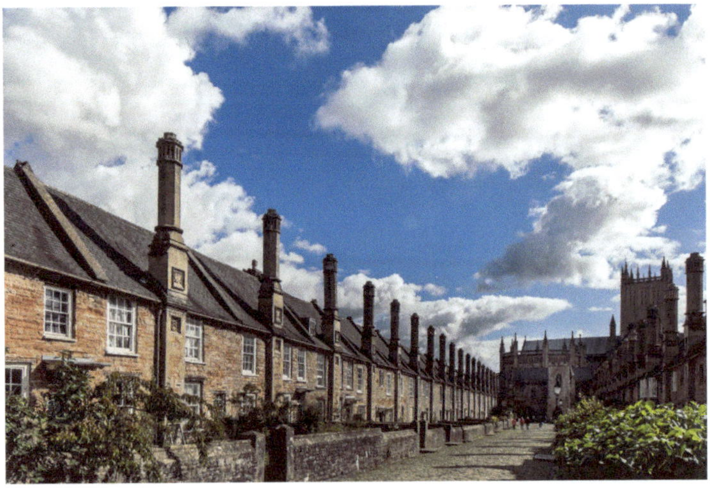

Below right:
In this urban landscape shot in Wells, it was essential to get the whole row of houses sharp, so I used f11 (with the hyperfocal distance technique - more below). If I had also wanted to blur the clouds, I would have needed a shutter speed of 4 or 5 seconds, which would have meant using a neutral density filter (see Chapter 2 - Kit).
5DIV, 11-24mm at 24mm, ISO100, f11, 1/320th

For a shallow depth of field

Choose a wide aperture (e.g., f2.8 or f4), and accept that if it's a bright day you may reach the mechanical limits of your camera – the shutter speed won't go faster than its maximum. If your image is still too bright, you'll need to use a neutral density filter to reduce the amount of light reaching the sensor from outside the camera.

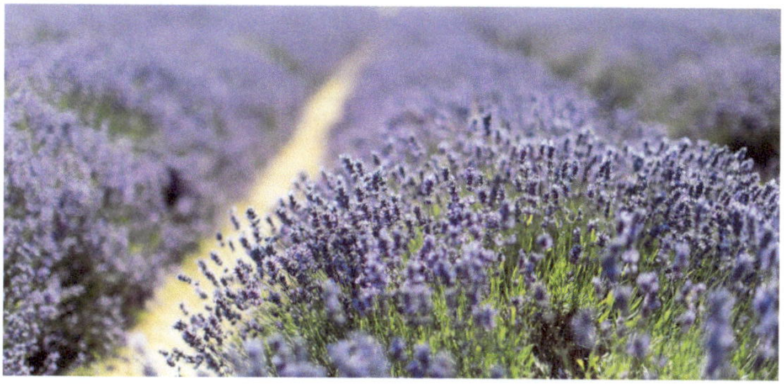

Left:
For this very, very shallow depth of field, I chose an aperture of f1.2. Because it was a bright day, this meant the shutter speed went to 1/8000th and there is nowhere else to go after that without using an ND filter. The original shot was slightly over exposed but I was able to bring it back a bit in editing.
5DIV, 50mm, ISO100, f1.2, 1/8000th

For motion blur

Choose a slow shutter speed (1/30th or slower), and then use a narrower aperture or neutral density filters to prevent over-exposure.

To freeze the action

Choose a very fast shutter speed (1/1000th or faster, for fast moving subjects), and then settle for a wider aperture or a higher ISO than you might otherwise have picked. With a wider aperture your focus will have to be spot-on, as you will have limited depth of field.

Bottom left, motion blur:
5DIV, 50mm, ISO100, f16, 140 seconds
Bottom right, frozen action (on a windy day):
5DIV, 50mm, ISO100, f1.2, 1/8000th

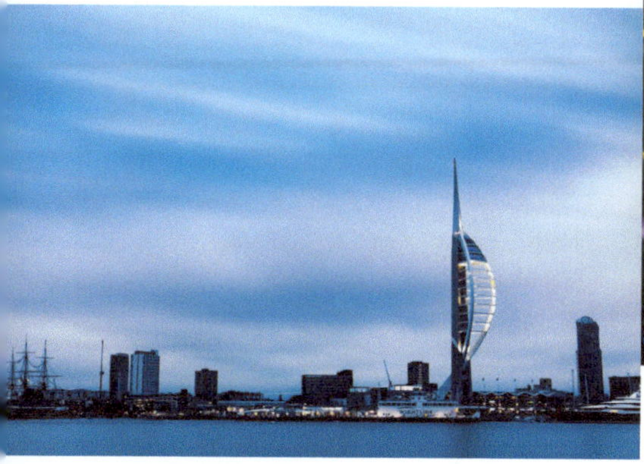

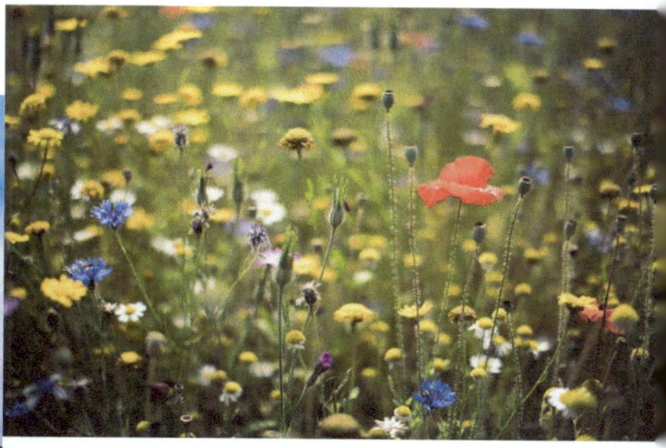

DYNAMIC RANGE

The eye sees things differently than the camera and this is probably the main reason people are disappointed with their landscape photos. You need to start seeing as your camera sees and understand that, when it comes to exposure, the dynamic range of your camera is far less than that of your eye.

Dynamic range is the difference in light intensity from the darkest part of an image to the lightest. Remember stops, the measure of light we looked at earlier in the chapter? Your eye can see up to twenty stops of light, but (depending on who you believe), the camera can only see up to around ten. The numbers aren't so important – it's the principle that matters.

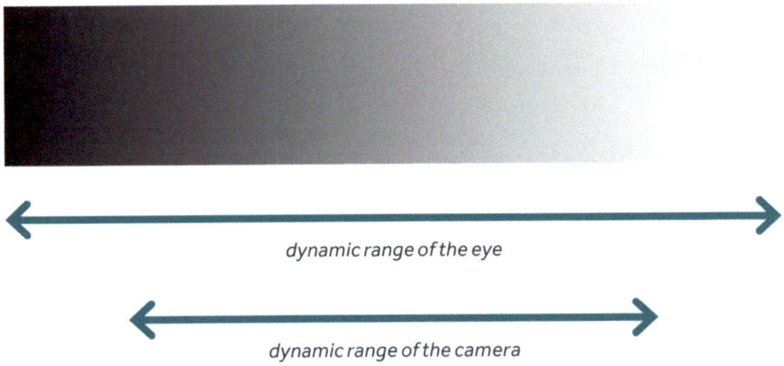

If you are looking at a scene with a high dynamic range (one with dark shadows and bright highlights) your eye will still be able to see details in those shadows and highlights. Your camera won't – it will record the shadows as blocks of black, and the highlights as blocks of white.

The reason this is such an issue for landscape photographers is that we are almost always working with high dynamic range situations: the sky will have bright highlights and the land will have deep shadows. The only exceptions are when you are working under a grey sky, at night, or when the sun is very low in the sky. To combat dynamic range issues, you either need to reduce the dynamic range of the landscape, or you need to increase the dynamic range of the camera. We'll look at these in turn, but first you should understand the histogram.

Histogram

Your camera will have a setting that lets you preview exactly what it is seeing, in terms of dynamic range. It is called the histogram and it is a small bar graph showing the distribution of tones all the way from pure black on the left to pure white on the right:

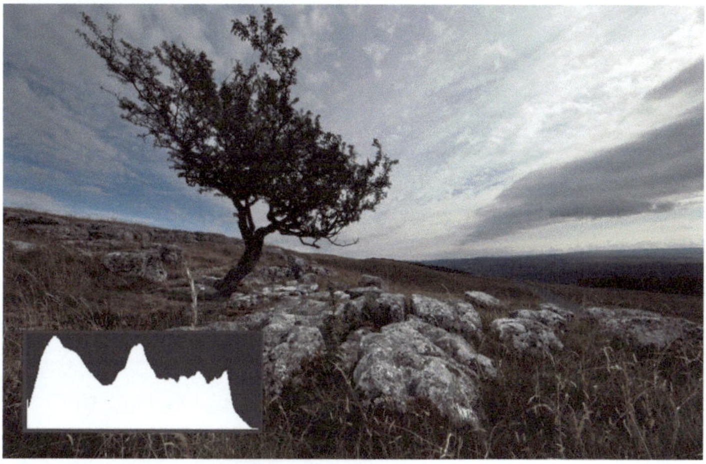

Top left:

This is how the human eye sees this tree in the Yorkshire Dales (the shot is over-edited: this is not what the camera saw).

The histogram (overlaid) is evenly spread throughout the range, indicating that you can still see detail in both darks and lights. It is climbing the wall on the left a little, showing that some shadow detail has been lost.

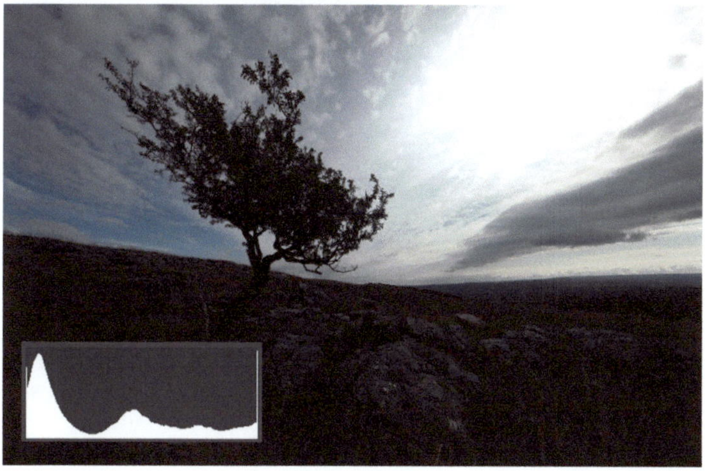

Bottom left:

This is how the camera (with its reduced dynamic range) sees the same tree. Notice the blown highlights in the sky, and the dark shadows with no detail.

The histogram is climbing the wall on the right and the left, indicating that there is no more information to show – and that corresponds to the blown highlights and lost shadows.

When working in potentially high dynamic range situations, always turn your histogram on so you can preview what the camera is seeing. If your camera doesn't let you have it on before you take the shot, it will let you overlay it as you review your images. If you see the histogram climbing the wall at either end, you know that you have lost all further information at that end, and you will have blocks of pure black or pure white in your shot (which is to be avoided).

If you have established that the dynamic range of your landscape is more than the camera can cope with, you have three choices: one, work with what you have; two, reduce the dynamic range of the landscape; or three, increase the dynamic range of the camera.

1. Working with what you have

Sometimes you just have to pick between two evils: keep the detail in the shadows and let the highlights blow out to white, or vice versa. If you hear photographers talking about "exposing to the right" or "exposing to the left", this is what they mean. If you "expose to the right", you are choosing to keep the detail in the right of the histogram, i.e., keep the details in the highlights at the expense of the shadows.

There is no correct way to expose (in spite of what they tell you in camera clubs). It all depends on what is in front of you. If you have a predominantly dark shot, with lots of detail to see in rocks and shadows, you would probably want to expose for the shadows. If your shot is mostly sky or brighter areas, you would want to keep the detail in the highlights. Always keep an eye on the histogram. The minute it starts to touch either the left or the right end you are beginning to lose information.

2. Reducing the dynamic range of the landscape

If you were a portrait photographer, you would be able to pop a little fill-flash onto your subject to reduce the dynamic range in a natural way. But with landscape photography, your subject is way beyond the reach of any flash. Your only option is to use a graduated neutral density ("ND") filter to reduce the dynamic range of the scene, and this only works if the shot has a nice, clean horizon.

A graduated ND is a filter which is clear on the bottom and tinted with a neutral tone on the top. You line the join up with the horizon and it reduces the brightness of the sky whilst leaving the land unaffected, reducing the dynamic range of the whole shot to something that the camera can cope with. Look closely at the second shot below and you can see where the join on the ND filter has caught the cliff as well as the sky and darkened it unnaturally.

Below:
Exactly the same shot of Durdle Door, with a 6-stop graduated ND filter used in the second shot.
5DIV, 11-24mm at 14mm, ISO100, f11, 0.8 seconds.

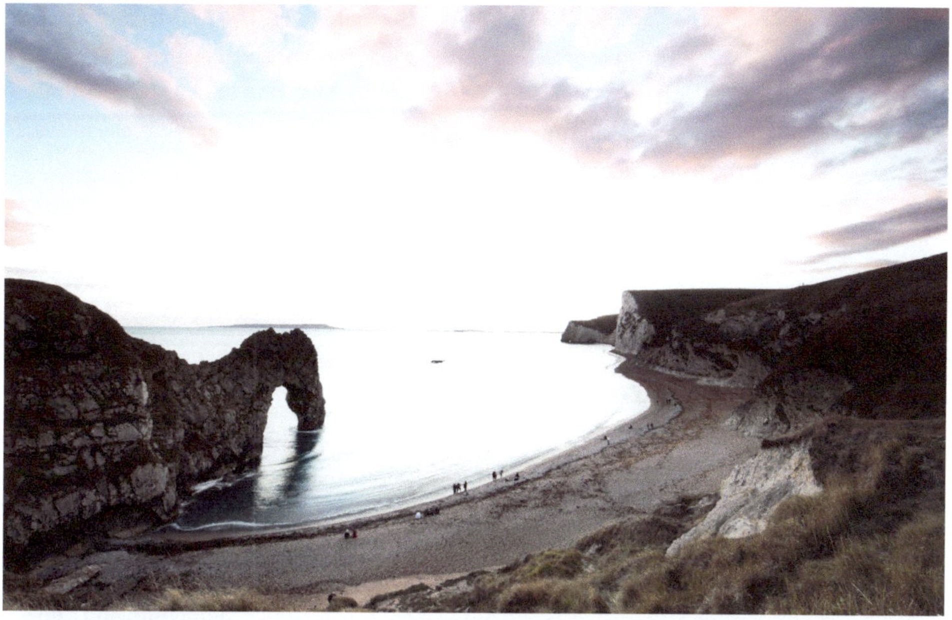

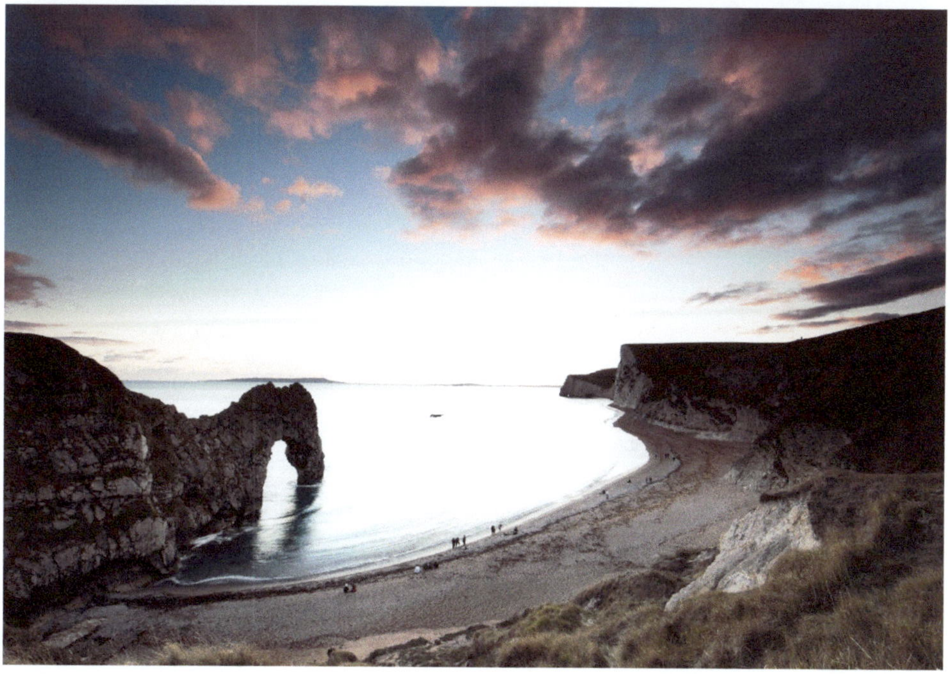

3. Increasing the dynamic range of the camera

The more expensive your camera, the better the sensor will be and the greater its dynamic range. Short of upgrading your kit, there are two techniques you can use to extend the dynamic range of your camera. The first is something I hope you're doing already and that is to shoot RAW, and rescue detail in editing. A RAW file is one that keeps every single piece of information that the camera can see. A JPEG file only keeps the information it needs to produce a ready-to-use image, and discards the rest. With a RAW file you can use post processing to coax out a lot of the detail in the shadows and the highlights that is initially hidden from view. There is more on this in Chapter 6.

The second option is to merge more than one shot into one single image. To use this high dynamic range ("HDR") merge technique, set your camera on a tripod so nothing moves between shots. Then take a series of shots (usually at least three) – one which exposes the shadows correctly, one which exposes the highlights correctly, and one in between the two. You can use the exposure bracketing setting on your camera to do this automatically without you needing to change settings between shots.

Using Adobe Lightroom, or another dedicated HDR software package, you merge the resulting shots into one single image. The software takes the detail from the shadows, highlights and mid-tones respectively and creates an image with no blown highlights or lost shadows. The final image can look unrealistic if overdone, but if done with a light touch, the results can be spectacular. This is a very useful technique to practice and learn.

Glen Coe, 6D, 11-24mm at 21mm, ISO100, f14, 1/5 sec (exposed for the landscape/shadows)

Glen Coe, 6D, 11-24mm at 21mm, ISO100, f14, 1/20th sec (exposed for the sky/highlights)

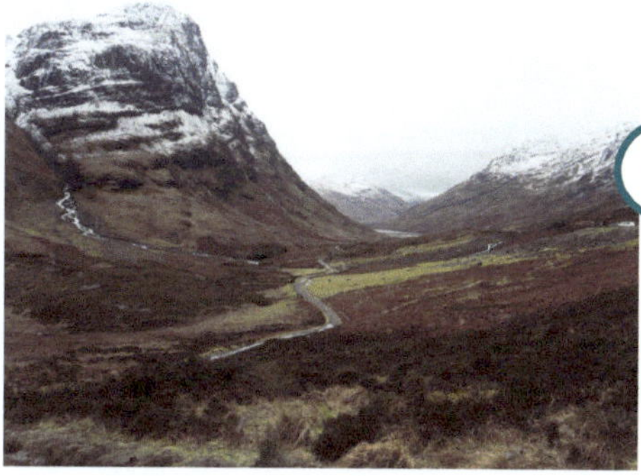

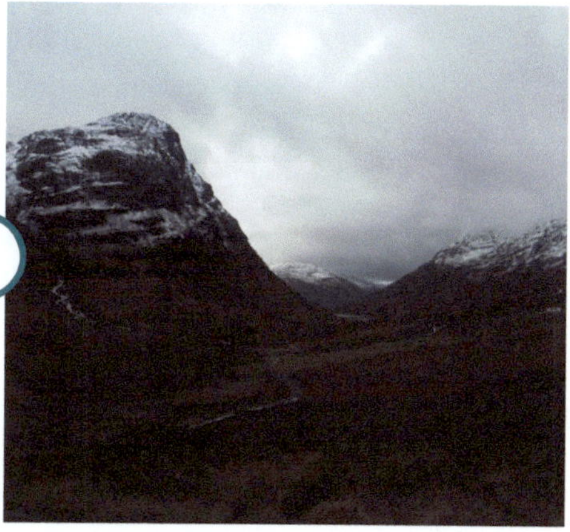

Final image, merged in Adobe Lightroom

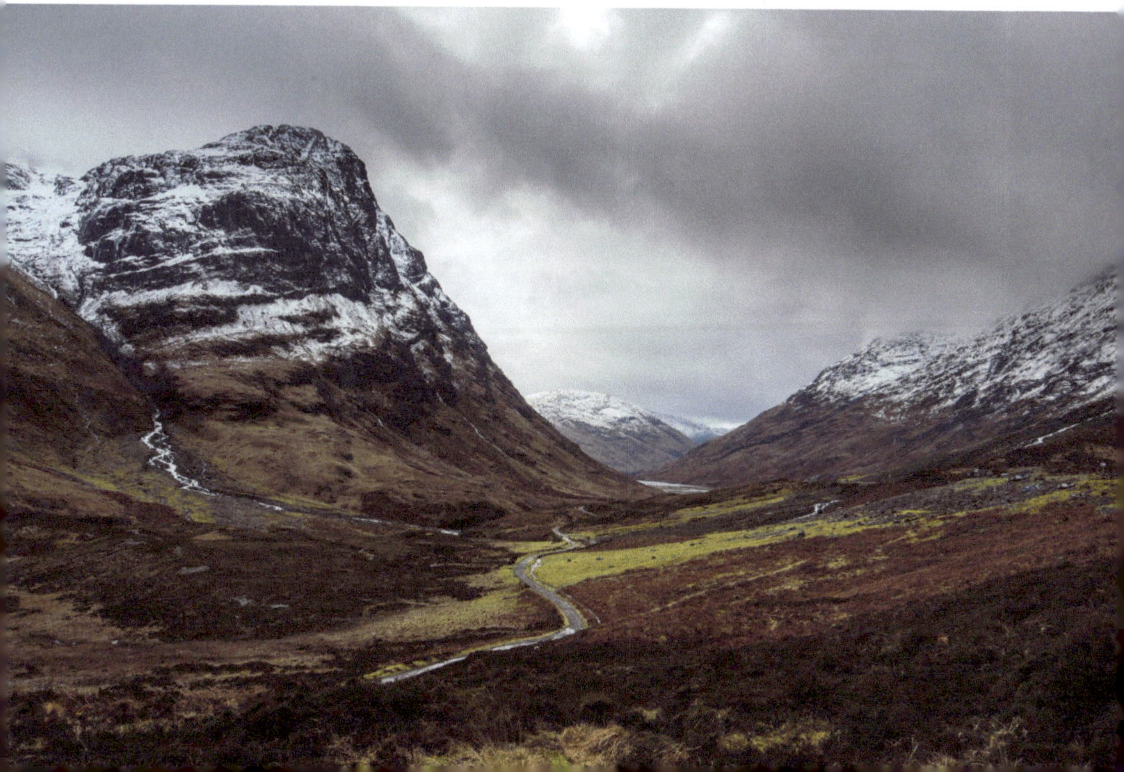

SHARPNESS

The goal of many landscape photographers is to achieve a shot which is perfectly sharp, from camera to horizon; a goal which seems unobtainable once you start to review your images at home and realise either the parts closest to the camera or those furthest away are not actually sharp.

If you look online and in exhibitions, you will see many shots that *do* achieve front-to-back sharpness. Before you hang up your camera in despair because you can't seem to replicate those shots, be aware that the photographer may have been using a tilt-shift lens (which changes the plane of focus – enabling camera-to-horizon sharpness – that is just not possible with a normal lens) or they may have used focus stacking. The latter is a similar technique to the HDR merge: you take two or more shots, where you move the focus point gradually through the frame from front to back. You then combine these shots in editing, taking only the in-focus parts of each image.

It is also often tempting to reach for your smallest aperture first, to increase the depth of field and get the sharpest possible image. But be aware that the smaller apertures start to introduce diffraction to your shots and you often end up with less sharp images as a result. Every lens has its "sweet spot" – the aperture at which it has the least diffraction and therefore produces the sharpest photographs. You should aim to shoot as close to this as possible, whilst still achieving the depth of field that you want. The sweet spot is usually around f8, but it depends what the range of apertures is – you can look it up online for your particular lens, if you are curious.

Hyperfocal distance focussing

Because depth of field starts from the point you focus on and extends in front of and behind that focus point, you can extend the depth of field in your image by bringing your focus point forward. This is called using "hyperfocal distance" focusing.

If you want to be incredibly precise about exactly where in an image to focus in order to optimise the available depth of field, you can use free hyperfocal distance calculators which you can find online (see Annex – Resources). But if you just want to extend the depth of field approximately, all you need to do is focus midway between the camera and the horizon, instead of automatically focussing on the furthest thing in the frame.

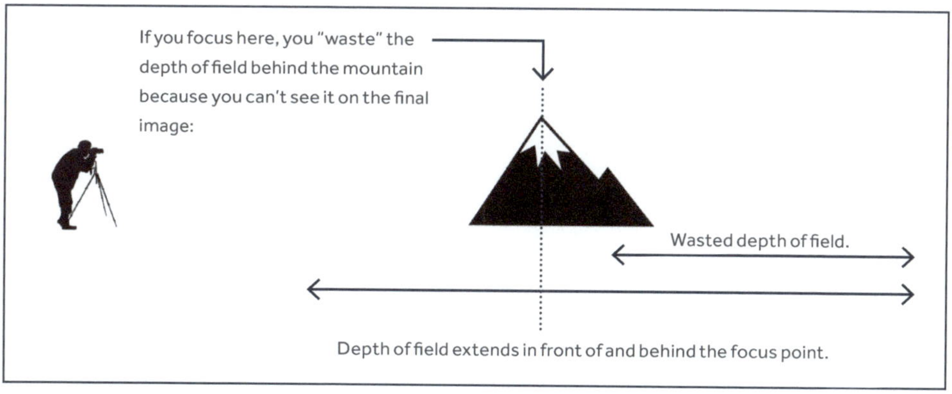

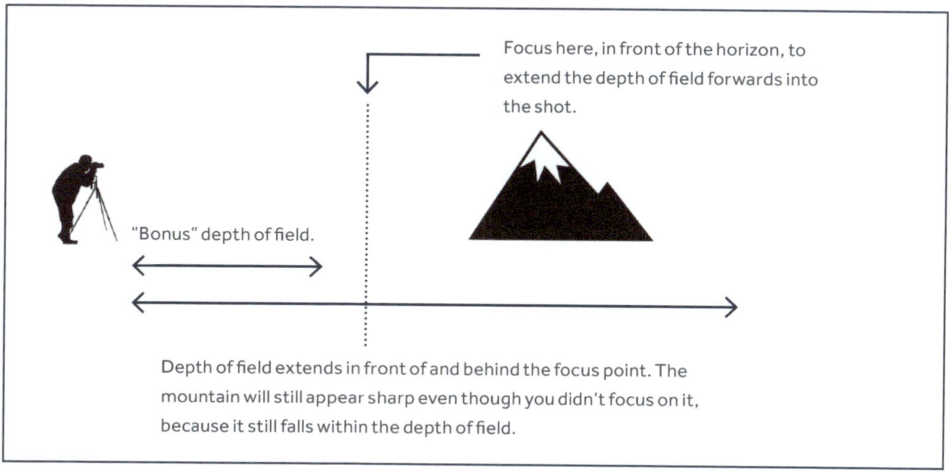

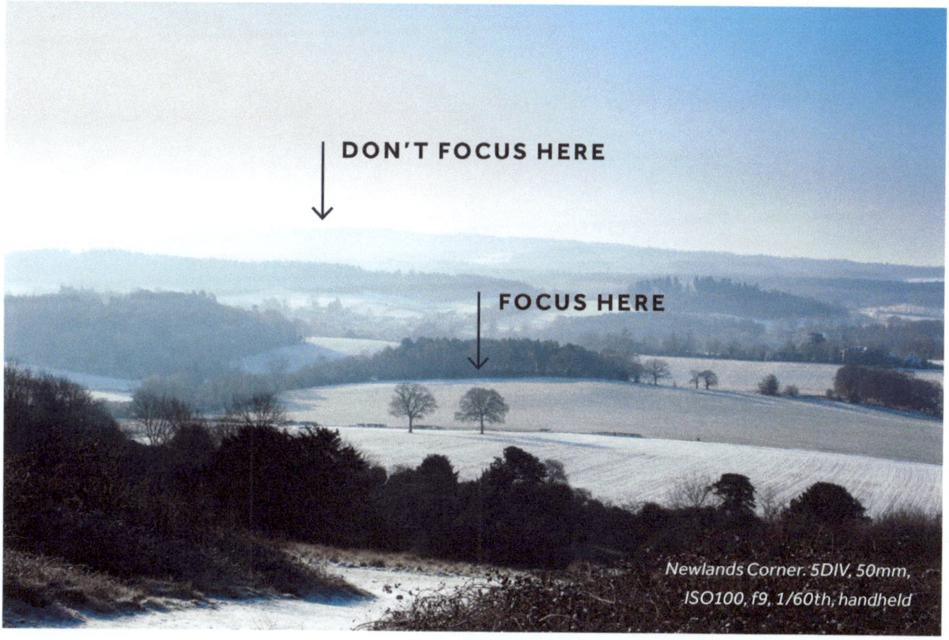

Newlands Corner. 5DIV, 50mm, ISO100, f9, 1/60th, handheld

A miserable, grey, rainy day with a five-minute window of epic light. You never know when it's coming, but with experience you can train your eye and learn to look for the signs. Pay attention to the weather even when it starts out grey.

Loch Assynt, Scotland. X-T1, 50-140mm at 50mm. ISO200, f2.8, 1/2400th, handheld.

4

LIGHT

All those incredible landscape images you see in calendars, on Instagram and winning all the competitions have one thing in common: epic light.

You can take a good landscape photograph in less than epic light, but you'll never take a great one. Your most disappointing landscape photographs are probably disappointing because of the mediocre light.

What is epic light?

You are looking for light that touches the landscape and brings it to life. It's not so much the light itself you are on the lookout for, it's the effect it has on the land. This is possibly the most important piece of information in this book: stop looking at the sun and start looking at what it looks like as it meets the ground.

Epic light will look like the breath of angels touching the ground and bringing it to life. It's more easily found when the sun is low in the sky and the light rakes across the land painting anything it touches gold. But you can also find it in driving rain, when the clouds break for a moment. Or when a cloudy day meets a textured landscape that would be overpowered by any kind of direct light.

There are no short-cuts here. You need to understand exactly what the light will look like as it meets the ground at all points of the clock, in all the seasons, and in all the weathers. Start by looking up every day. Look in the opposite direction to the sun, and see what is going on in the sky.

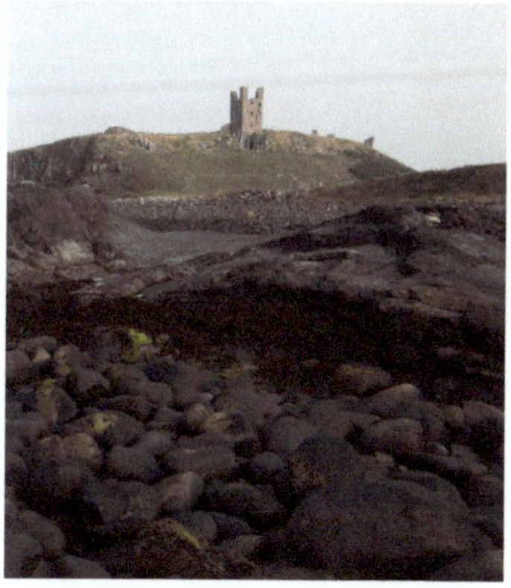

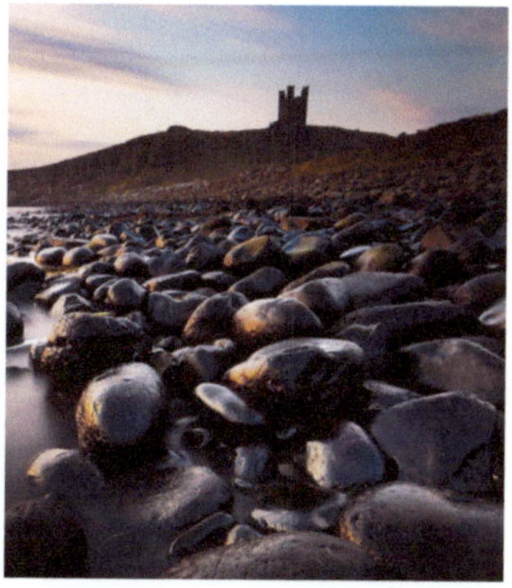

Bottom left:
Dunstanburgh Castle shot at 7pm in July - the sun is still high in the sky (it didn't set until 9.30pm). There are no clouds to catch the sun's rays and the light falls from above on the stones making them utterly uninteresting.
5DIV, 11-24mm at 11mm, ISO100, f8, 1/80th.

Bottom right:
The same place, shot at 6am the next morning. The sun had been up for one hour, but it had only just broken above a layer of clouds on the horizon. This is epic light because of the way it catches the clouds and bathes the stones in pink. Only half an hour later and all the colour had gone.
5DIV, 11-24mm at 20mm, ISO100, f14, 65 seconds.

TRY THIS

Start a collection of photographs of all kinds of light (not just ones that include epic light). You can just use your phone for this – this is your library of ideas, it's not going to be seen by anyone else. It will take you up to a year to finish. Aim to get a shot of the land and the sky at these different times of day throughout at least the four different seasons:

the hour before dawn
dawn
the hour after dawn
midday
the hour before sunset
sunset
the hour after sunset
heavy rain
mist or fog
as many different clouds as you can find

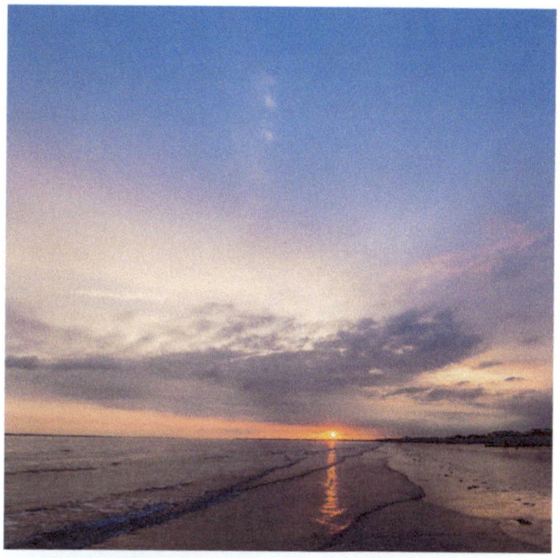
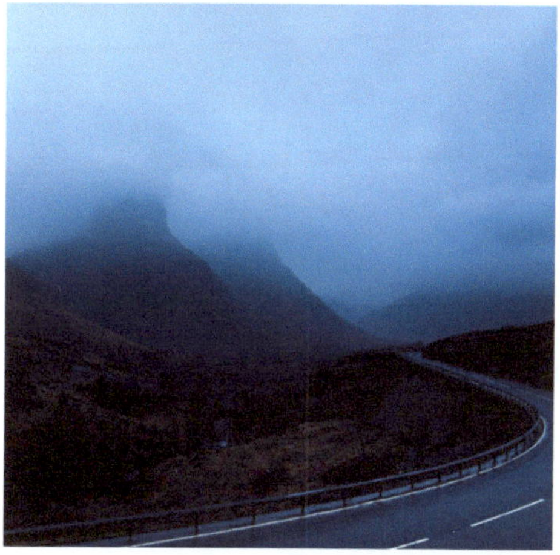
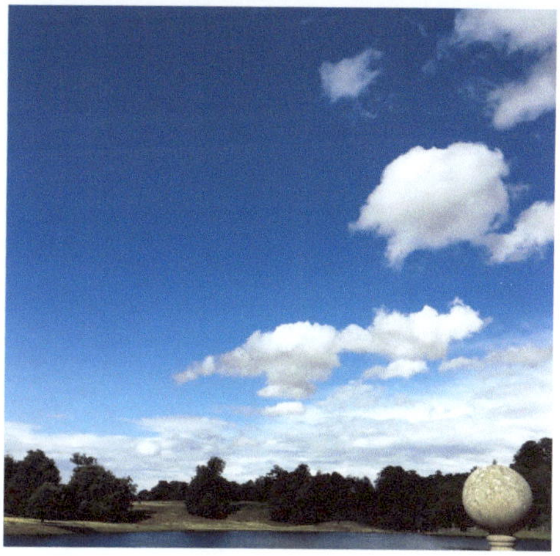
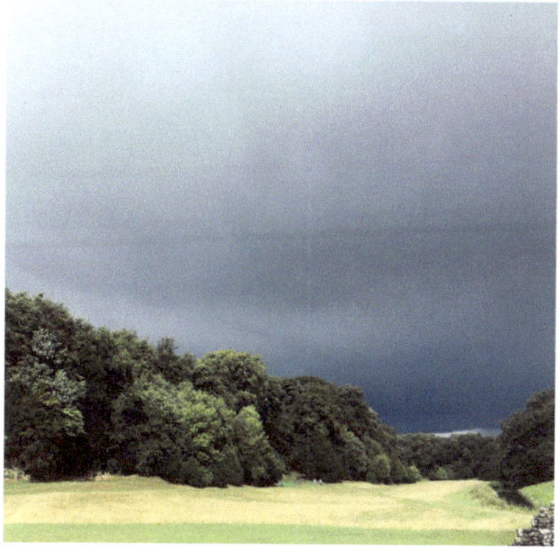
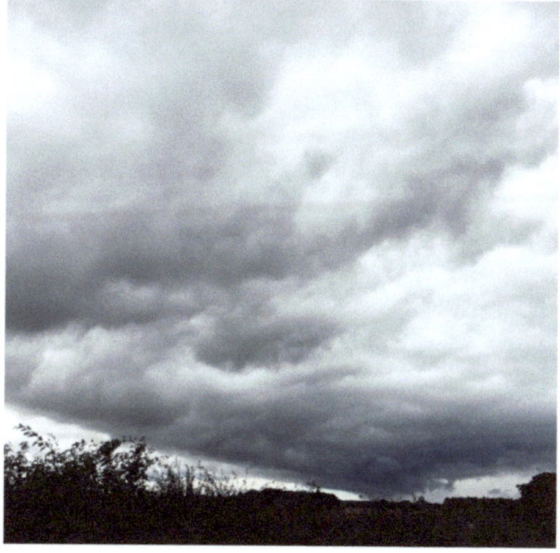

TIME OF DAY

The direction, colour and intensity of light changes minute-by-minute throughout the day. And if you are shooting away from the Equator, it also changes dramatically through the seasons.

The blue hour

The light just before dawn and just after sunset is very soft, indirect light with a blue tone. It doesn't actually last exactly an hour although it's referred to as "the blue hour". Depending on the time of year and your latitude, it can last only ten minutes, or it can last for a couple of hours.

You really need a clear sky to make the most of this time of day – the light filtering through a very cloudy sky before dawn is pretty much the same as a very cloudy sky just after dawn.

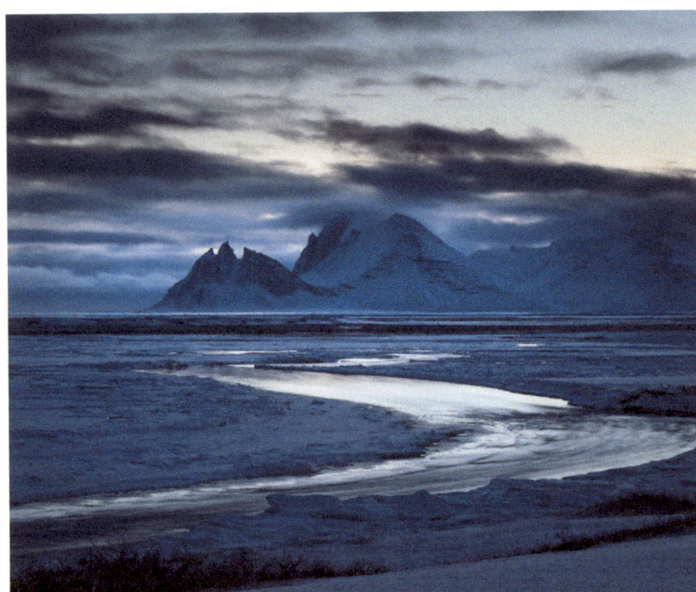

Right:
Southern Iceland at 5.25pm in early December: 2 hours after sunset and the blue hour is still evident.
X-T1, 50-140mm at 70mm, ISO200, f18, 8.5 seconds.

The golden hour

If the sun is in the sky but only just above the horizon, it creates very, very beautiful light for landscape photography. The light might be anything from gold through to dark pink and is seen at its best when there is a high layer of clouds to catch it. This light lasts until the sun rises (or sets) to about ten degrees above the horizon. This can take less than an hour after sunrise or before sunset if you are close to the Equator, or it can last all day if you are closer to either of the poles.

Watch out for clouds sitting low on the horizon – they will cut your golden hour short as the sun dips behind them ahead of the official time of sunset (or remains hidden after sunrise).

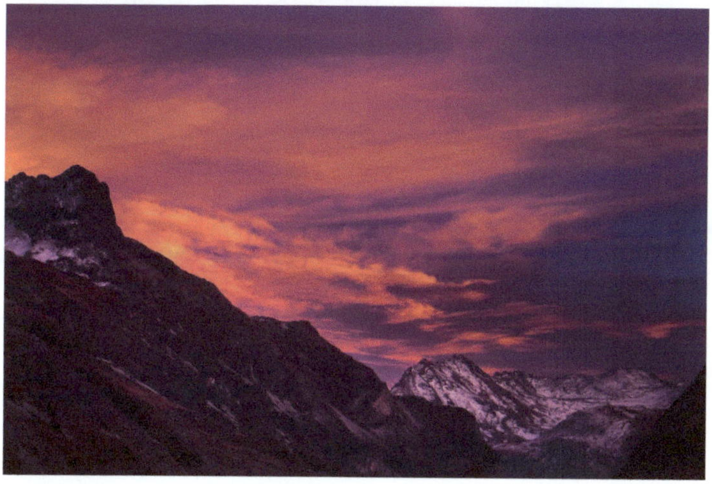

Left:
The golden hour that was actually pink: 5.30pm at the end of October in the French Alps.
X-T1, 50-140mm at 50mm, ISO200, f2.8, 1/100th, handheld.

Midday

Traditionally, midday is a time for landscape photographers to stop shooting. High contrast, blown highlights, oversaturated colours and no texture make for dull photographs. But harsh midday light just means you have to work harder to find your image. Get close, find a strong shot, work with the light you have rather than fighting against it.

And don't forget that midday in the height of summer can be very different from midday in the depths of winter. Pay attention to how high the sun is in the sky, rather than the absolute time of day.

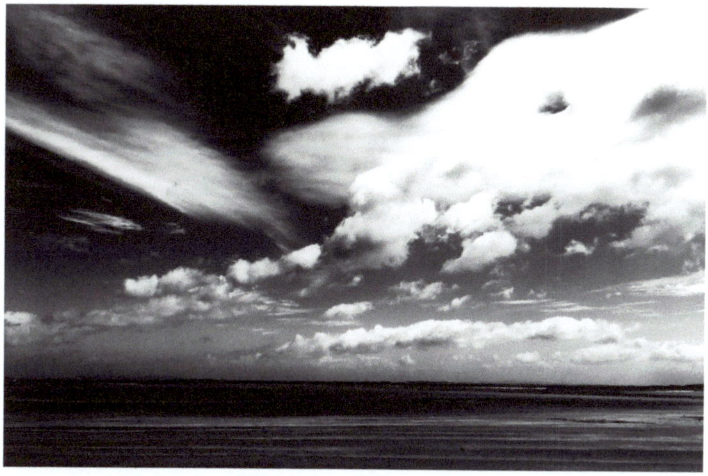

Left:
12.30pm in July on the west coast of Ireland. Bright blue skies, high contrast light and flat landscape: poor conditions for a traditional sweeping landscape shot, but perfect for a bold black and white shot of the sky. Work with what you have, not against it.
iPhone 6S.

HOW HIGH IS THE SUN?

High in the sky

When the sun is high in the sky your shots will suffer due to high contrast (the difference between the lightest and the darkest parts) and unforgiving shadows. But there are a few things you can try even in the midday sun:

- Bright colours set against a blue sky, silhouettes, or a perfect reflection of the blue sky in a still lake.
- Head into the trees to diffuse the strong light.
- Get in close and shoot intimate landscapes.
- Work with the hard shadows – create a strong composition where the shadows form an integral part of the shot, maybe shooting with black and white in mind.
- Wait for the sun to dip behind a cloud and work with the softer, diffused light.

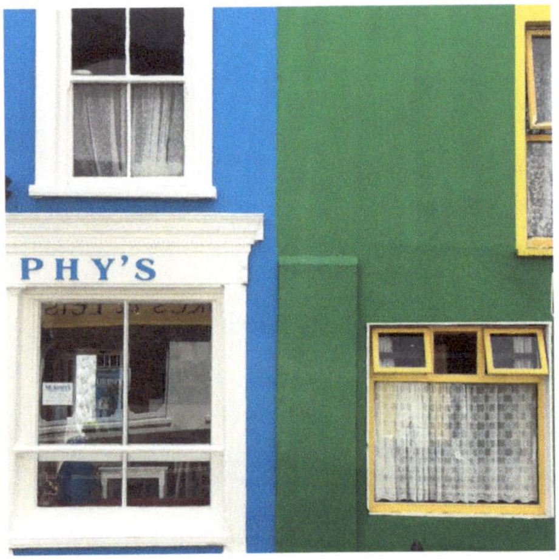

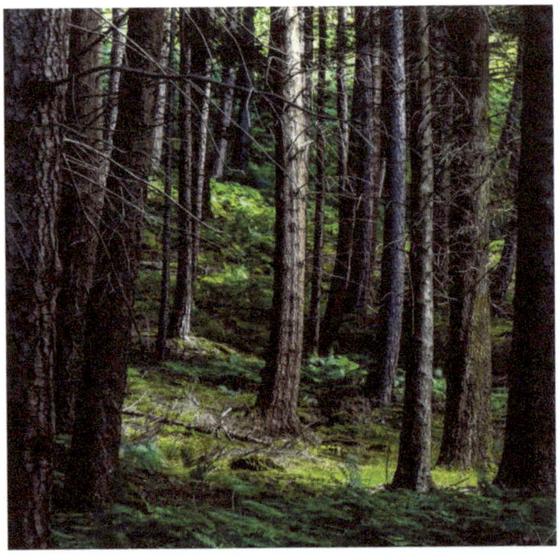

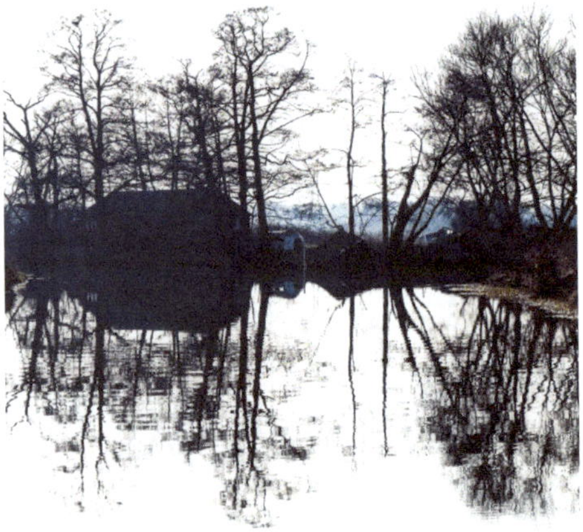

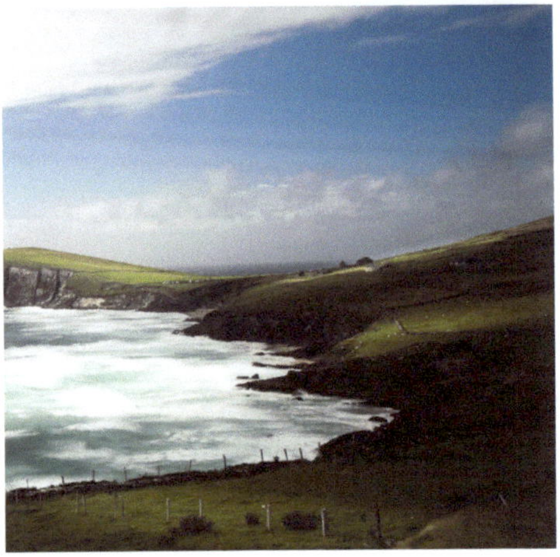

Low in the sky

When the sun drops lower in the sky you should seize your chance for the textbook landscape shot: beautiful low light catching the landscape, revealing texture and mood. Always remember to look where the sun is falling as well as at the sun itself. The sunset (or sunrise) may be spectacular, but the light on the landscape behind you might be even better.

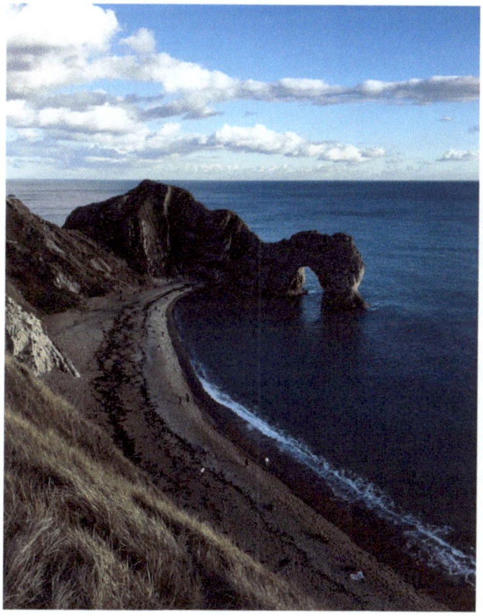

Above:
Durdle Door (on the south coast of England), shot at 5:38pm in September, about two hours before sunset, with the sun to the right behind a cloud.
iPhone 6S

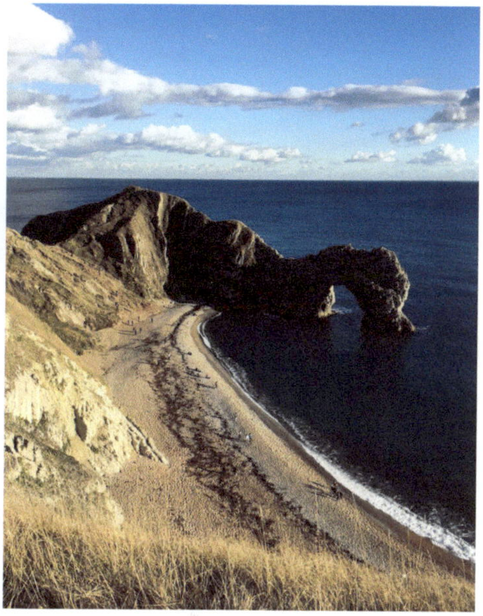

Above:
Contrast the previous image with this one, shot at 5:39pm, only one minute later. The low sun has emerged from behind its cloud and is now bathing the landscape with late evening light. Note the shadows and texture that have emerged that would have been lost if the sun was directly overhead.
iPhone 6S.

CLOUDS

Sooner or later you will realise that the state of the sky is going to make or break your landscape image. The better you are at recognising an interesting sky, and more importantly being able to forecast one, the better your landscape shots will become.

A clear blue sky might be what we all dream of, but it makes for a reasonably dull landscape shot. Break it up with fluffy white clouds though, and you have something interesting and evocative. Depending where you live, you might be familiar with those days or weeks of unending flat, grey skies that deliver neither sunshine nor storms. These will show as pure white in your landscape photography and need to be avoided or cropped out of frame.

I learnt everything I know about clouds from the very easy to read book, The Cloudspotter's Guide, by Gavin Pretor-Pinney. It's equal parts geeky, entertaining and fascinating, and it stays in my car at all times to be pulled out when an interesting cloud formation appears.

High clouds

The high clouds are the ones that will catch the sun's rays as it rises or sets, and be lit up with colour for a brief moment. If you can learn to predict when they will arrive, you can plan your sunrise and sunset shots more effectively. There are a multitude of weather apps, many of which will include current and forecasted cloud cover by height.

The illustration opposite shows some common cloud types along with their approximate height (heights shown refer to the base of the cloud).

Dramatic skies

Don't discount cloudy days. A sky full of drama is usually preferable to a dull blue sky with no cloud detail.

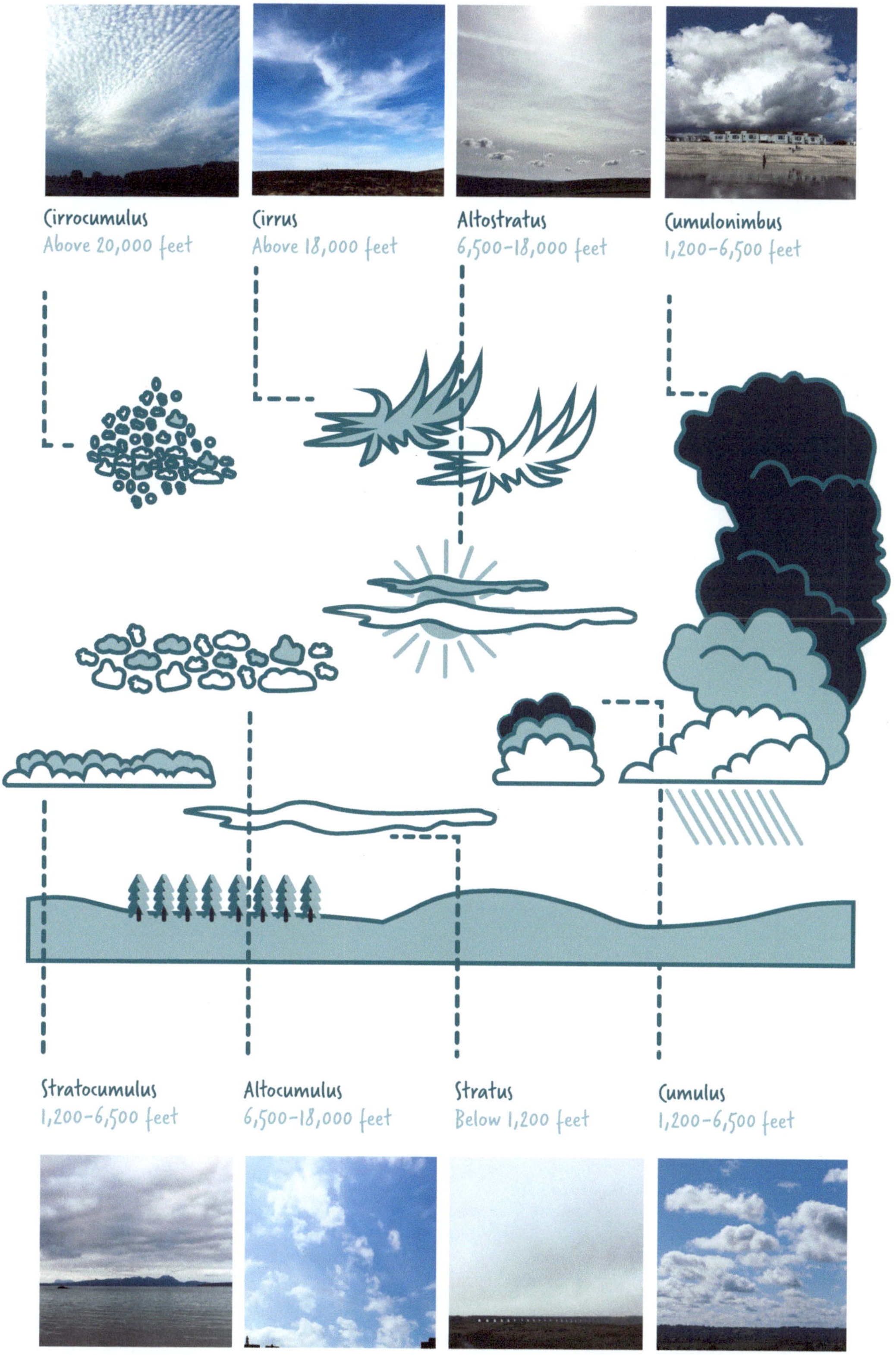
Cirrocumulus
Above 20,000 feet
Cirrus
Above 18,000 feet
Altostratus
6,500–18,000 feet
Cumulonimbus
1,200–6,500 feet
Stratocumulus
1,200–6,500 feet
Altocumulus
6,500–18,000 feet
Stratus
Below 1,200 feet
Cumulus
1,200–6,500 feet

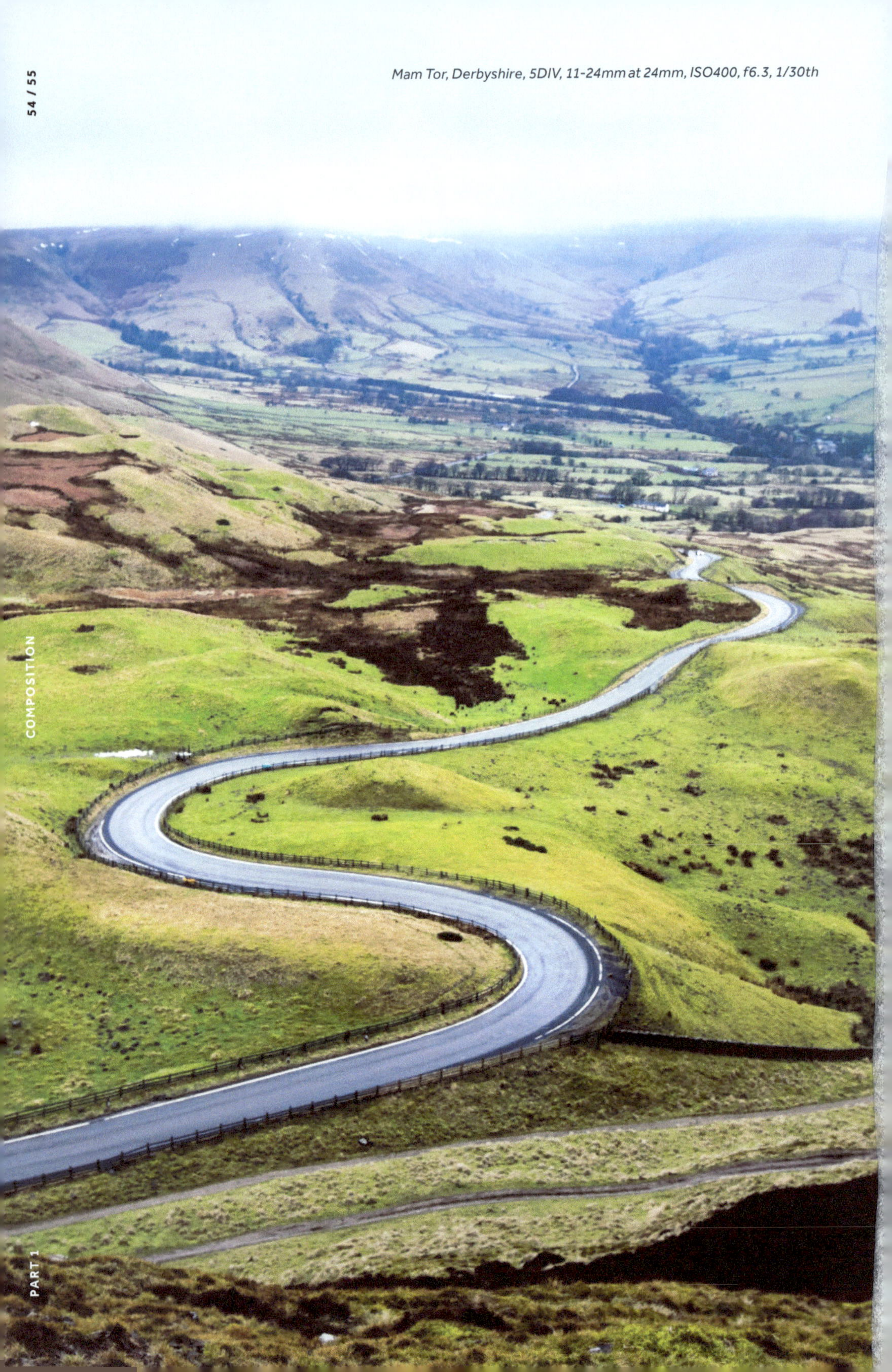

Mam Tor, Derbyshire, 5DIV, 11-24mm at 24mm, ISO400, f6.3, 1/30th

5

COMPOSITION

Where will you stand?

Landscape photography is essentially the art of compressing a three-dimensional scene into a two-dimensional representation by choosing carefully where you stand. The place you choose determines how every element in your shot relates to every other element when it is crystalised into those two dimensions.

In the shot (below) of the lone tree at Llyn Padarn, if I'd stood a little further to the right the tree trunk would be lost in the mountains. A little further to the left and I'd lose the 1/3: 2/3 balance between the background each side of the tree. Higher, and you'd lose that sense of being "at eye level" with the tree. Any lower and the tree would start to loom over you.

When you look at a view without a camera, your brain interprets things for you. It conveniently skips over a huge foreground. It finds the tree or the distant mountain and makes that appear bigger in your imagination that it really is. You need to learn how to be objective if you are going to take an epic landscape shot. Starting with where you choose to put your feet.

This chapter is divided into two sections: the first takes you through the basics of composition and helps you start to look at a landscape dispassionately so that you can be a better judge of how that compression from three to two dimensions will actually turn out once you press the shutter.

The second moves you to a more advanced level of photography by considering how to compose a truly dynamic shot.

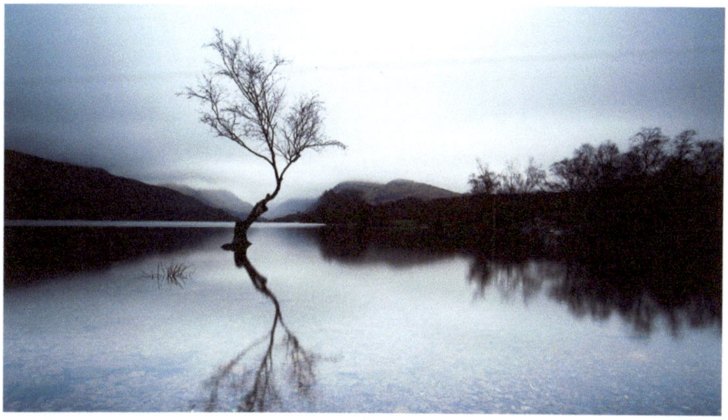

Left:

The lone tree of Lyn Padarn. *11-24mm at 20mm, ISO100, f14, 15 secs.*

SECTION 1: BASIC LANDSCAPE COMPOSITION

1. Viewpoint

Look up from where you are right now. What's in your field of view? What's overlapping with what? What bits of the background are obscured by the foreground?

Now move your head very slightly. What's changed? What can you see that you couldn't before? What's now hidden?

Next, try and move your head so that something in the foreground is lined up exactly with something in the background – their edges are touching. If there's nothing in the foreground lift up this book (or whatever device you are reading it on) and arrange it so one edge of it just touches the edge of something in the distance. You may need to close one eye to do this.

Finally, imagine you are not simply trying to line a book up with a window frame. Imagine you are outdoors confronted with a view that starts at your feet and finishes at the horizon. You have to line everything up so that it falls into place. You can't move anything in the shot – the only thing within your control is where you put your feet and which way you tilt your camera.

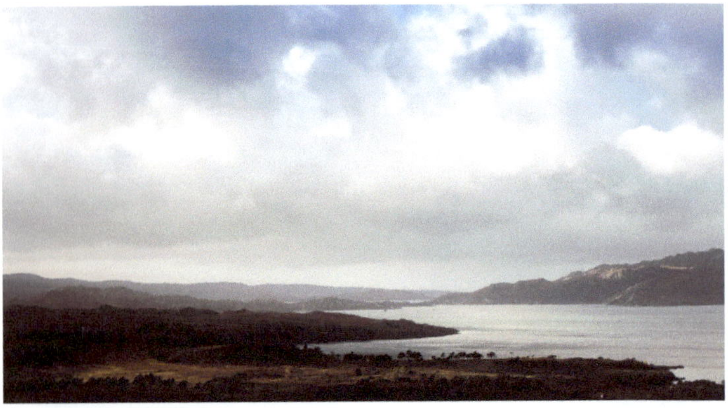

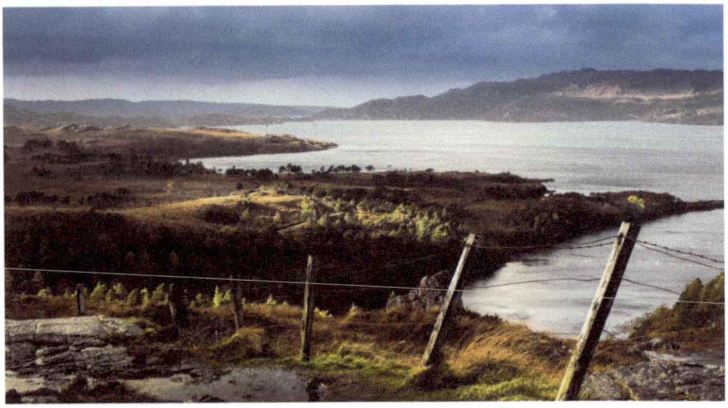

Top:
This shot of Loch Torridon makes the most of the changing light and the billowing clouds. But in the next shot I did nothing other than tilt the camera down slightly and raise it up about a foot, to include the stretch of fence in the foreground. The composition is now lifted from nice enough to slightly more epic.
6D, 50mm, ISO100, f10 1/80th.

Bottom:
6D, 50mm, ISO100, f10 1/60th.

Adult head height is not the only place to take a photograph from. In fact it is rarely the best place. With landscape photography a lower viewpoint often helps you include some interesting foreground, or a higher one will open up the shape of the landscape in the distance.

TRY THIS

- Find a view outdoors. It doesn't have to be epic light or a beautiful vista.
- Stand in one place and take a series of shots, starting at your head height and continuing following a vertical line down to ground level. You can use your phone camera for this.
- Examine the photos and see how the relationship between all the elements in the shot changes as you move your viewpoint. As you did for the first exercise, see what is hidden or revealed as you move your viewpoint.
- Now do the same exercise one step to the right. And then one step to the left.

There are an infinite number of places for you to put your camera as you approach a landscape. Look at the view first. Look carefully. Try to imagine how it will look compressed to two dimensions. Where do you want to put everything in the frame? And where do you need to stand to achieve that?

2. Rule of thirds (and breaking the rule of thirds)

A basic rule of composition is that if you avoid putting your subject right in the middle of your photograph, you will probably create a more interesting shot. The "rule of thirds" is more specific, stating that you should place your subject (or anything interesting, like the horizon), on one of the implied lines that splits the frame in three, horizontally and vertically.

This is a good rule to adopt, most of the time. An off-centre composition is more dynamic and more engaging. But there is always a time and a place to break the rule. Aim to be aware of the rule, but be ready to break it if you want to create a calmer, more static shot:

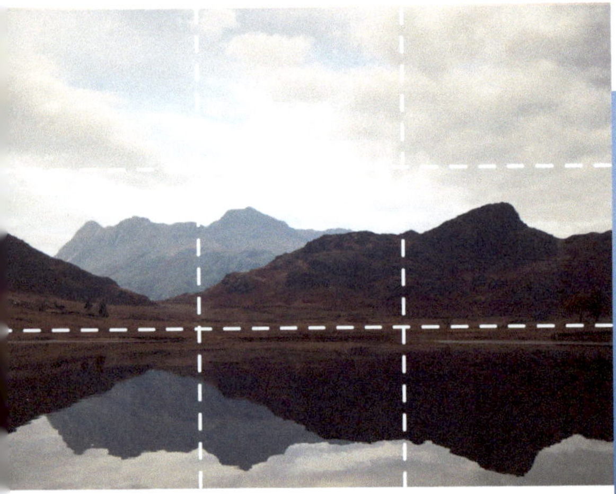

Above left:
Placing the point of interest on one of the rule of thirds lines. Blea Tarn, the Lake District. *5DIV, 24mm, ISO200, f8, 1/320.*

Above right:
Breaking the rule of thirds. The sky behind Jökulsárlón glacier lagoon. *5DIV, 100mm, ISO100, f2.8, 1/125th, handheld.*

3. Focal point, background, foreground

As you begin to pay attention to where everything falls in the frame, you may notice that you can usually split the elements of your image into three: the focal point, the background and the foreground. Not all shots divide neatly this way, but it can be a useful way to make sure your shot has a suitable balance.

Focal point

With portraits or still life photographs, the focal point is easy: it's the person or the main thing the viewer looks at. The term is often used interchangeably with another; the "subject" of the photograph.

With landscape photography you can't always use "subject" and "focal point" to mean the same thing, because often the *entire landscape* is the subject of your photograph. But you should still aim to have a focal point: where your viewer's eye comes to rest. If you have competing focal points (e.g. a castle and a lighthouse both on the horizon), the viewer continually jumps between them and finds the image unsettling.

Background

Again, with other genres of photography, the background is easy to pick out: it's anything behind the subject. With many landscape photographs there is no background in shot as the whole view is the subject, with no space for anything beyond that. But if you shoot intimate landscapes, or more two-dimensional shots, you may find you can start to pay attention to your background. In these cases you should make sure it doesn't distract from the subject (see "the art of alignment" below).

Foreground

Foregrounds are often critical in landscape photography. This is the area of the image that starts at the photographer's feet and leads the viewer into the shot, towards the mid-ground. It can be a fine balance to create an engaging foreground that introduces the shot, but doesn't overwhelm it.

Below:
The whole image forms the subject in this shot, but there is a focal point (where the eye settles) in the valley. The trees framing the shot form the foreground. The background is less certain, but you could argue the sky and the distant mountains form a background. Equally, you could say there is no background because the whole image forms the subject and there is no space for a true background. Bormio, Italy. *iPhone 6S.*

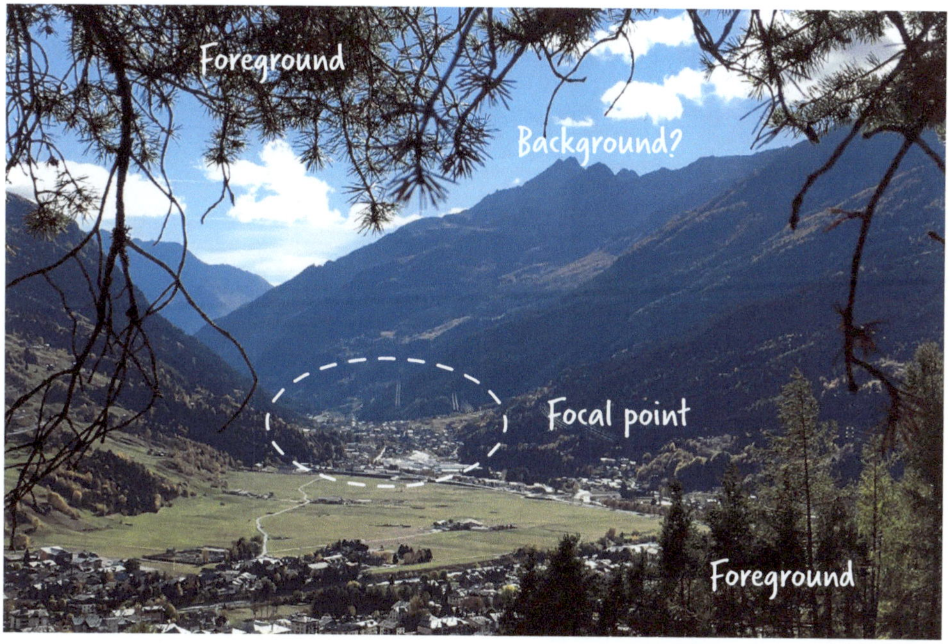

4. The eye's journey through the frame

Nothing in an epic landscape photograph happens by accident. The photographer thought carefully about the placement of every single element within the frame. It gets easier the more you try it and you find that you can decide where to stand more quickly – but, to start with, it is an objective, careful exercise in graphic design.

With a good composition you are aiming to take your viewer by the hand and guide them through your image. You need to take control of their eye's journey through your frame – don't leave it to chance. This might sound contrived, but when you strip back photographic composition to its bare bones, this is what you find: the photographer taking control of the image and giving the viewer subconscious cues as to where to go next.

As you are weighing up your choice of viewpoint, you should ask yourself four questions:

1. Where does the eye go first?
2. Where will it settle?
3. How does it get there?
4. What happens after it has arrived?

Take the shots below and opposite as an example. In the first shot your eye goes straight to the horizon. That's all three questions answered in a single step (marked 1,2,3). Your eye might stay there, or it might come forward and have a look at the patches of light (marked 4), before going back and forth between those and the horizon. But it never really travels very far around the frame:

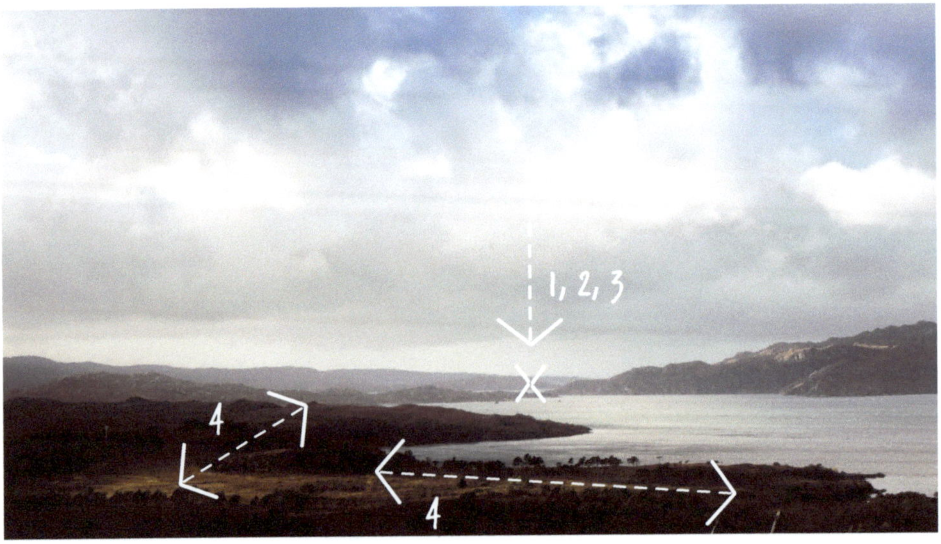

But with the second shot you are introduced to the image much more slowly and this makes it a more engaging, interesting shot. There is more for the viewer to unpack. If the first image were a book the whole plot would be set out on the first page. With the second shot you'd have to keep reading to find out what happens:

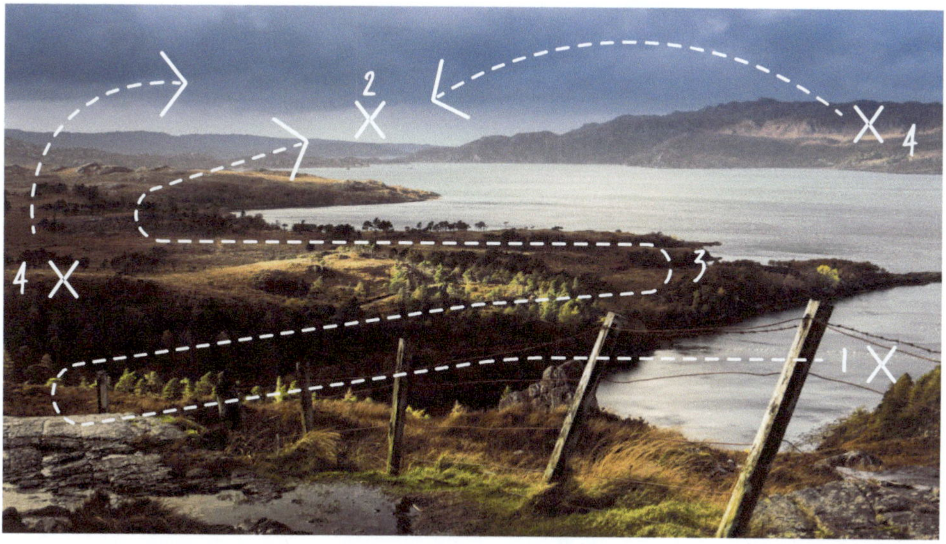

How to guide your viewer's eye through the frame

1. *Where does the eye go first?*

If you want it to step gently into the frame instead of running straight to the back, you need to give it something to latch on to.

2. *Where will it settle?*

Every image should (usually) have a single focal point. This is the eye's destination. If you have more than one, the eye will not settle – it will keep jumping between them. If you choose not to have a single focal point, be deliberate about it, and recognise you will be creating a more unsettled image.

3. *How does it get there?*

You use simple cues within the image to nudge your viewer through the frame. And importantly, you avoid distracting them on the way (more on this later in this chapter). Footpaths and roads are obvious route markers, but the shape of the landscape, a shadow, or anything with an edge can be used to help the viewer travel onwards.

4. *What happens after the eye arrives?*

Is there something else competing for the viewer's attention? Does the viewer go back to the beginning and start again? Can you offer a balancing element that doesn't distract from the focal point but adds something of interest to the shot? (A balancing element is a kind of "supporting act". It is something that adds support and context, a counterweight to the focal point, but without competing.)

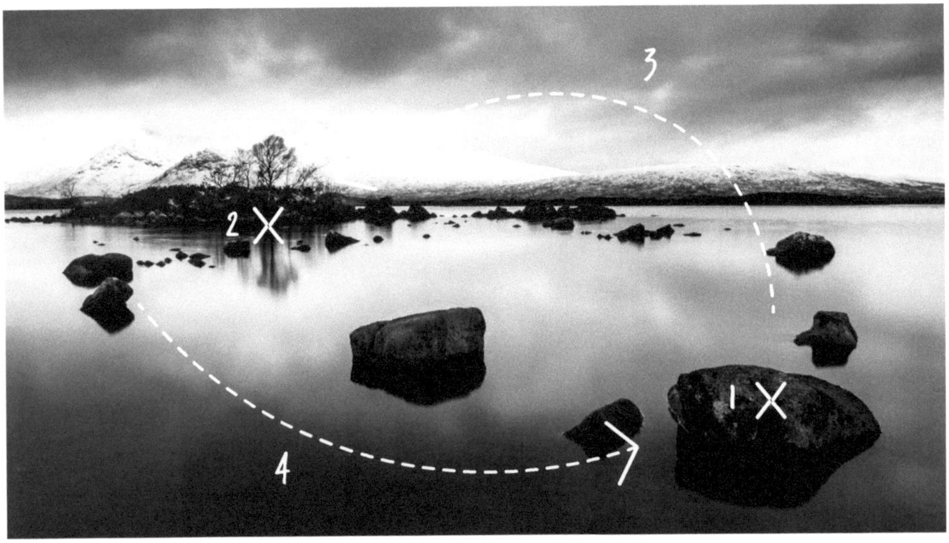

Above:
Lochan na h-Achlaise.
X-T1, 18mm, ISO200, f22, 1.5 secs.

In this shot on Rannoch Moor (above) there is a literal stepping stone to help the viewer into the frame. The focal point is clearly delineated by being the only living thing in the shot, silhouetted against the background. There is nothing to compete with it. There are a helpful set of stones to take the viewer from the foreground to the focal point and then another set to bring them back to the start. Notice how your eye continues to circle the image, occasionally taking a diversion to look for a detail, but always coming back to the trees.

Contrast the shot of Buttermere on the following page. Here there is a very strong leading line taking the viewer into the shot and leaving them at the focal point. But what happens next is less certain. I find myself simply scanning left and right along the line of the mountains. It's a nice enough shot, but compositionally it is split into two definite halves which makes it less strong.

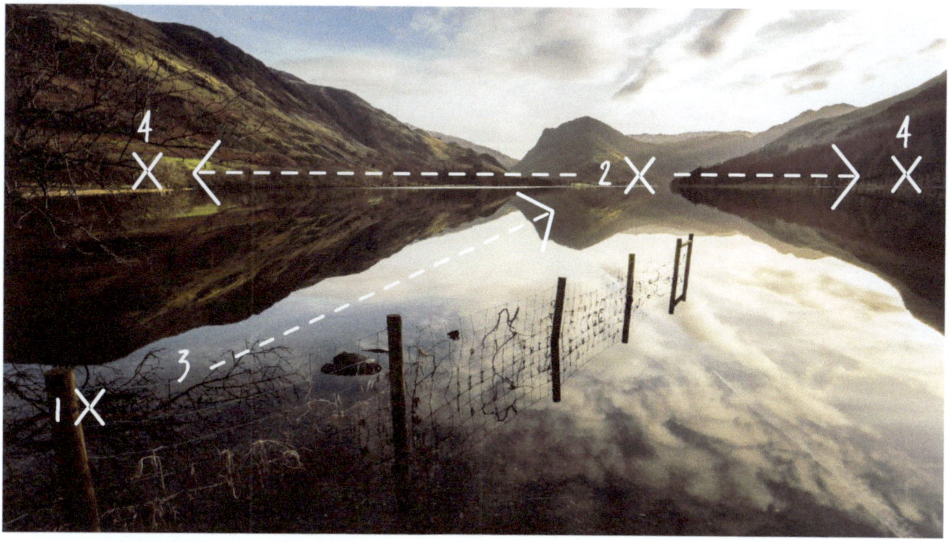

Above:
Buttermere.
6D, 11-24mm at 16mm, ISO100, f22, 1/15th.

5. How to stop your viewer wandering off

Building a strong composition is more than just helping the viewer through the image in a positive way. You also need to avoid distracting them. We've already mentioned not having a competing focal point, but there are a few other pitfalls that can suck their attention and you should aim to exclude them from your landscape photography at all costs – by moving or waiting.

The things to avoid listed below all draw the viewer's attention because they have what is known as a lot of "visual weight" (anything that draws the eye). You usually want your focal point to have the most visual weight, with everything else playing a supporting role only in the overall composition. This list is not exhaustive, but outlines the most common distractions that a beginner landscape photographer accidentally includes in their photograph.

Black holes

Remember dynamic range? The fact that your eye can see a wider range of tones than your camera? This has implications when it comes to unintended distractions. As you look at a scene that includes both shadows and highlights, your eye will pick out details in both. But when the camera takes the shot, you often find that all the shadow detail has disappeared, leaving only large areas of darkness – "black holes". These black holes suck the viewer in, adding nothing to the image.

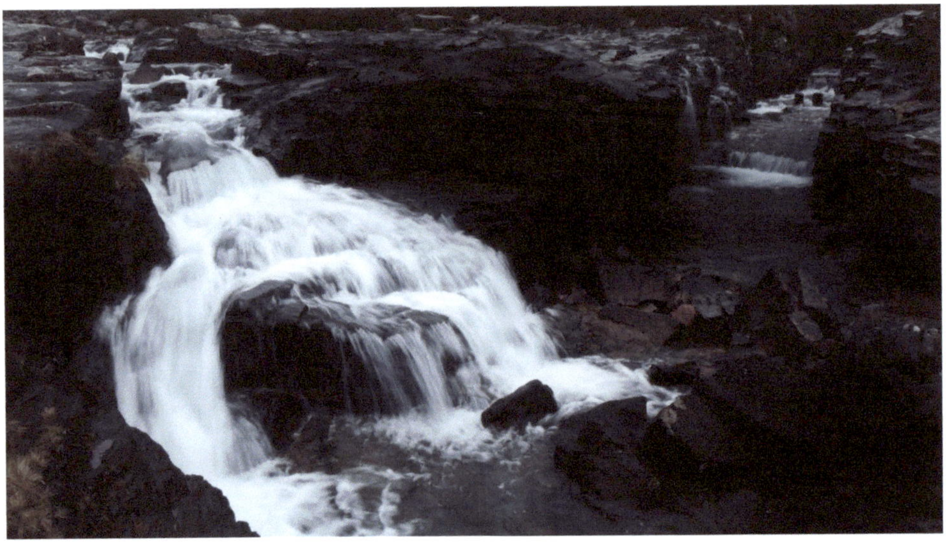

Above:
Glen Coe
X-T1, 18-135mm at 18mm, ISO200, f22, 1/10th.

This shot of a waterfall has four areas of distracting black holes that pull the attention. The eye is attracted to them because it needs something to hold on to - it wants to search through the shadow and see if there is any detail at all.

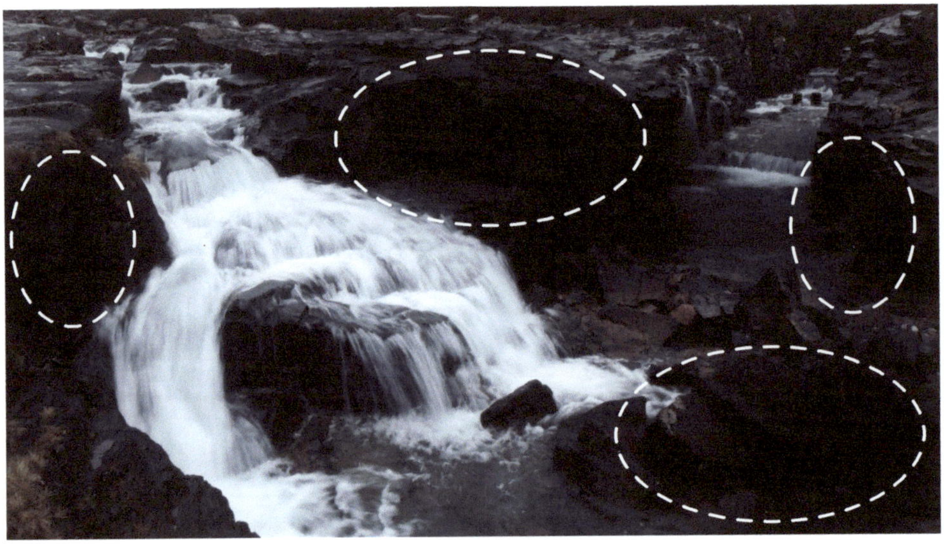

High graphic contrast: bright lights and red stuff

Anything that has a high contrast will jump out and draw the viewer's attention. The most common instances are something white against a dark background or something sharply in focus when all around it is blurred. Be aware that anything red, no matter how small in the frame, will have a disproportionate amount of visual weight in any shot. Red draws the eye at the expense of everything else in the image.

In this shot, York Minster with the western facades caught by the setting sun, should be the undisputed focal point. But your eye is continually drawn down to the red car and the red clothes in the bottom right. The pedestrian in the white T-shirt bottom left also draws the eye because of the high contrast against the dark background.

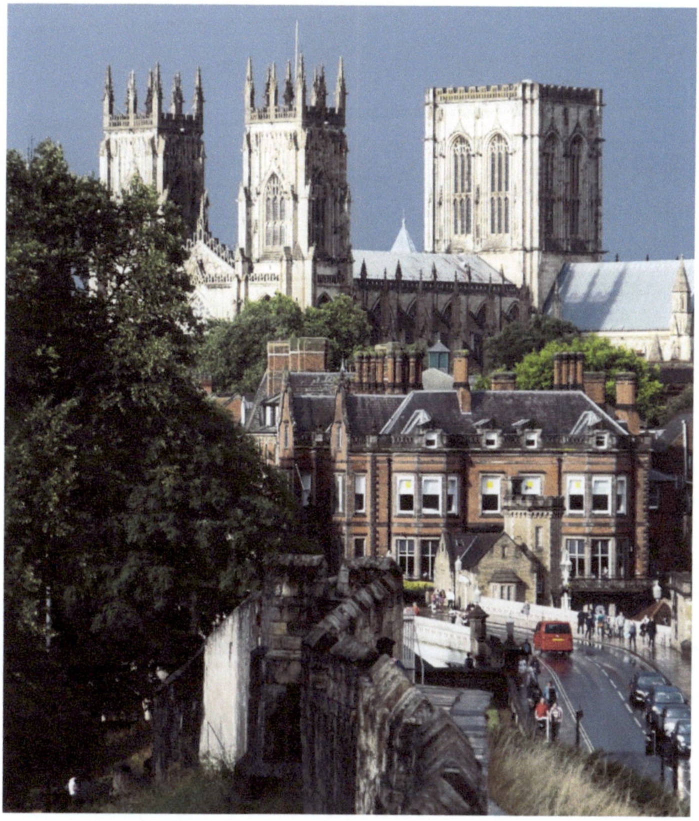

Left:
York Minster
X-T1, 18-135mm at 78mm, ISO200, f5.3, 1/240th.

People and faces, even things that just look like people or faces

Any hint of a person will draw the eye immediately. It doesn't have to be as obvious as the person in the shot below – even a rock or a cloud that looks a bit like a face will act like a magnet to the human eye.

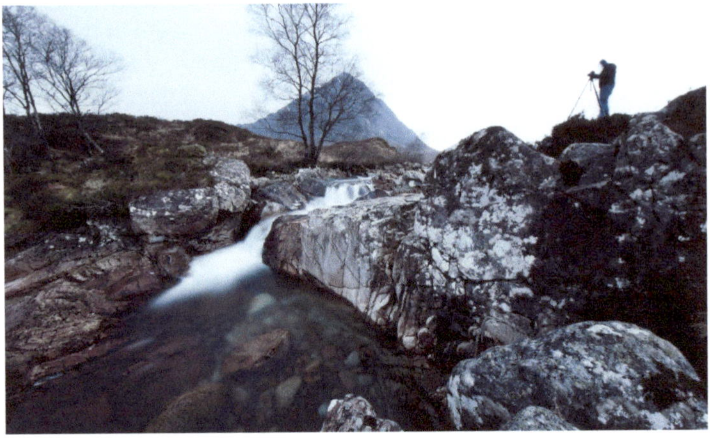

Right:
Buachaille Etive Mor.
6D, 11-24mm at 11mm, ISO200, f22, 20 secs.

Text

Any letters, numbers or symbols, whatever language they are in, will attract attention. We just have to try and read what's been written down. And even once we've read it, it's still in the corner of our eye. Try and avoid having any text or signposts in your landscape shots.

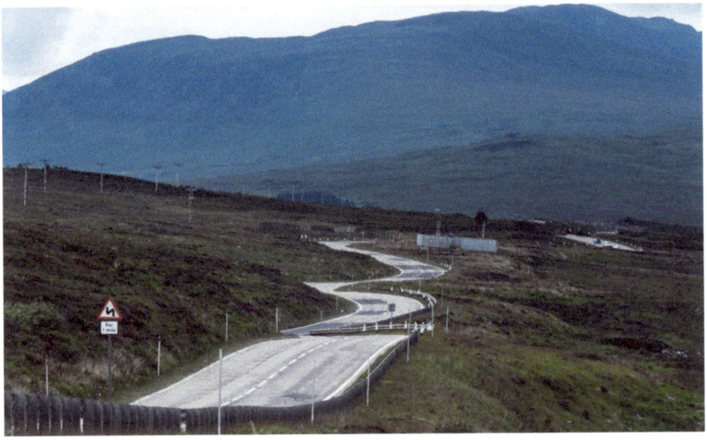

Right:
The A835 next to Loch Glascarnoch.
X-T1, 50-140mm at 140mm, ISO200, f8, 1/90th.

Incongruence

Incongruity is simply abstract contrast – something in shot that draws attention by virtue of the contrast it has to the rest of the image. The most common incongruities for landscape photographers are traffic in wilderness areas or wildlife in urban ones.

Below: a classic shot of Glen Coe spoilt by the car. Roads through landscapes seem reasonably in-keeping, but add any traffic and it starts to jar. And in the following shot, any sign of human thoughtlessness spoils a peaceful village scene.

Below, top:
Glen Coe
X-T1, 14mm, ISO200, f11, 1/80th.
Below, bottome:
John O'Groats
X-T1, 50-140mm at 140mm, ISO200, f8, 1/180th.

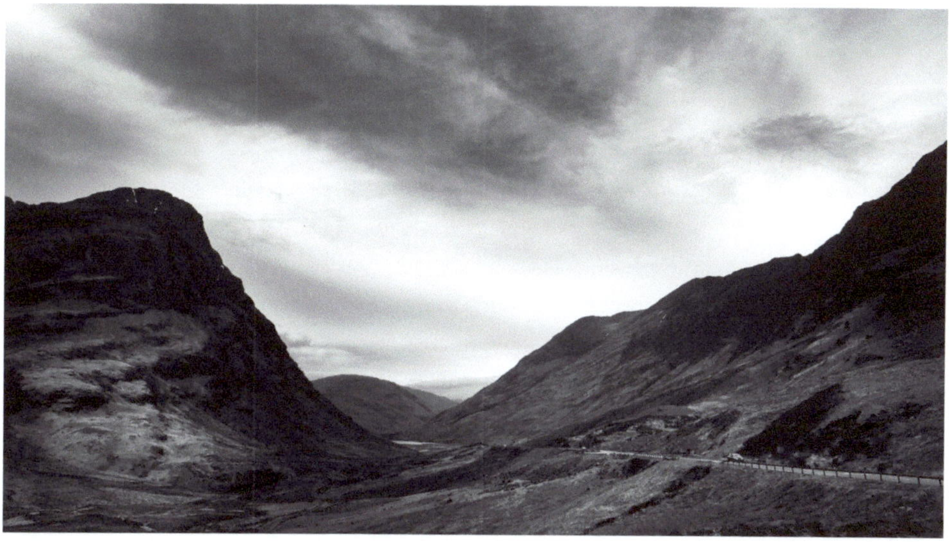

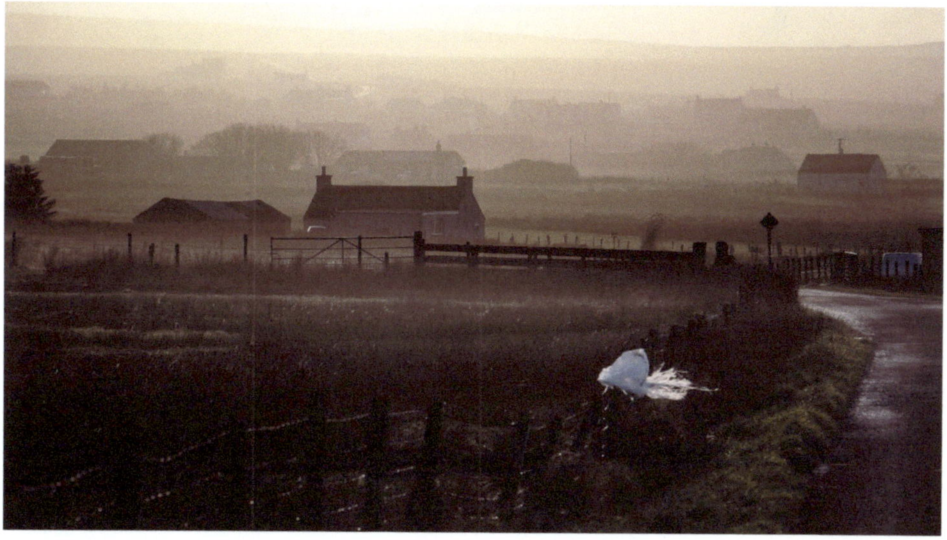

6. The art of alignment

The most epic landscape shots will be clinically planned. A photographer might visit the same spot over and over again until they have isolated the viewpoint they want, at the time of day they want, with the direction and quality of light that they want. They will be continually looking at every separate element in the frame and checking how it lines up with everything else. What is touching what? What needs more breathing space? Is everything lined up in a pleasing way?

The art of alignment in photographic composition is an exercise in precision and patience. You will be tempted to take a "good enough" shot from time to time and there's no shame in that. But to create your best work you need to scrutinise every single thing in your shot and decide if it would be a better shot if you moved slightly. This is easier in warm weather, after a good night's sleep and a hot lunch. It takes some grit to keep trying alternative viewpoints when you've been up since 4am, your socks are wet, your feet are cold, you can't feel your fingers and you ate your last bag of snacks three hours ago. This is why landscape photography is such hard work. And why, when you finally nail that shot, it is so much more satisfying than any other genre of photography.

The shots that follow all demonstrate how tiny movements in camera position can have a disproportionately large effect on the alignment of elements in the final image. As you are composing your shot you need to continually and dispassionately examine where every element of the image rests in the frame and whether or not it is touching or overlapping anything else in the shot. And if it is, would it be a better composition if you moved? And, if you do decide to move, you then need to check everything again. I never said it would be easy.

Combining background and foreground

Here's a textbook example of poor alignment to get us started (opposite, top). When any element in a shot overlaps with any other element, the two become a single unit. If the two things are from the same category – two trees for example – it *might* not matter. But when they are unrelated like our cow and pole example, if the two elements have no similarities to each other, and it wasn't done deliberately, then it can make a very poor shot.

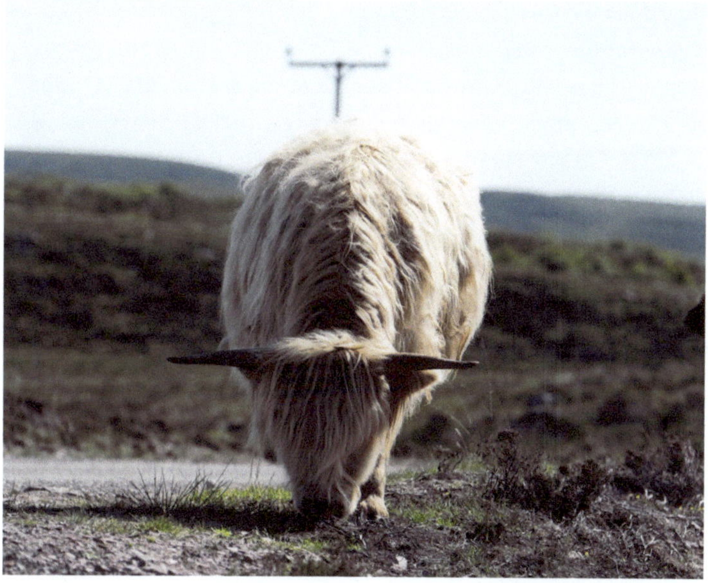

Left:
Highland cow north of Applecross.
X-T1, 50-140mm at 100mm, ISO200, f3.2, 1/1500th.

Avoid this by scrupulously scanning the edge of your viewfinder before you press the shutter. Your brain is very good at filtering what you see and you need to consciously override its tendency to prioritise the subject or the foreground over the rest of the shot.

What's leaving the frame?

Watch what is going on at the very edge of your frame. Is something touching the edge or leaving the frame that shouldn't be? Would the composition be stronger with more breathing space around the edges?

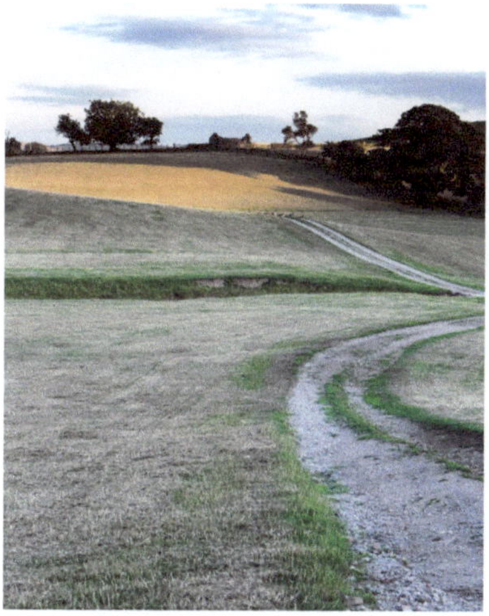

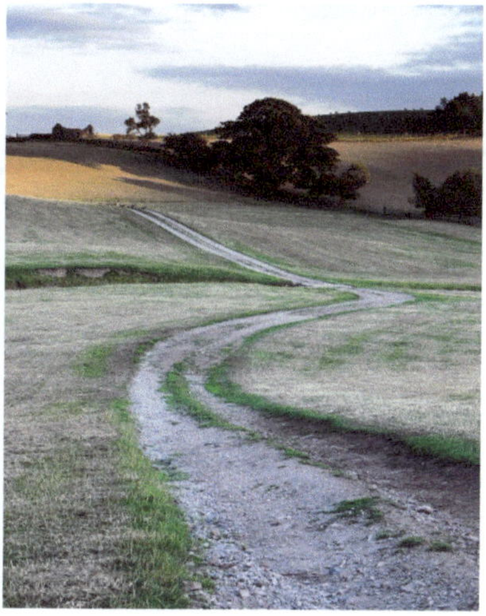

Below, left:
This track leaving the shot interrupts the eye's journey through the frame. Yorkshire Dales.
iPhone 6S

Below, right:
Ensuring the track is all safely in the shot permits a smooth journey up the image to the focal point on the horizon
iPhone 6S.

How does the foreground overlap?

If your foreground overlaps with your subject (rather than being simply a stepping stone into the shot at the bottom of the frame) consider carefully how it sits graphically with the finished image.

The two images below were shot from virtually the same place. In the second I dropped my viewpoint and moved slightly to my right, to allow the flowers to take a more prominent role in the shot. The flowers in the second shot form a more triangular, dynamic shape in the bottom left of the frame, breaking up the very linear left-to-right composition of the original image.

Below:
Roseberry Topping from Clay Bank.
X-T1, 50-140mm at 95mm, ISO200, f22, 1/70th.

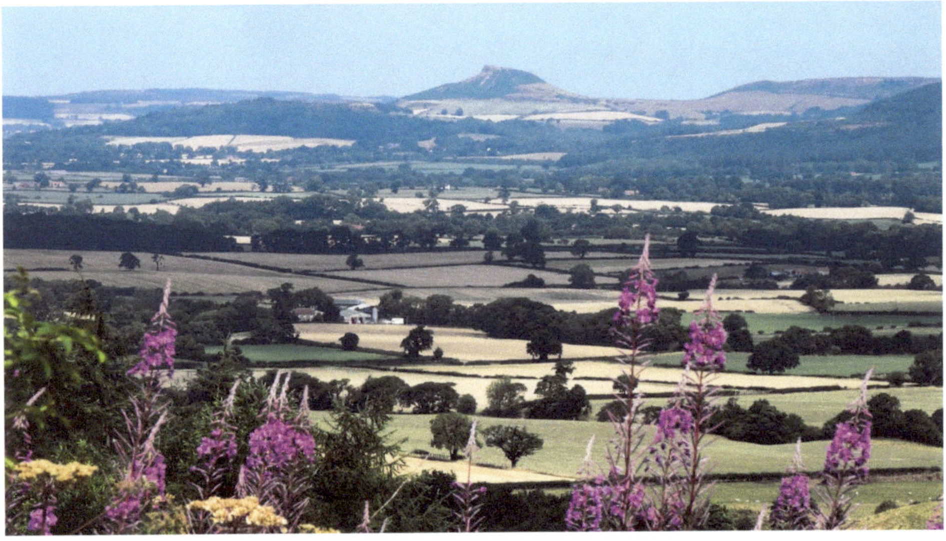

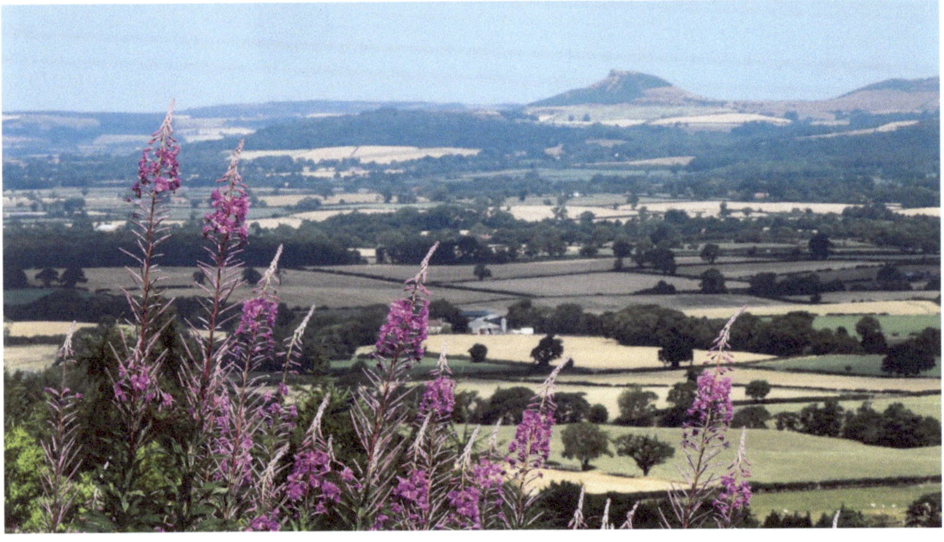

Losing the subject in the background

Just as the foreground overlaps with the subject/background, so the subject itself may overlap with whatever is behind it.

In the first shot below, the tree is lost to the similar-toned background. A better alignment would be the second shot, where the tree is shown clearly against the lighter sky:

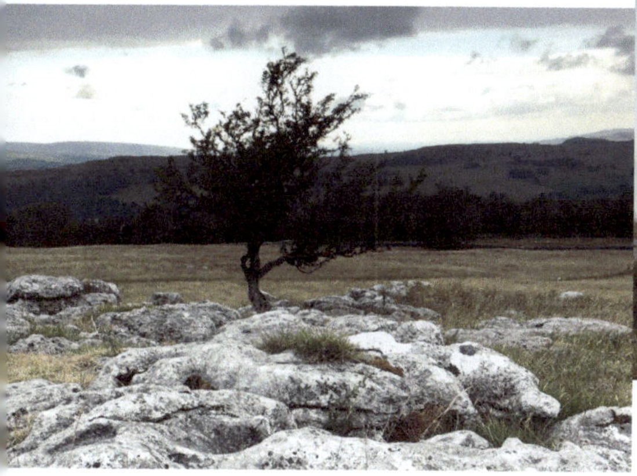

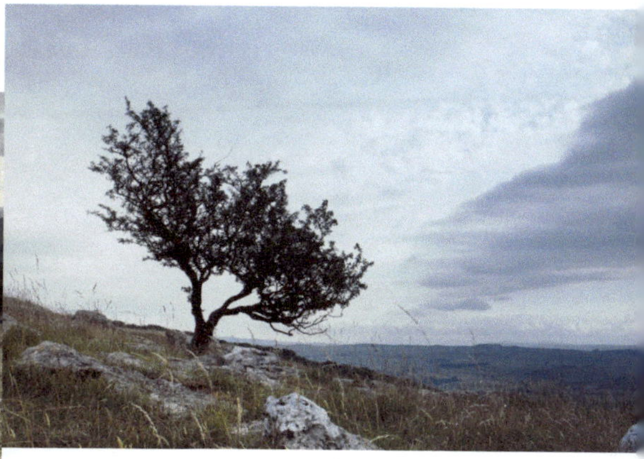

Above left:
Limestone pavement, Northumberland.
iPhone 6S

Above right:
5DIV, 50mm, ISO100, f16, 1/160th

Can you make a stronger composition just by moving?

Take your shot and review it objectively. What would happen if you moved, even slightly?

In the shots below, by moving closer to the sticks so that they take up more space in the frame and extend into the sky, I was able to make the composition stronger and more eyecatching:

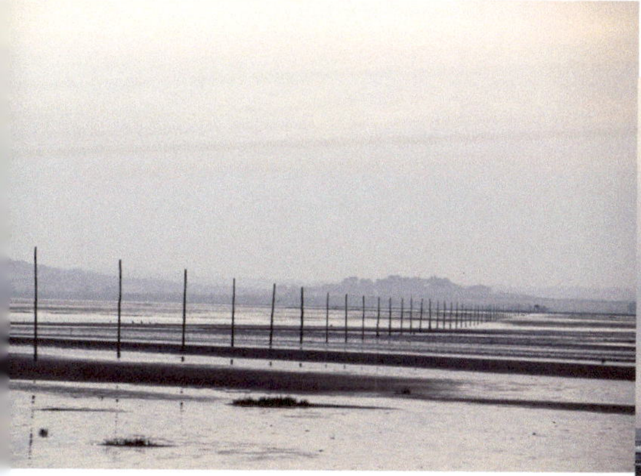

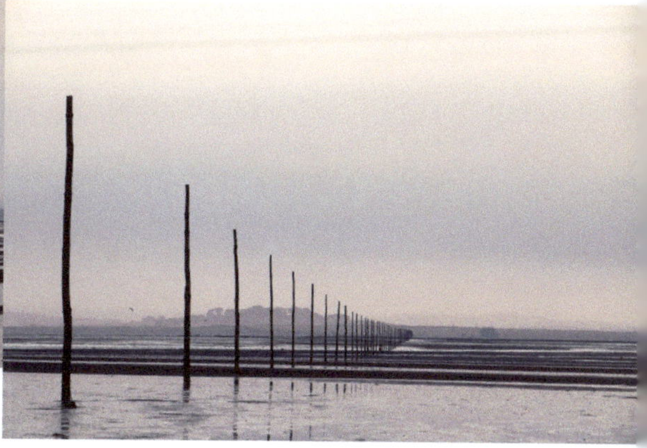

Below left and right:
Lindisfarne causeway.
X-T1, 50-140mm at 140mm, ISO200, f8, 1/950th.

TRY THIS

Find some professional landscape photographs. The Landscape Photographer of the Year website "Previous Winners" pages are a good place to start. Pay attention to where your eye goes first when you look at a photograph.

- Where does your eye settle?
- How did it get there?
- Does it wander off again?
- Are there any distractions?
- Which elements overlap with which other elements?
- What's touching, and what has space to breathe?
- Can you work out how high above the ground the photographer placed their camera?

Now try the same exercise but with less polished landscape photos. Try looking on Instagram or 500px for classic landscape destinations like Buttermere, Bamburgh Castle, St Michael's Mount, the Lake Bled boardwalk, Giant's Causeway or Durdle Door. Search out the least popular images. What is it about the composition that lets these shots down? And how many distractions can you find?

SECTION 2: ADVANCED LANDSCAPE COMPOSITION

The ideas explored in this section will help lift your images from being simply snapshots. A truly epic shot will reach out and touch the viewer emotionally. The shot might trigger a memory – a hope, an anxiety, a fear, or it may bring peace. Or the viewer might simply be moved by the beauty of the photograph.

In the three types of advanced composition that follow there is no "right" or "wrong" way to do things. No one idea is better than another. One is not more clever or more sophisticated. They are just different – but it's important you know what options are available to you. Also, there's a degree of overlap between the concepts: you can have a flat, closed image for example, or a dynamic, open one.

1. Images with depth vs flat images

The classic landscape shot will be overflowing with depth. Think of the covers of outdoor photography magazines – bold foregrounds with visual cues taking you all the way through the image to the horizon. But there is plenty of space for quieter images in the landscape genre. Photographers such as Michael Kenna are known for their sparse, two-dimensional shots that lack depth but are graphically engaging.

Start to pay a bit of attention to the style of landscape photography you are drawn to. Remember, you don't need to pursue a particular style just because it seems to be the "right" way to do landscape photography.

Below:
An image with depth: the shot starts at your feet and carries on all the way to the horizon.
The Stacks of Duncansby.
6D, 11-24mm at 11mm, ISO100, f8, 1/125th.

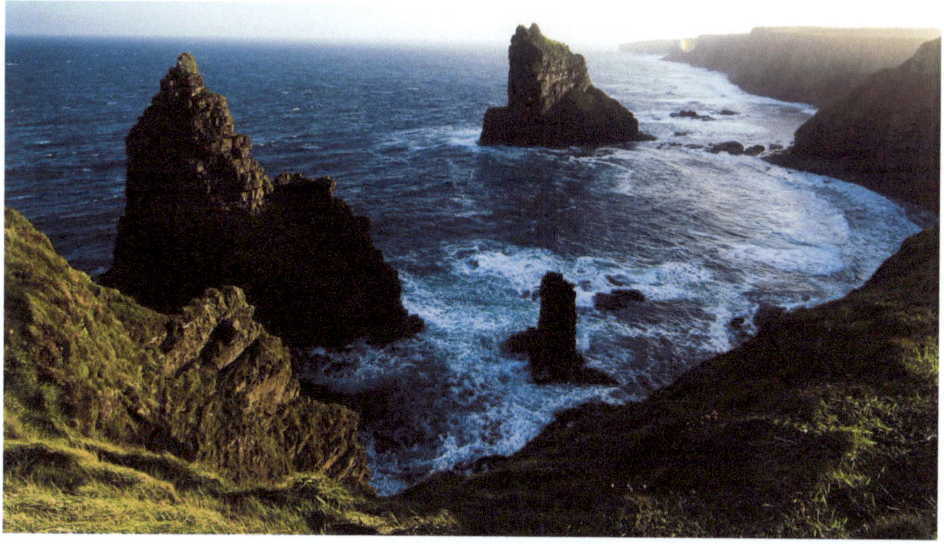

Right :
A flat image: there is minimal depth in this two-dimensional graphic shot.
Hemsedal.
iPhone 5S.

2. Static vs. dynamic images

If most of the lines in an image (actual lines or implied lines) are vertical or horizontal, it is said to have a static composition – one that is calm and still. If most of the lines are diagonal, it is a dynamic composition – one with more energy and movement.

Static compositions tend to be predictable. Dynamic compositions add a splash of tension. Don't forget – neither is "better" than the other; which style you pick will depend on the kind of mood you want to convey.

Dynamic images
Below left:
Lillehammer.
X-T1, 14mm, ISO200, f22, 1/340th, handheld.
Below right:
The Gap of Dunloe.
X-T1, 50-140mm at 55mm, ISO200, f2.8, 1/400th, handheld.

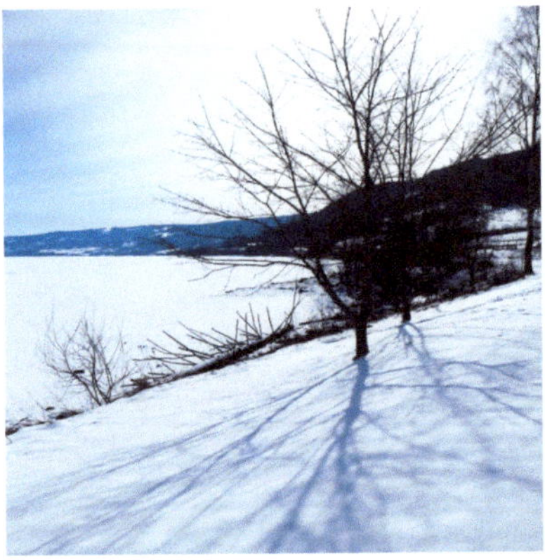

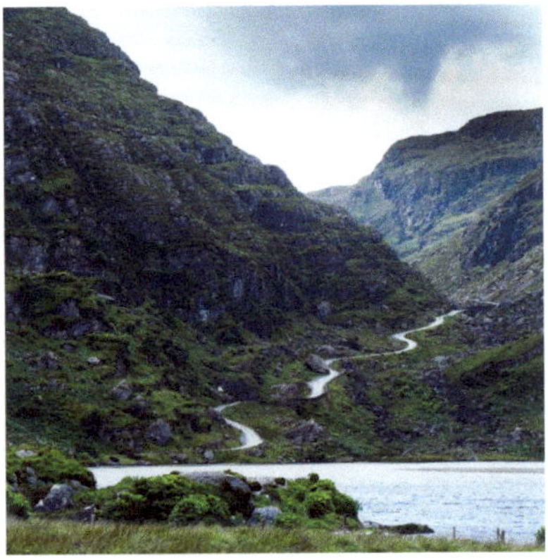

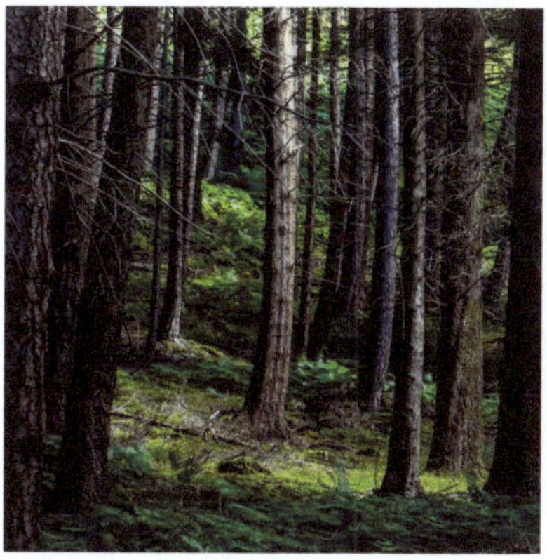

3. Closed vs. open images

A closed composition is where an image is neatly arranged within the frame. It usually has a clean subject positioned centrally or slightly to one side and it's clear straight away what is going on – there is no ambiguity. Closed images tend to be static, calm and complete.

In contrast, open compositions leave more room for the viewer to engage and explore the photograph. There will be no framing of the subject and the shot will not feel constrained by the boundaries of the image. Questions will remain unanswered in the image, and the viewer is invited to imagine the back story or the action going on out of shot.

If the image feels very stable and balanced, or like it could have been shot in a studio, or is more like a still life, then it is probably a closed composition. If it feels like it is window on the world, bursting out of the frame, it is probably an open composition.

Most landscape shots are open, but it is an interesting exercise to try and create a closed composition outdoors and an open one indoors.

Static images
Above left:
Glendalough.
X-T1, 50-140mm at 100mm, ISO200, f17, 1/10th.
Above right:
Seascape.
X-T1, 50-140mm at 140mm, ISO200, f22, 1/15th, handheld panned.

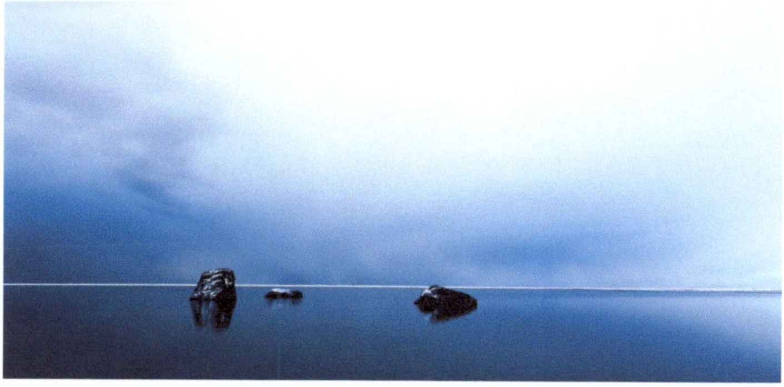

Left:
A closed image, Iceland.
6D, 11-24mm at 24mm, ISO100, f22, 1/5th second.

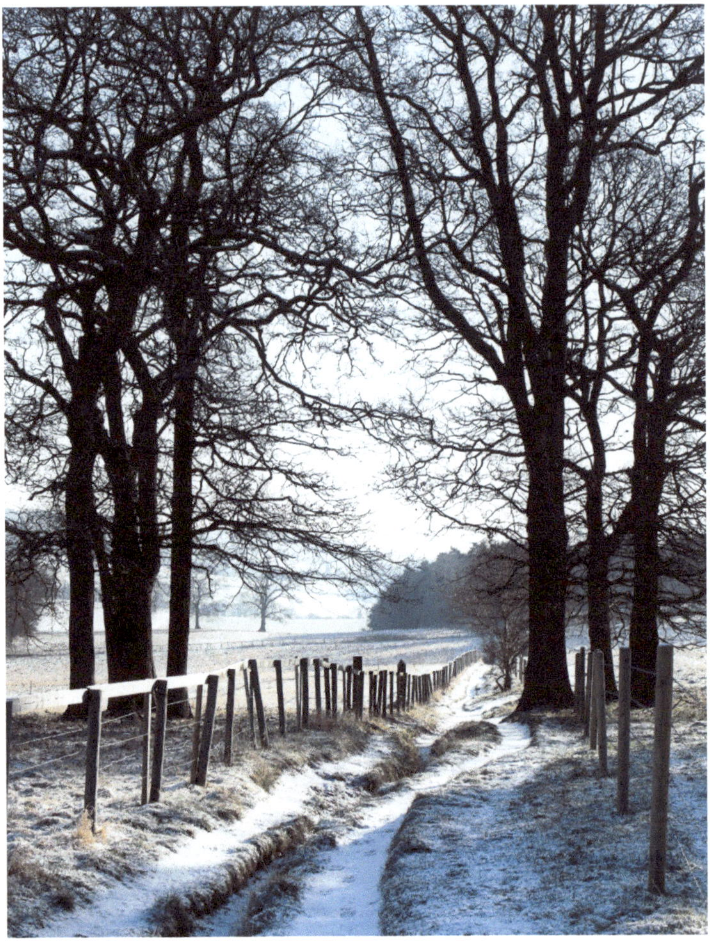

Right:
An open image, Newlands Corner.
5DIV, 50mm, ISO100, f11, 1/125th, handheld.
Below left:
A closed image, Derbyshire.
X-T1, 50-140mm at 140mm, ISO200, f4, 1/600th, handheld.
Below right:
An open image, the Langdale Valley.
5DIV, 11-24mm at 17mm, ISO100, f5, 1/80th.

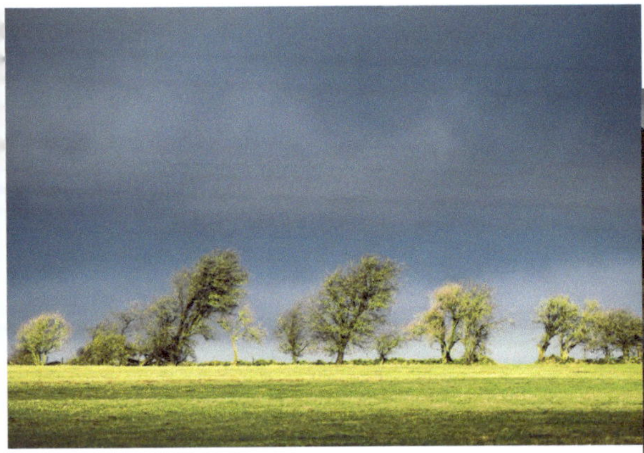

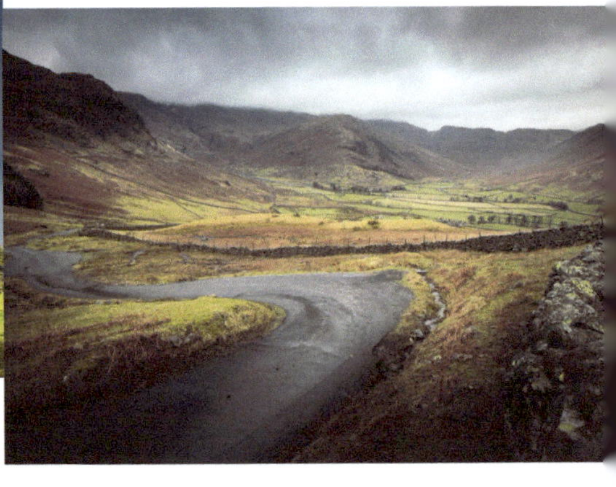

TRY THIS

Using tracing paper and a soft pencil, trace over the main elements of a few images – either your own or other peoples'. You can also do this exercise with famous landscape paintings (look online or search a museum's catalogue).

- Look at the tracing. How has the photographer or artist arranged everything in the frame?
- How precise have they been with every element in the frame – is it clear whether anything was accidental?
- How do the marks lead you through the frame?
- Is the image open or closed, static or dynamic, flat or with depth?

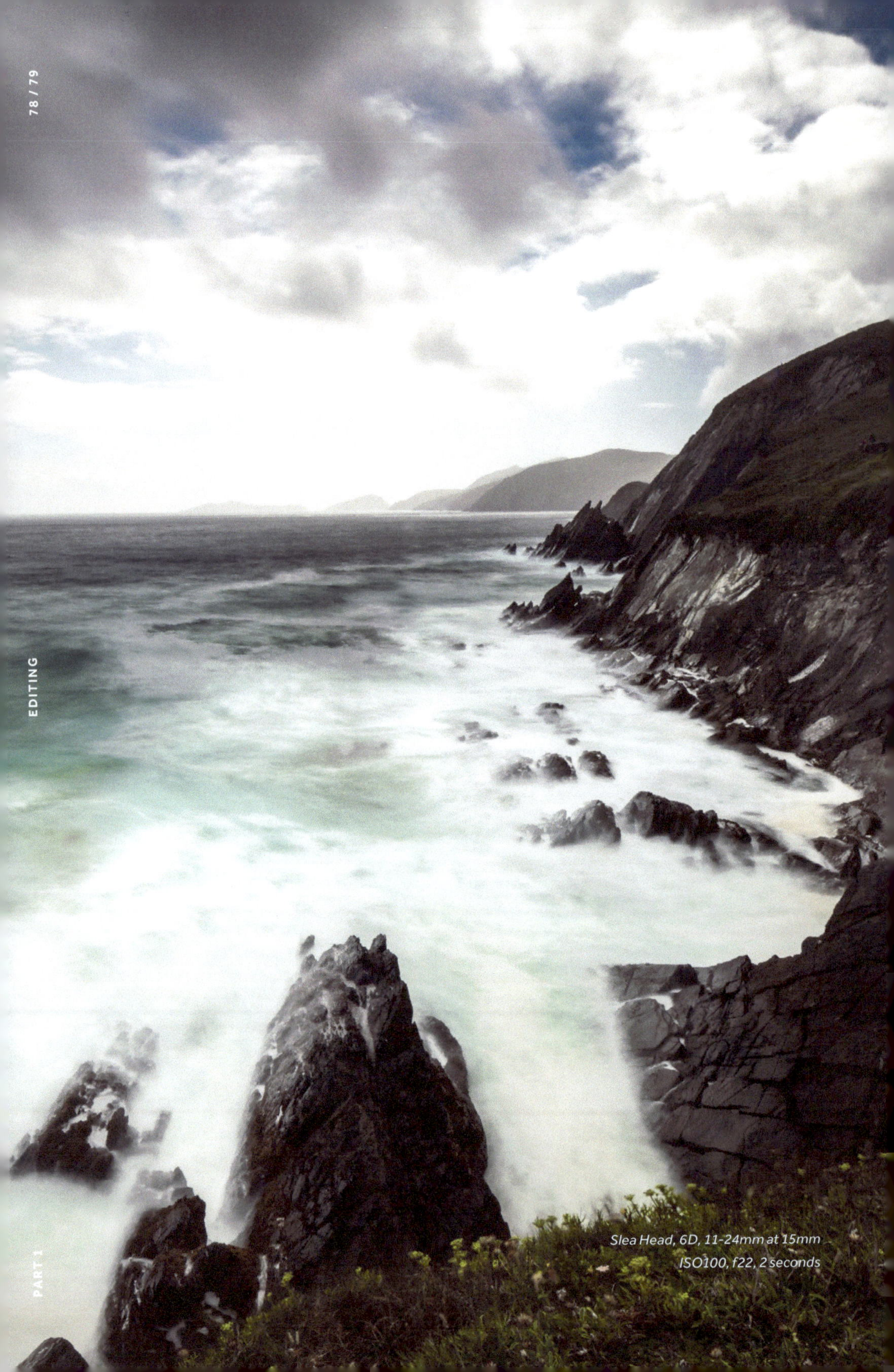

Slea Head, 6D, 11-24mm at 15mm
ISO100, f22, 2 seconds

6

EDITING

Editing a digital image is as much a part of the final photograph as it was when photographers shot film and printed their images in a darkroom. One of Ansel Adams' more famous quotes is, "The negative is the equivalent of the composer's score, and the print the performance." The same holds true for digital files: you use editing to create the performance you saw when you took the shot. On a different day, with a different performance, you can create something more dramatic, or with less contrast – the only limit is the line you personally will not cross (more on that later).

To take epic landscape shots you need to shoot RAW and you need to edit.

It's worth saying that by "edit' I don't mean "change". I'm not talking about cloning out telegraph poles, or creating a shot that wasn't there (although you *can* do either of these things in Photoshop). Editing for landscapes in my book means coaxing out of the digital file all the tonal relationships and contrasts that are there but hidden, in a way that realises your own vision for the shot.

In this book I can explain only the very basic principles of editing landscape shots. It is often easier to watch someone editing whilst they explain what they are doing. If you prefer to learn this way, keep an eye on EmmaDaviesPhotography.com/landscape-links for details of when my Lightroom for Landscape Photographers video course will run. Alternatively, a quick search on YouTube for the edit you want to make on your particular editing software will bring up plenty of examples. This chapter will explain what is possible, but I don't have the space to show you exactly how to make every edit on every piece of software.

RAW vs. JPEG

Your image goes through a few stages between you taking the photograph and you sharing the photograph. First the sensor records all the information about the light that hits it when you press the shutter release. The camera's computer saves this information – this is the RAW file.

Then the camera's computer processes the RAW file – it makes assumptions about the white balance, boosts the contrast and maybe the saturation, applies a bit of sharpening. It throws away all the information it doesn't need, compresses the file and saves this processed information as a new file, a JPEG.

Now, depending on how you have your settings configured, the camera will save just the JPEG (this is usually the default setting), save both the RAW and the JPEG, or just save the RAW. So when you download your photographs from your camera, you will be saving either just a JPEG file, both, or just a RAW file.

The downside of the JPEG file is that you can never get the information that the camera discarded back. You've just paid a fortune for a great camera, and now you are only using a third of its capacity. And with landscape photography in particular, you really need all that original information to solve the dynamic range issue described in Chapter 3 – Camera Controls.

With RAW files, you have three times the data to play with in post processing. You can make your own decisions about white balance, sharpening, exposure, contrast and saturation (instead of relying on the camera's preset JPEG settings). And you can do all this without degrading the photograph, which just isn't possible when you are starting with an already compressed and pre-processed JPEG file.

Your camera probably came with just JPEG set as the default file format. You will need to go into the settings and change it to shoot RAW, if that's what you want to do. Be warned that your file sizes will be larger, so your memory cards will fill up faster.

The first time you shoot RAW, be ready for very, very disappointing images straight out of camera. Don't forget, this is the file without all the camera's preset JPEG edits already made. But don't panic. You only need to make a couple of edits and you will have an image that is better than anything the camera could manage shooting JPEGs.

Below left:
Brough Bay, RAW file straight out of camera. In reality the stormy skies were much darker. *6D, 11-24mm at 18mm, ISO100, f8, 1/160th, handheld.*

Below right:
The same shot, with only tonal edits made: the dark tones were reduced significantly, and the light and highlight tones reduced slightly. The white point was adjusted.

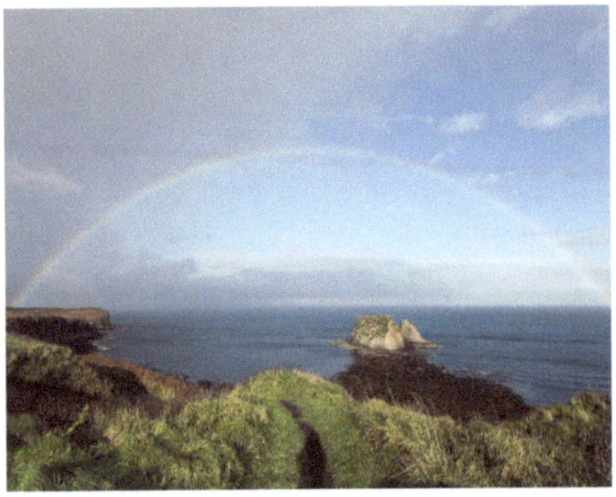

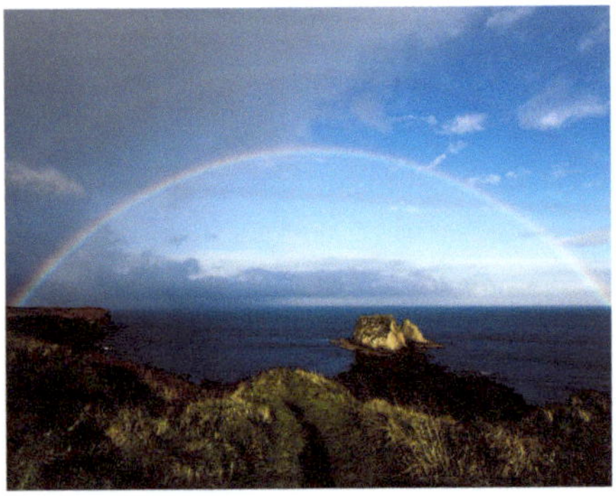

BASIC EDITS

I use Adobe Lightroom to edit my shots, but any software will be able to make the basic edits. Many people like to use Affinity as it is a robust editor which is available to purchase up-front instead of the subscription model that Adobe uses. Check your software has a RAW convertor before you buy and that your camera's RAW files are supported.

Cropping

The purists say you should compose in-camera, and never crop. I don't subscribe to that. I say if you want to crop, crop. Just be aware how much of the file you are cropping away, especially if you want to print your shot – it's easy to be left with a very small file size if you crop radically.

Tonal edits

Have a look at your histogram when you open up your file – if it falls short at either end you will find you have a low contrast image because no information has recorded in the extremes of light and dark of your shot. Can you see how the histogram below left, both at the black and the white ends, doesn't touch the limit of the scale at either end? This means there are no pure blacks and no pure whites in the shot. If there *should* be pure blacks and pure whites, you would correct your exposure (if you were still out shooting) or fix the tonal range in editing, until the histogram looked more like the one on the right:

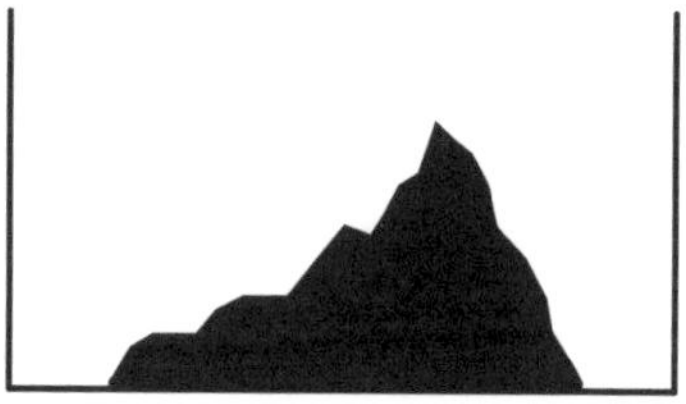

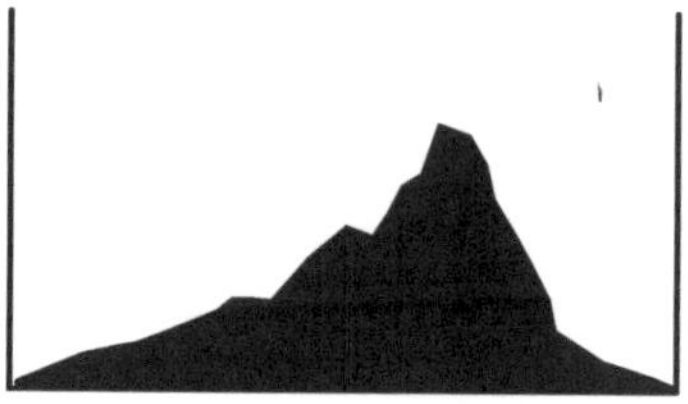

The benefit of using software like Adobe Lightroom is that you are able to do "local" adjustments rather than "global" adjustments. This means you can manipulate small areas of the shot instead of having to make a heavy-handed adjustment to the whole image. For example, with tonal edits you can brighten or darken the shadows, mid-tones and highlights separately. In the rainbow shot on the previous page, I was able to darken the shadows (dark tones) by a much higher proportion than the lights and highlights. And I was able to leave the midtones untouched. This was all achieved using the "curves" tool. Most intermediate level editing tools will have this tool and it is very easy to use. Drag the sliders or move the curve itself and see what happens to the tonal values of your shot.

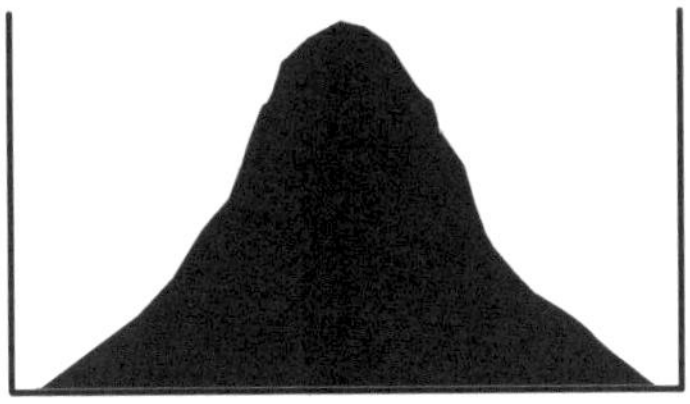

Below left:
This histogram would indicate a low contrast shot: the difference between the darks and the lights is relatively narrow.
Below right:
This histogram would indicate a higher contrast shot: there is a greater difference between the darks and the lights.

Sharpening

Sharpening an image is the process of increasing the apparent sharpness by increasing the contrast at the edges of the elements in your shot. All RAW images need a degree of sharpening but, if you shoot JPEGs, your camera will do it for you.

The ethics of editing

Everyone has a line they won't cross when it comes to post-processing. Mine is simply this: I imagine that my mother was with me when I took the shot. If I then showed her my edited image, would she be proud of my shot? Or would she be disappointed that I had used trickery? For example, I wouldn't take the star-trail sky out of one shot and put it behind a famous landmark in another shot. But I would increase the contrast in a stormy sky, bring out lost shadow detail or emphasise shafts of sunlight raking across the mountains.

What other people do or don't do, doesn't affect *your* photography. You can waste a lot of energy being angry that some people do very extreme post-processing, creating shots that bear little resemblance to the landscape in front of them when they pressed the shutter. You can't change the world on this one: better just to accept it and focus on your own work.

Competition entries

The line you will not cross doesn't mean anything when it comes to competitions. If you enter a shot for a competition, read the rules very, very carefully – it's their line that counts now, not yours. The more professional competitions will ask shortlisted entrants for the original RAW files so they can check whether any edits were within the rules, before they announce the winners. One thing to watch out for in particular is whether merged shots (HDR merges or focus stacking) is permitted.

Before and after

You can see below some of the before (on the left) and after (on the right) editing of shots used in this book. I shoot RAW so that I keep all the data available at the time I took the shot. Every single shot I publish, whether just on Instagram or in print, has been processed.

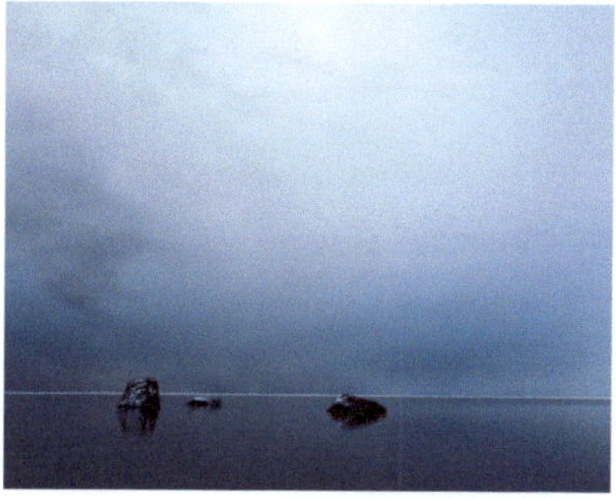
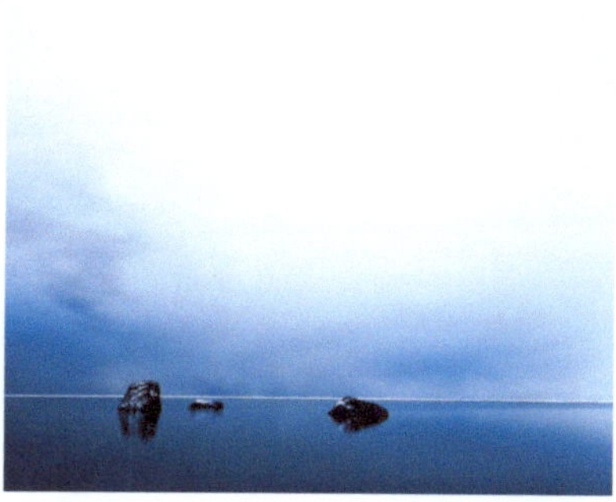
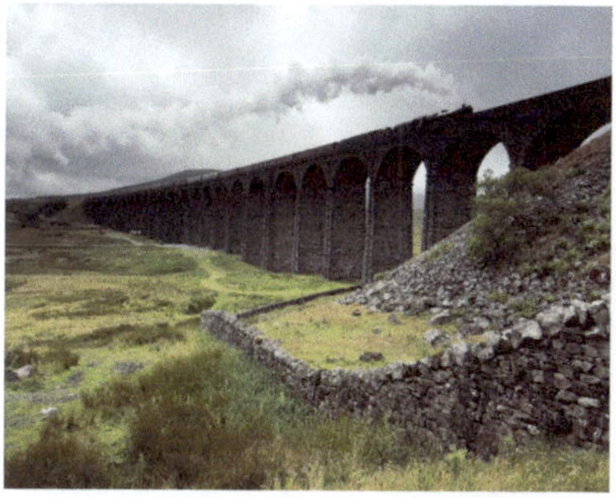
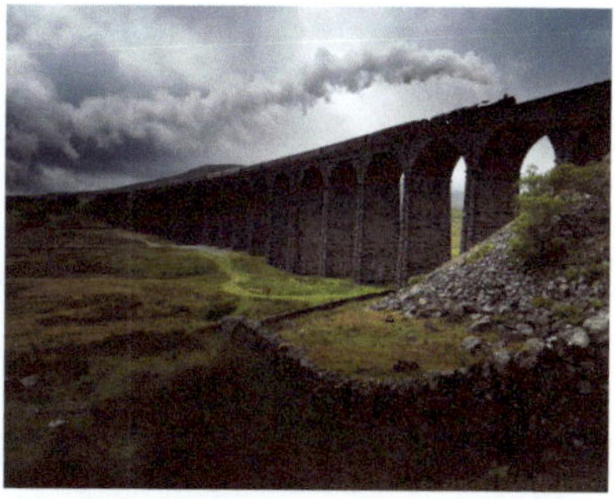
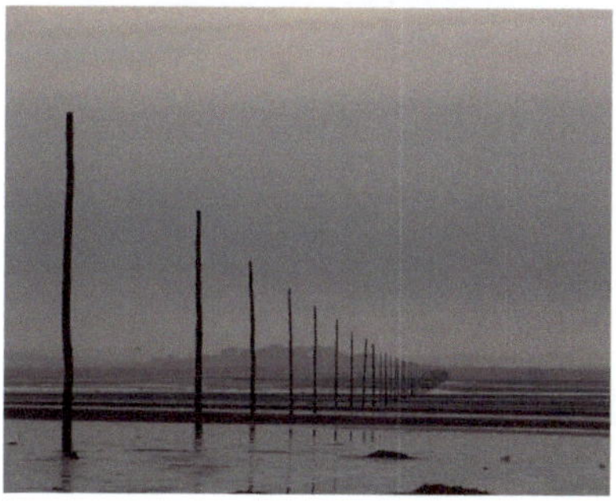
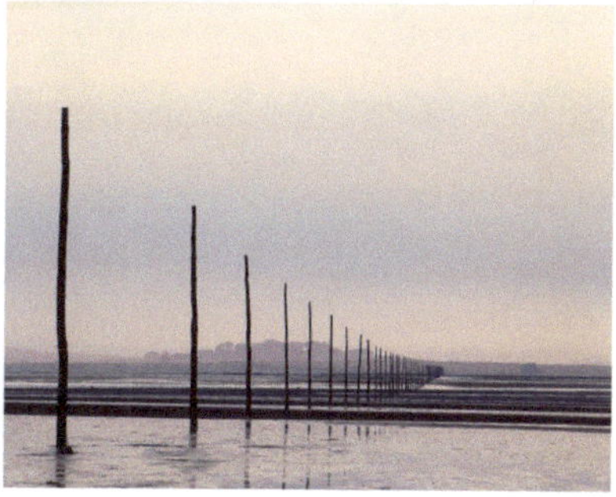

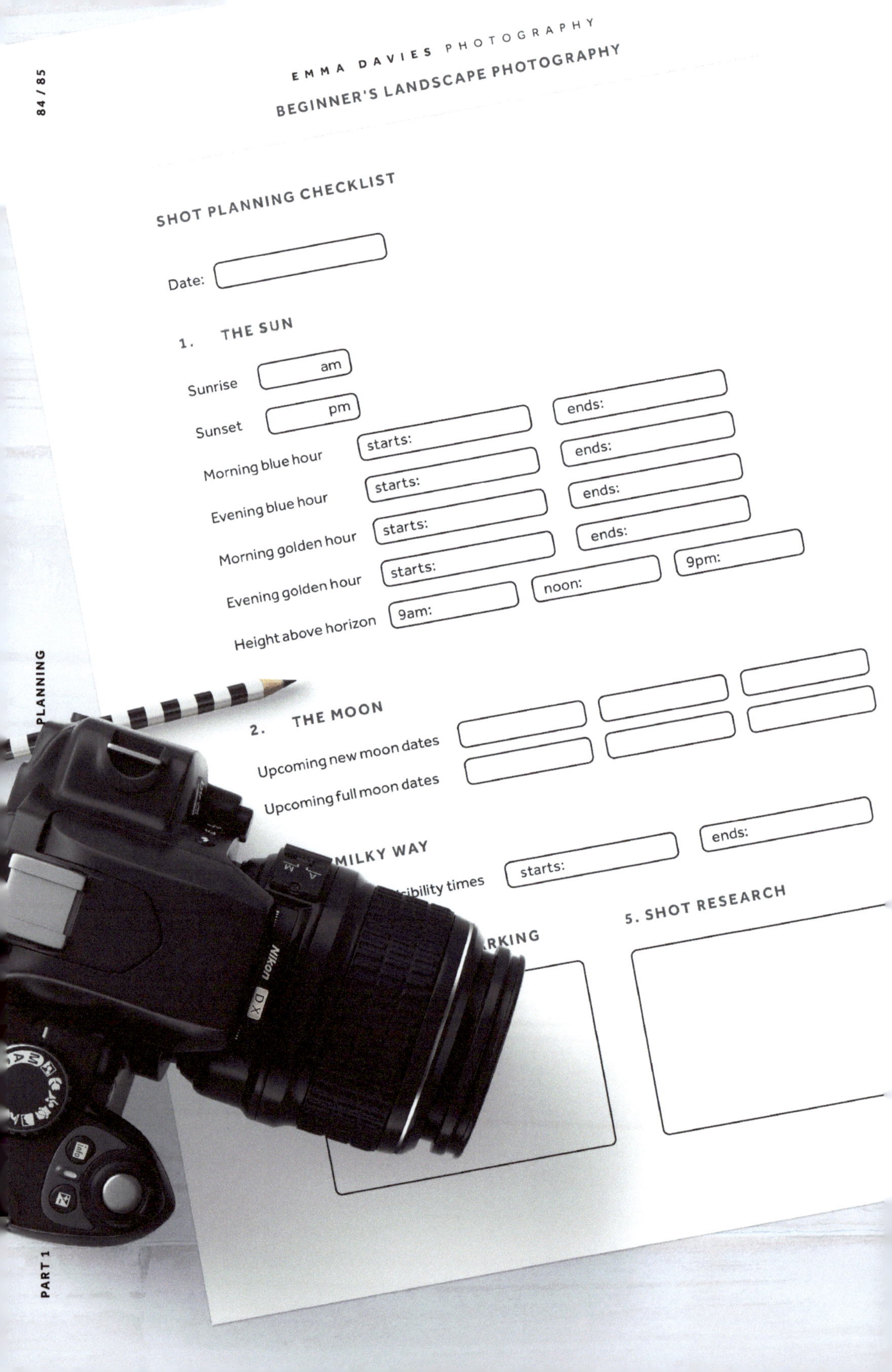

EMMA DAVIES PHOTOGRAPHY

BEGINNER'S LANDSCAPE PHOTOGRAPHY

SHOT PLANNING CHECKLIST

Date:

1. THE SUN

Sunrise am

Sunset pm

Morning blue hour starts: ends:

Evening blue hour starts: ends:

Morning golden hour starts: ends:

Evening golden hour starts: ends:

Height above horizon 9am: noon: 9pm:

2. THE MOON

Upcoming new moon dates

Upcoming full moon dates

MILKY WAY

...ibility times starts: ends:

...RKING

5. SHOT RESEARCH

7

PLANNING

At EmmaDaviesPhotography.com/landscape-links you'll find a downloadable pdf to help you plan your next shoot.

You can do a lot of research before you arrive at your shoot location, but I would always suggest scouting the area in person before the time you want to shoot to look for viewpoints and sightlines. You should expect to revisit a place three or four times at least before you know it well enough to take an epic shot.

The sun

During the day, the sun will be your light source. You need to know exactly how it will illuminate your landscape.

There are many things you can plan months or years ahead of your proposed shoot:

- Time of sunrise?
- Time of sunset?
- When does blue hour start/finish?
- When does golden hour start/finish?
- How high does the sun get above the horizon?
- Which direction will the light fall on the landscape at different times during the day?

Based on all your research you can work out (from your desk) at what time on what day the sun will be producing the kind of light you want for your shot.

For example, if you want a golden landscape you'll need a golden hour shoot. If the landscape you have in mind faces west, then you'll need an end-of-day golden hour so the sun's rays fall where you want them – if you turn up at dawn to a west-facing landscape, everything will be in the shade.

In the week leading up to your shoot you can start to check the cloud forecast. You'll remember from Chapter 4 that a clear sky is not always the best for landscape photographers. A flat, grey sky is probably not the most epic either. High clouds that catch the sun and provide interest are usually the best – but don't rule out stormy weather and other impressive cloud formations.

For night photography

If you want to shoot the stars (starscapes, star trails and the Milky Way) you will want a new moon (no visible moon) to avoid light pollution from the moon itself. This immediately reduces your options to only twelve nights each year of optimal night sky conditions; a few more if you are happy to shoot each side of a new moon.

If you want to shoot nightscapes lit by the moon, then you would opt for nights closer to a full moon.

The Milky Way

To shoot the Milky Way including its galactic core, some careful planning will be required. The core is visible only for about 7-8 months of the year and is always seen in a southerly direction. The months it is visible depends on your hemisphere: in the northern hemisphere you can see it from March to October, and in the southern hemisphere from February to October. Finally, it will only be visible all night during the middle of the viewing season. For the rest of the season you will only be able to see it either earlier in the night or later on, towards dawn, depending on your hemisphere.

So for an epic Milky Way shot, you'll need a time of year when it is visible, a time of night when it is above the horizon, a day during the month when you have a new moon, and a night of no cloud. And that's before you start planning your composition.

Transport and parking

How will you get there? How long will it take you to hike to your exact viewpoint, if needed? Where will you park? You can use Google Maps to find car parking spaces.

Shot research

Will you look at what other people have done in a particular location? Or will you turn up with no preconceived ideas? You can use sites like 500px and Instagram to search for images by location, but you do risk losing that "fresh eyes" perspective you get when you arrive at a place for the first time.

If Google Street View is available for your location, it enables you to get a three-dimensional viewpoint which is useful for seeing how distant objects will line up with your foreground.

If you plan your composition ahead of time, you can make sure you take the right kit with you.

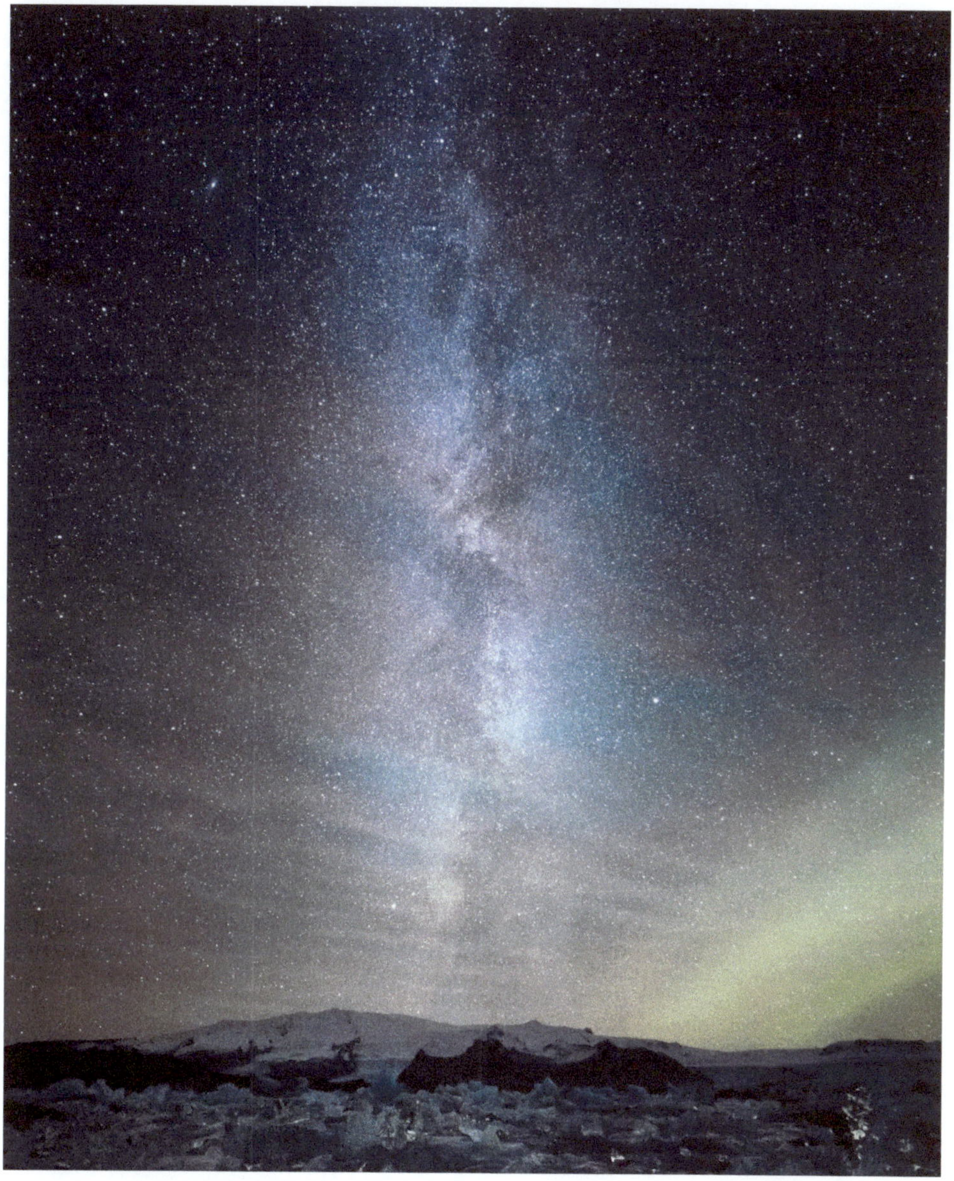

Above:
The Milky Way shot in Iceland at 10.30pm four days ahead of a new moon (waning crescent moon, 24%) with a small touch of aurora borealis in the bottom right corner.
5DIV, 11-24mm at 11mm, ISO6400, f4, 20 seconds.

Goals

The better you get at landscape photography, the fewer images you expect to come away with. One good shot per location is all I aim for. If you've done the planning, and the weather behaves as you expect it to, you can get the shot you want first time. Then you can spend some time reviewing your shot and making changes to viewpoint and exposure, for as long as the light lasts.

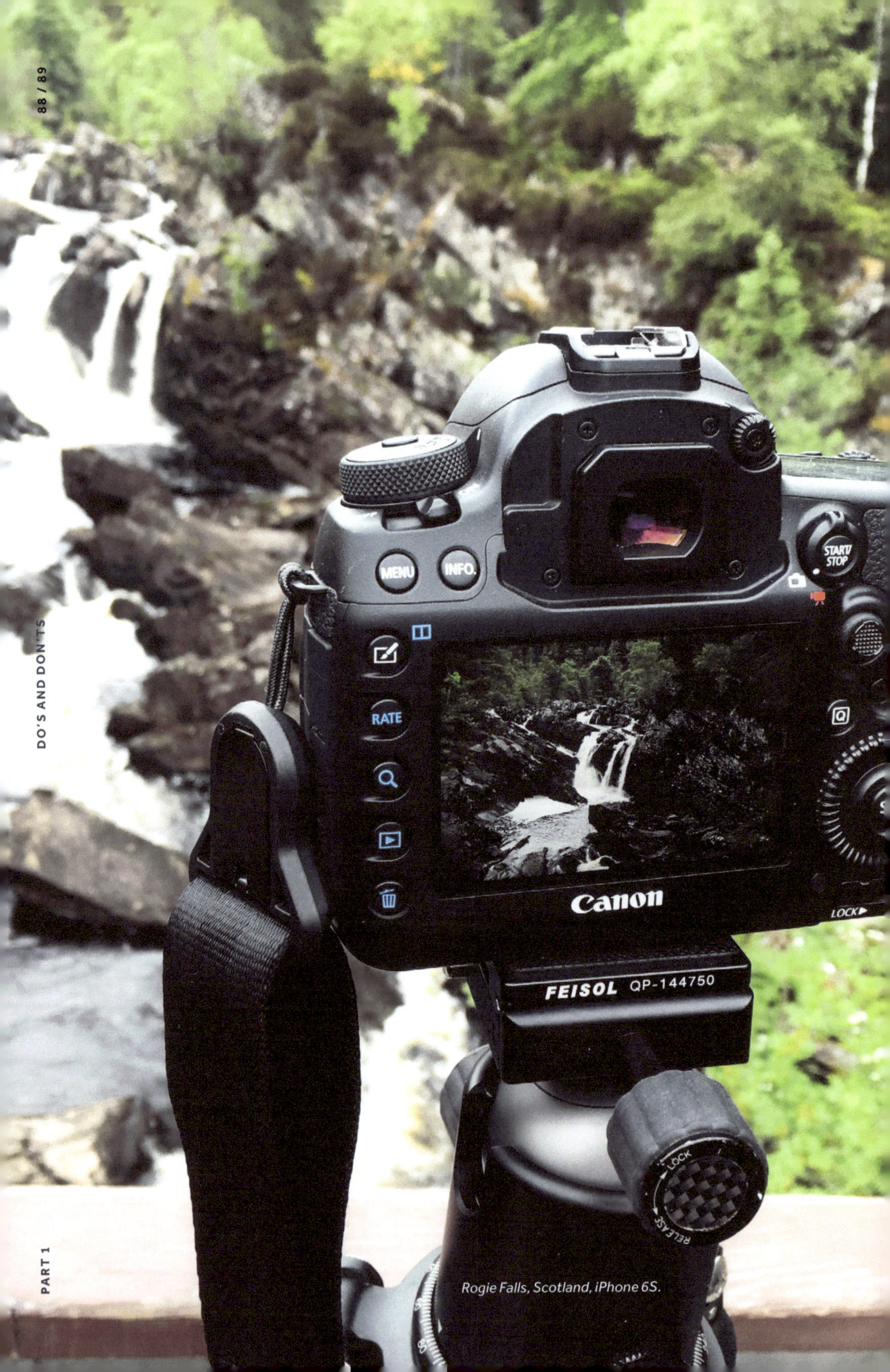

Rogie Falls, Scotland, iPhone 6S.

8

DO'S AND DON'TS

This short chapter is for beginners who have booked onto a landscape photography workshop and are worried they will stand out by doing something "wrong". In an ideal world, no one would judge anyone in situations like this, but I know how competitive groups of photographers can get and, if I can help you relax and enjoy the workshop, then I'd like to.

First, there are only a few truly "wrong" things you can do and I list these below. They are wrong because you risk damaging your kit or spoiling someone else's shot. But when it comes to things like what lens to use, or where to stand, then you can be confident in making your own creative choices (there is no right or wrong). Photography is not a science. There is no perfect shot. It is an art and, in the words of Ansel Adams, "You bring to the act of photography all the pictures you have seen, the books you have read, the music you have heard, the people you have loved." Your shots *should* be different to everyone else's.

1. Never carry your tripod with the camera attached. I know it's a pain, but always detach the camera from the tripod and carry it separately, preferably secured on your body.

2. Don't rely on the tripod to hold your camera. Always keep the strap around your neck or wrist. It only takes one gust of wind or an unexpected wave to knock your camera flying. I saved a £2,000 lens because I had the strap round my neck when one of the tripod legs slipped off a rock in the river I was standing in.

3. Don't leave your camera bag closed but unzipped. If someone picks it up thinking it is zipped closed, all your kit will fall out. Your bag should either be zipped closed, or completely open.

4. Don't wear red. You'll show up in everyone else's shots.

5. Do look around from time to time, to check you are not spoiling someone's shot. This is especially important if you are part of a workshop, as you'll be spending the rest of the day with the group and would probably prefer to be on good terms.

6. Don't extend the middle column of your tripod to get extra height – you'll look like a beginner. If you do, you then effectively just have a monopod on top of a tripod, and you lose all the benefit of having the three stable legs. (It's OK to use the central column in a studio, because there's no wind.)

7. Don't leave footprints in the sand – always walk behind everyone shooting, so you don't put your footprints in their foreground.

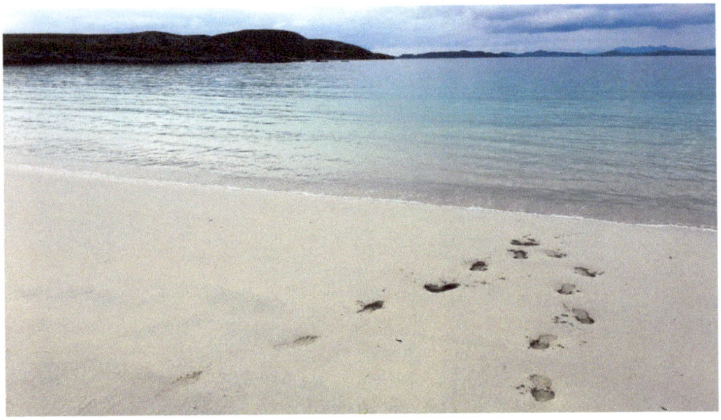

How to overcome the fear of shooting in public

The next few tips are optional extras and mindset hacks. When I started doing landscape photography seriously I was already an award-winning photographer in my own genre (garden photography). Nonetheless I was still terrified of doing something wrong, or standing out, or being found out as a fraud in this new world of landscape photography. I wrote this whole book to help others in the same situation get over the awkward first few trips out. These are a few miscellaneous tips that might help, but don't really fit in anywhere else in the book.

If you arrive at a popular landscape viewpoint, chances are there will already be photographers set up and shooting. As a novice, it is tempting to stay in the car, shoot through the window and drive off before anyone sees you. But you really do have as much right to be there as everyone else. As long as you don't set up in front of them, it's up to you how much you engage. It's fine to start a conversation – although it will usually be about kit, being the only thing most photographers have in common. If you are not feeling outgoing, here are my top tips for minimising any interaction:

1. Wear headphones.

2. If asked, say you are a student. Or a tourist. This diffuses any threat you might present to their desire to be the best photographer present. Or try being honest. You never know, you might meet someone nice, or someone who can give you tips.

3. Have a plan. Start with one shot you can take. Stick with one lens and one setting. Get that shot before you try different viewpoints.

4. Remember, what people think of you is none of your business. They probably haven't even noticed you. And if they do, and they are patronising and condescending, then that's their problem. They won't all be. Some will be lovely, encouraging and enthusiastic. Some will look down on you (and they will look down on everyone who's not Ansel Adams, to be fair). Most will just want to get on and get their own shot in their own space – as long as you don't put on a red coat and sit in their foreground, they will be happy to ignore you.

5. If the worst happens, and you get cornered by a patronising, condescending, all-about-the-gear photographer who wants to show off, don't try and compete with kit. If you have better kit they will hate you. If you don't, they will be smug. So, take a moment for a little smugness yourself. Remember that unlike them, you aren't there to be the most experienced, to have the most kit or to know the most about the golden hour. You are only in that place to work on visualising an image, and then capturing it to the best of your current ability. If you come back in a month, you will probably do it better, but right now, who you are is good enough. Write this on a piece of paper and stick it in the top of your camera bag in case you ever forget: "I am enough. I belong here. I can do this."

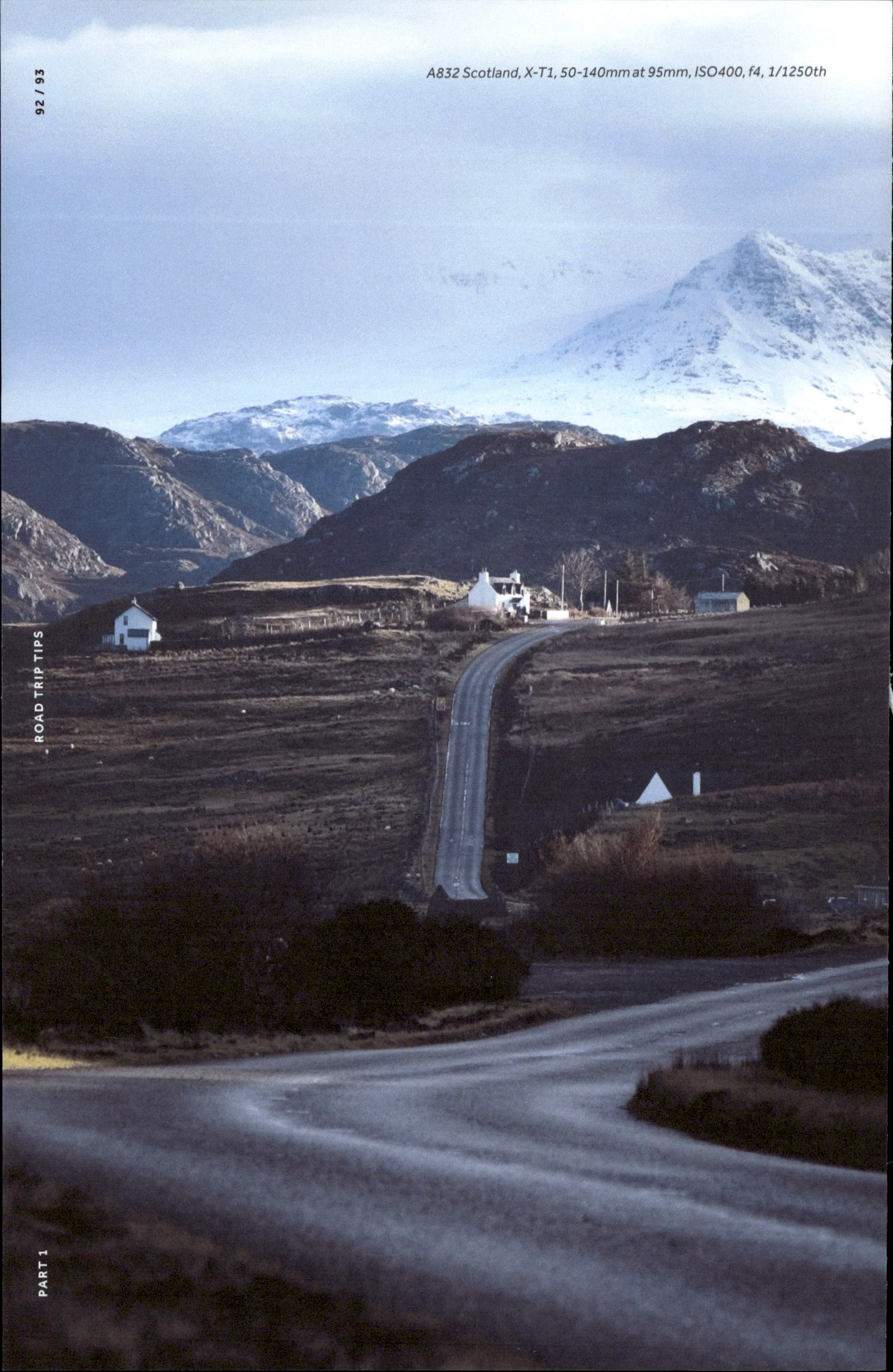

A832 Scotland, X-T1, 50-140mm at 95mm, ISO400, f4, 1/1250th

9

ROAD TRIP TIPS

An epic road trip through a remote landscape brings you close to a constantly changing panorama ready to be caught by your camera. The tips in this section are designed to keep you shooting: you need to be physically ready to get in the position you need for the shot, but you also need to be mentally ready to make decisions about settings and creative composition. I've also included a description of my on-the-road workflow, to minimise backup disasters.

Mindset

You don't just need to be on the lookout for a shot, paying attention to the changing weather and the changing backdrop, you also need to *care* about the next shot. From the comfort of your front room, with a hot coffee and the anticipation of a trip to come, this might sound like the least of your worries. But when you've been on the road for four days, you're driving through a drizzle, with a string of disappointing shots and a few uncomfortable nights behind you, it takes a lot of willpower to get yourself into a creative frame of mind.

Above all, you mustn't forget you're a landscape photographer, not a tourist driving through on your way to somewhere else. The journey really is your destination. Enjoy the moment you are in, give it your full attention, and be aware of how your mental energy ebbs and flows through the day.

- Drive with the window open to reduce the feeling that you're in a bubble. Smell the landscape. Feel the weather on your skin.
- Be open to serendipity. You will have your skeleton route plan, with some viewpoints and stops pencilled in, but be ready to go where the light is.
- Have a technique to get yourself out of the warm car and into the cold weather (or out of the air conditioning into the stifling heat). I have a simple rule: I can only eat chocolate outside.
- Have a day off. I can keep shooting for six days maximum on a road trip. On the seventh day I know I won't care where I am and there's no way I'll want to take my camera out.

- You will have the most mental energy on your first couple of days. Plan the pre-dawn shots for these days if you can.
- Don't be afraid to turn the music off and leave the podcasts quiet for a while. Driving with no auditory input allows your creative brain to percolate ideas, in the absence of distractions.
- When you are shooting, allow yourself the luxury of no time pressure. Even with another stop planned, if the light is right where you are, stay there and immerse yourself in the moment.
- If it does all come together for you for one epic shot – the view, the light, the weather – be ready for the reaction afterwards: from the high of getting the shot, to the low of leaving it behind. But just keep going. Get out and take photos with your phone. Dial your expectations down a little for a couple of hours. Think Instagram instead of Landscape Photographer of the Year. You'll get back into it.
- Don't expect fabulous shots around every corner. If I get one usable shot per day, I'm happy.

Keeping yourself comfortable

- If you're driving yourself, make sure you have your sat. nav. destinations ready before you leave, so you aren't tempted to start using your phone while you're driving.
- Stop regularly. No one (unless they have narcolepsy) ever falls asleep at the wheel out of the blue – everyone feels tired beforehand. If you need to stop, stop.
- It's easy to forget to drink enough on a road trip. Fill up a bottle and make sure you keep sipping from it throughout the day.
- It's also easy to eat snack food all day and not actually eat a fruit or vegetable all week. A carbohydrate-based diet makes your brain sluggish. Keep a varied diet to make sure you stay creative.
- Having said that, have plenty of snacks packed in your camera bag so that if you're away from the car you can keep your blood sugar levels up and stay out for the good light. I need constant refuelling when I am on a road trip otherwise I get irritable and just can't keep shooting.
- My luxury items are a car kettle and a supply of dehydrated camping food, so I can have a hot lunch. (Yes, I mostly shoot landscapes in winter.) The kettle plugs into the car's

cigarette lighter socket, and means you can boil water away from mains electricity. (I've also been known to settle for a dehydrated dinner back at my bed & breakfast, if I arrive back late and too tired to find somewhere to eat.) I've included list of my favourites over at EmmaDaviesPhotography.com/landscape-links.

- Be considerate and park carefully.
- Always take everything with you for the shoot when you leave the car – you'll never want to pop back for something you've forgotten or didn't think you'd need. Every time I'm tired and leave a long lens in the car rather than adding it to my bag, I always end up wishing I had it.
- Be ready. The light changes in an instant. Have your camera to hand on neutral settings and ready to shoot (for me, that's on auto focus, ISO200, aperture priority mode, f5.6, auto white balance, lens cap off, clean lens, exposure compensation back to zero, exposure bracketing back to none, battery full and space on the memory card.)
- Stretch at the end of every day.

Portable workflow

At the end of every day, no matter how tired you are, get your kit ready for the next day:

- Download and backup your shots.
- Charge your batteries.
- Clean your lenses and filters.
- Check your sensor for dust.
- Put all your settings back to neutral.
- Make a note of every single location you visited (you *will* forget).
- Make sure you've still got change for parking.
- Check the weather for the next day, and set your alarm if it will be an early start.

Even on the road you should aim to have two copies of every shot, ideally in different places. I don't like to fill up my laptop with images, so I bring a portable external hard drive. If you have wifi, you can upload images to the cloud. I don't format my memory cards until I'm home – they are my backup backup.

Loch Glascarnoch, X-T1, 50-140mm at 70mm, ISO200, f5.6m 1/400th

10

SHOOTING IN ALL WEATHERS

Looking after yourself in all weathers is taken as read. Take layers when it's cold, suncream and a hat when it's sunny, and head-to-toe waterproofs when it's raining. The idea is to keep yourself alive, obviously, but also keep yourself comfortable enough so that it's not the weather that sends you home; you are able to keep shooting as long as you want to. Looking after your kit may need a bit of extra preparation.

Rain

I'm based in the UK, so my prevailing weather challenge is always rain. Your first concern should be to keep the rain off your lens, and then to keep it off your camera. Any rain spots on your lens will show up as grey spots on your final image.

Tilt your lens downwards as much as possible, and all the time when you're not actually shooting. Although it makes you look like a tourist, holding an umbrella over your lens is actually the best way to keep the rain off it. If you can't bring yourself to use an umbrella, then a peaked cap also works well.

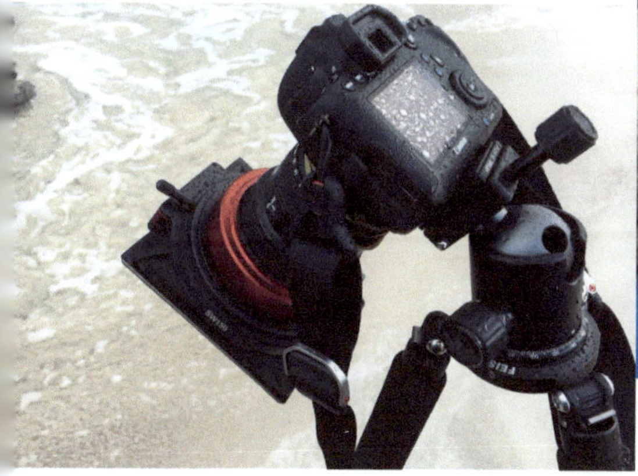

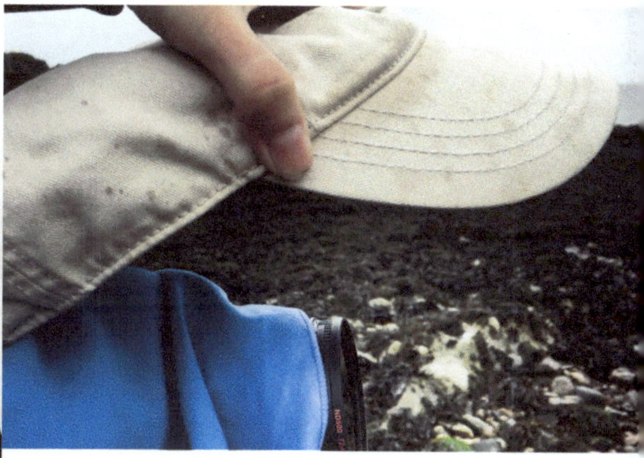

Check your lens before every shot, and have a lens wipe ready. Microfibre cloths can work well, but using alcohol wipes means your lens will dry much more quickly and they leave fewer smears.

No camera is actually waterproof (other than underwater cameras), but the more expensive ones are "weatherproof", which means the electronics won't fuse in a light shower. If your camera is not weatherproof, put it in a plastic carrier bag while you shoot – cut a hole for the lens to poke through, and leave the bag open at the back so you can operate the controls. Or you can buy tailor-made raincoats to fit any make and model (but you may need different ones for each length of lens).

Take one of those super-absorbent camping towels to protect your camera, even if it is weatherproof. Drape it over the whole set-up and keep wringing it out as it gets damper.
And don't forget – you can't auto focus on a rainbow. Focus on something close by, or use manual focus.

Cold

Sub-zero temperatures will affect you more than the camera. Know how to prevent hypothermia, and take plenty of provisions. Don't be tempted to take your gloves off – you'll risk frostbite. At the very least, have a pair of thin gloves under your thicker ones, and work quickly to change your settings. Keep hand-warmers in your pockets to warm up between shots.

If you're staying out to shoot after dark, don't forget that a warm evening can quickly turn into a very cold night.

The first thing to go will be your batteries – they drain much faster in cold weather. Take lots of spares, and keep the spares next to your skin to keep them warm (or wrap them next to a hand-warmer). Take the current battery out of your camera and keep it warm between shots.

If you are moving between cold and warm conditions, condensation on your lens will be a problem. Try to keep the camera at a constant temperature and, if that's not possible, keep it in a sealed bag until it has reached the warmer air temperature – this way the condensation will form on the bag, not on the camera. Keep any temperature transitions as slow as possible.

Shooting in extremely cold conditions needs a professional spec. camera. Any moisture inside the camera will freeze and can damage the electronics, the shutter and the sensor.

If you're shooting in snow, remember everything you know about how the camera exposes. On auto modes it will assume the snow is grey, and will underexpose. If your shot is mainly snow, you will need +1 to +2 stops over what the camera picks.

Fog

A fine mist rising up on an autumn morning is one thing – an impenetrable fog is another. I think thick fog is the only weather condition wholly unsuited to landscape photography. Your best bet is to pay attention to local weather forecasts and either move to where the fog is not, or be ready for when it lifts.

Heat

As with the cold, it's more likely that you will expire before your camera does in hot weather. Take steps to avoid sunburn and dehydration. Wear a hat and know how to prevent heat stroke. Heat often brings dust or sand with it. Protect your sensor at all costs – if you get dust on your sensor you'll either need to know how to clean it yourself, or find a camera repair shop to do it for you. To check whether you have dust on your sensor, take an out of focus shot of the sky or something plain and bright. If there are mysterious spots on the shot, that are in the same place whichever lens you use, you have dust on your sensor.

Dust only gets on your sensor when you take the lens off. Never, ever change lenses in a dusty environment. Always switch your camera off before you change a lens (the static charge will attract dust), and have everything ready to go before you start so you can work as fast as possible. Hold the camera pointing downwards for as long as possible whilst the lens is off.

Wind

Wind by itself isn't a problem. You will just need to use increasingly higher shutter speeds to stop anything blurring in your shot, as the wind picks up. If it is very strong, keep an eye on your camera and kit to make sure it is safe and steady.

If the wind blows stuff onto your camera, you will need to be ready with lens wipes and protection. Rain and sea-spray are obvious culprits, but look out for leaves and light debris that can lodge themselves in a shot. Clean everything carefully when you get home, especially if you were near the sea – salt residue will start to corrode any metal parts in your camera and tripod.

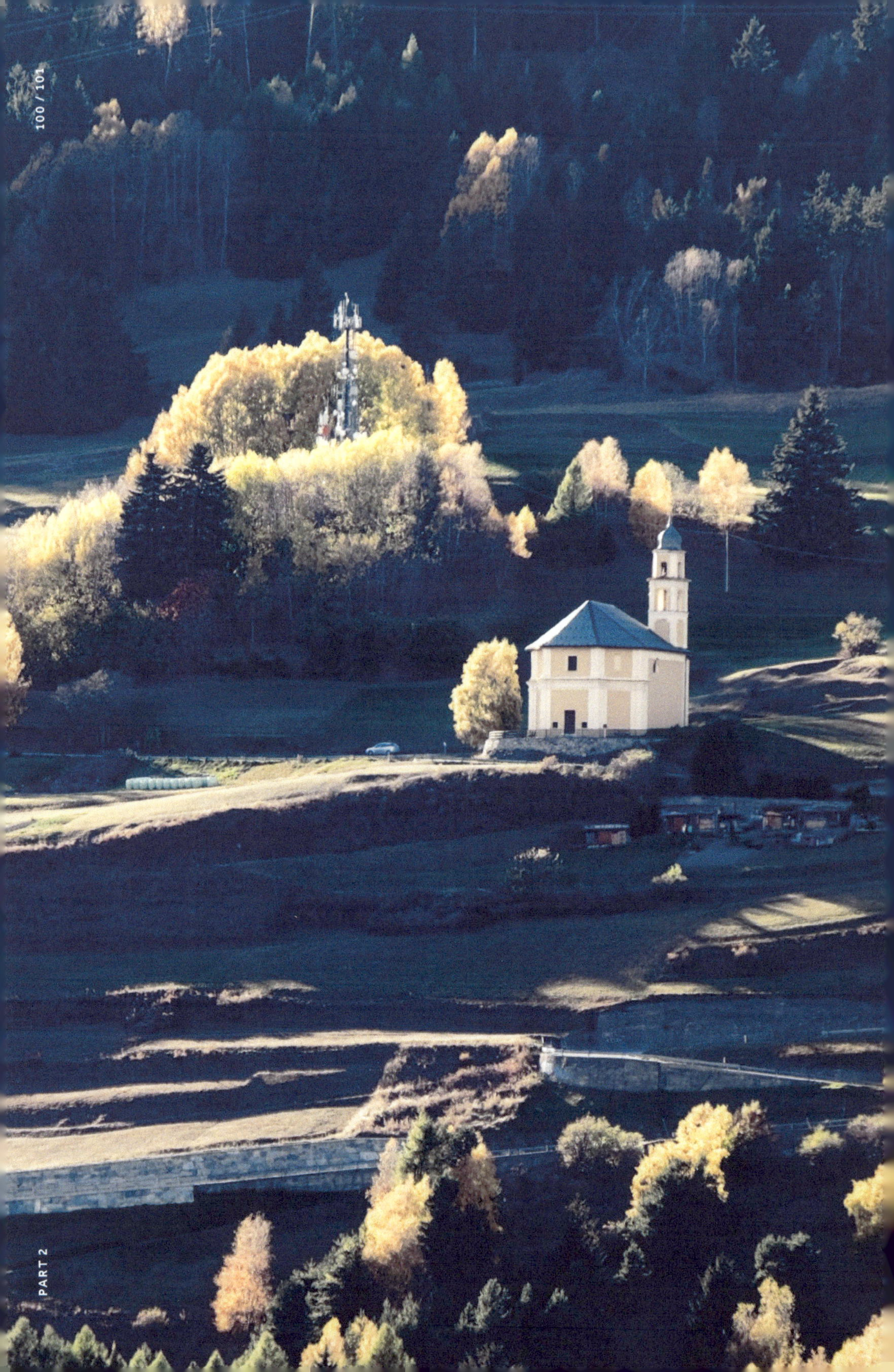

PART 2

When I started taking landscapes seriously (i.e. when I planned my trips instead of just turning up and shooting, and researched the weather instead of hoping for the best), I found I simply could not capture what I saw in front of me the way I wanted to. I had a vision, an idea of a shot I wanted to take, but I could not translate that into two dimensions. At first.

Many, many disappointing shots later, I began to make progress. I had to learn how all my different lenses compressed or stretched the scene. I needed to be disciplined in checking for distractions and alignment, and diligent about moving for a better viewpoint.

This section of the book has been designed for you to teach yourself by imitating what I did, hopefully make much more efficient progress than me, and ultimately be able to move beyond the book and shoot your own ideas.

How to use Part 2

Start by copying my shots (or someone else's). This is how fine artists and musicians learn their craft – by copying – and photographers should be no different. You don't need to go to the exact locations I did, but when you are at a beach for example, try and replicate the viewpoints in the Coastal chapter. When you are faced with a waterfall, use my settings and composition as a starting point.

Copying shots allows you to learn how to use your kit. You find out exactly what focal length lens you need to recreate a particular style of image. You are forced to deconstruct another photograph's composition and work out how to make something similar. You can analyse the depth of field a photographer used, and learn how to do the same with your particular camera and lens combination. You will pay very close attention to the way the light falls on someone else's image and then decide what time of day you would need to go out to find the same kind of light.

You might realise your kit has some shortcomings that mean you are limited in what you can do – this is when you start to embrace compromises, and find workarounds. (Please find out what you can do with your own camera first. Don't automatically think you need to buy more kit each time.)

You aren't going to be copying shots for long. Once you can more-or-less recreate an image you have seen, then you can start to decide what kind of a composition *you* want. You can let the landscape speak to you personally and create an image that reflects this.

If you don't want to start by copying images, then by all means jump right ahead and start creating your own work. You can still take all the information from this Part 2 with you, and refer back to it whenever you need a new idea or a reminder of some settings.

Finding your own light

I hope you will use this book as a starting point and ultimately be able to find your own landscape destinations, your own light, your own composition - not one of the clichéd locations, but something personal to you. Your shot is how the landscape speaks to you, not to someone else. Use long lenses, do intimate landscapes as well as trying the more familiar wide-angle epic vistas. Try everything. Read the light. Deconstruct your composition and try again.

Pay close attention to where you take your inspiration from, especially if you are frequently drawn to popular photography sites like Instagram or 500px. Stuart McGlennon who has a gallery in Keswick in the English Lake District (lensdistrict.com) put it well; "Instagram serves the fast food market of landscape photography with many in a race to produce instantly eye-catching images whilst quite a lot of the time sacrificing quality/originality." By all means start by taking your inspiration from popular places and compositions, but you will only grow as a landscape photographer when you start to find your own way.

MEASURE YOUR PROGRESS

As you make progress with your landscape photography, aim to tick off the following achievements:

Technical

1. Understand how to shoot on manual mode.
2. Be able to shoot on manual without thinking too much about it.
3. Be able to shoot manual in the dark.

Composition

1. Understand composition theory and ideas, and compose a shot using a single basic principle, e.g. the rule of thirds.
2. Be able to replicate a well composed shot.
3. Be able to make your own composition decisions in the field in a new location.

The why

1. You just want to stop being disappointed in your landscape shots.
2. You want to take a photo other people say "WOW" to.
3. You want to take a photo that represents how the landscape speaks to you.

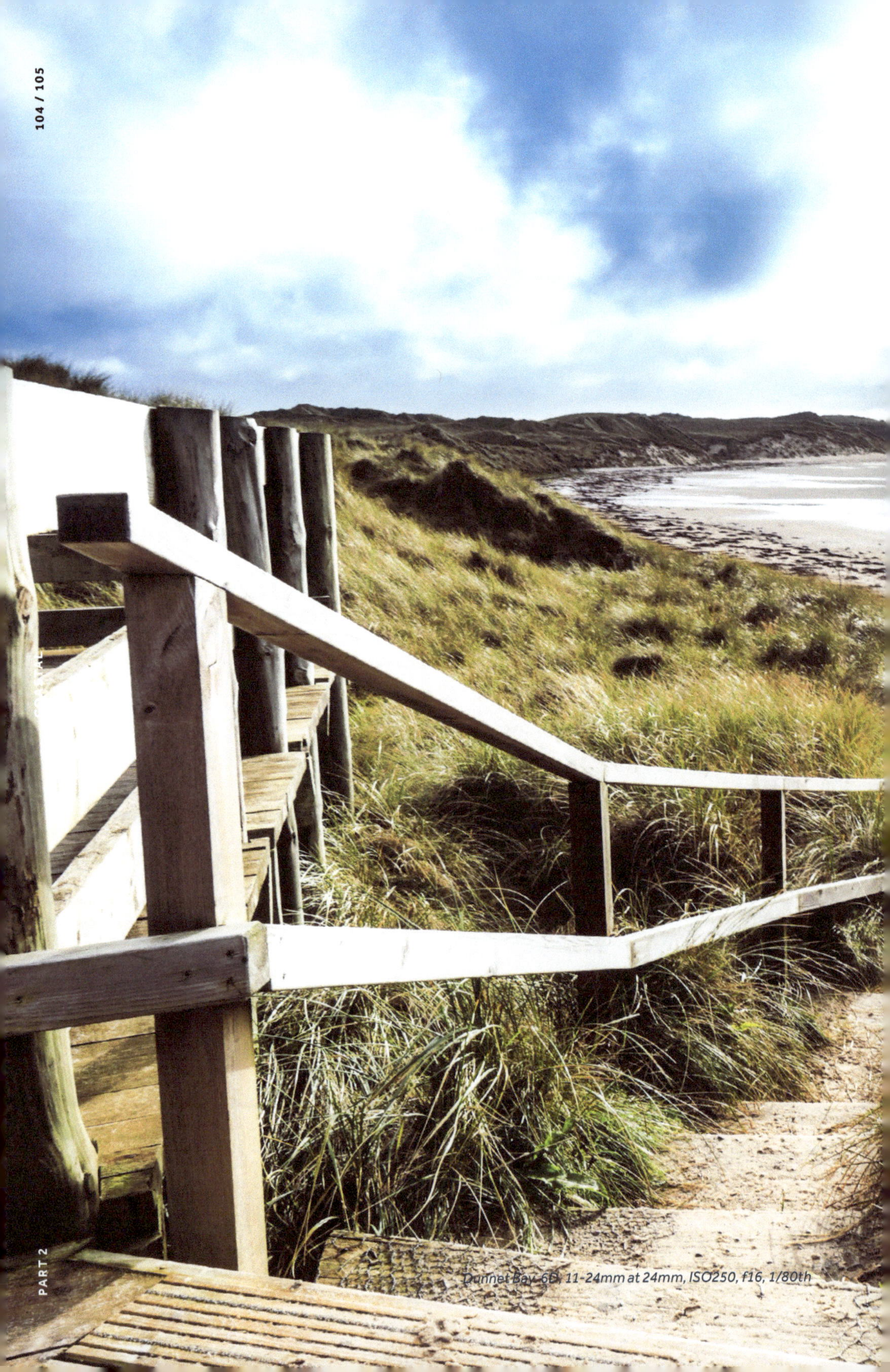

Dunnet Bay, 6D, 11-24mm at 24mm, ISO250, f16, 1/80th

11

COASTAL

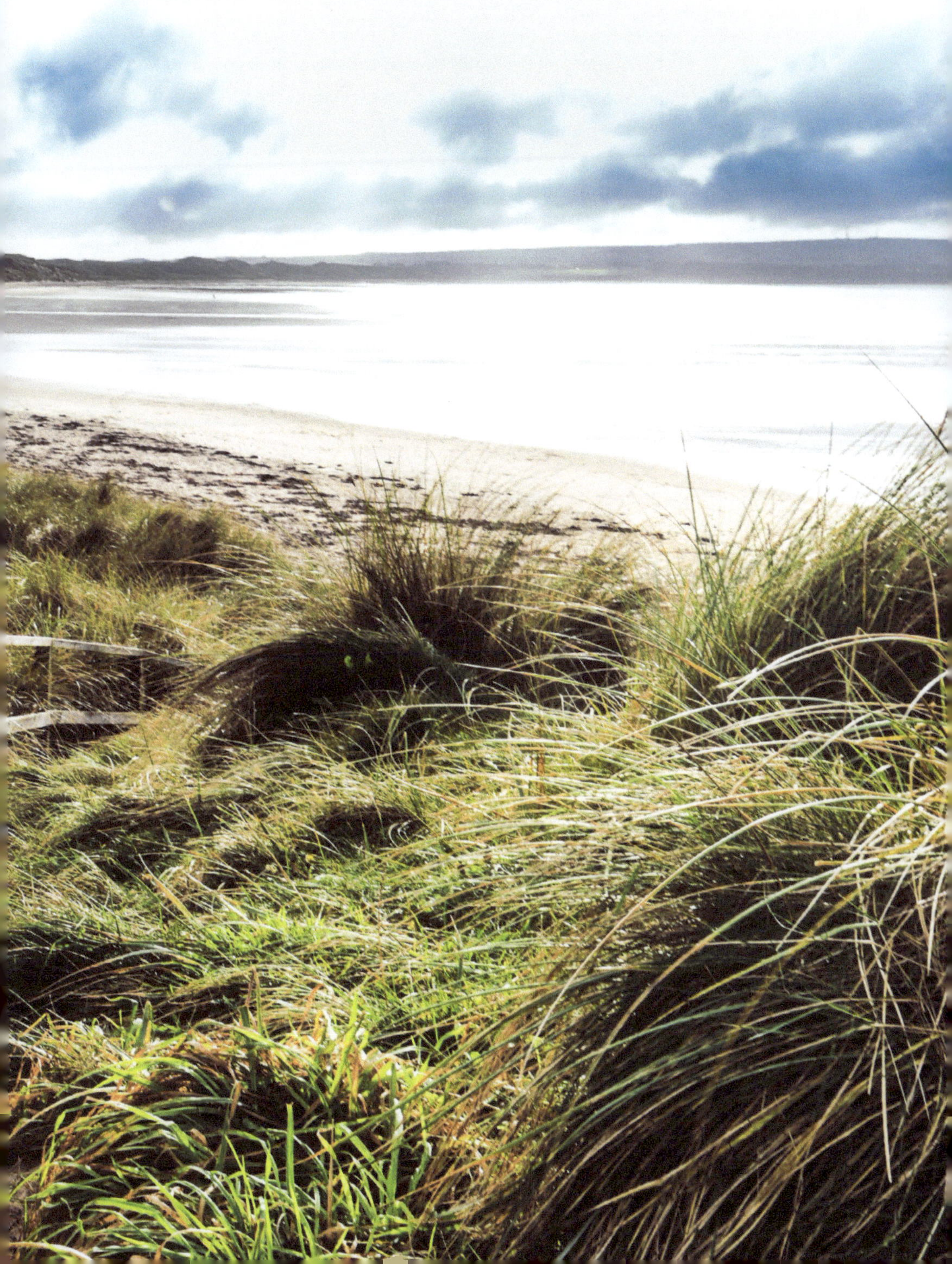

Photographs shot where the land meets the sea always have an edge-of-the-world feeling to them. You can imagine explorers of old setting off into the unknown. Often the waves are uncontrollable, and the tides are relentless. It's a place for humans to feel small: we are just passing through – the cliffs have been here for centuries, and will still be here for centuries to come. Depending on the weather that the day brings you, beaches can also conjure up thoughts of desert islands, peace, tranquility, isolation and contemplation.

COMPOSITION TIPS

1. Get up high

If you shoot a beach or shoreline at sea-level, you often end up with just a thin line of sea. But if you can look down from a higher vantage point, you can start to create a more dynamic composition:

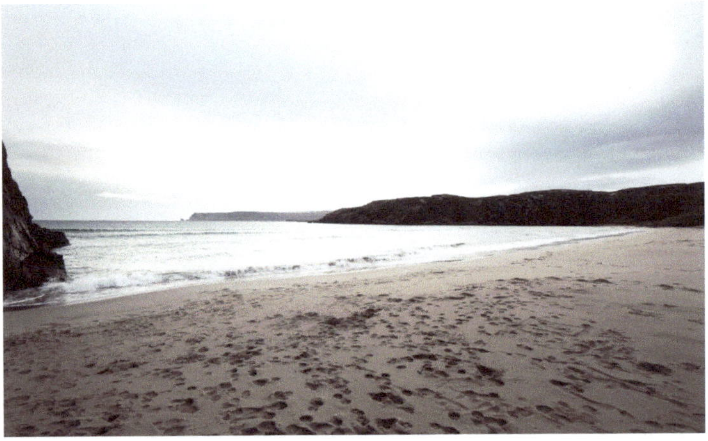

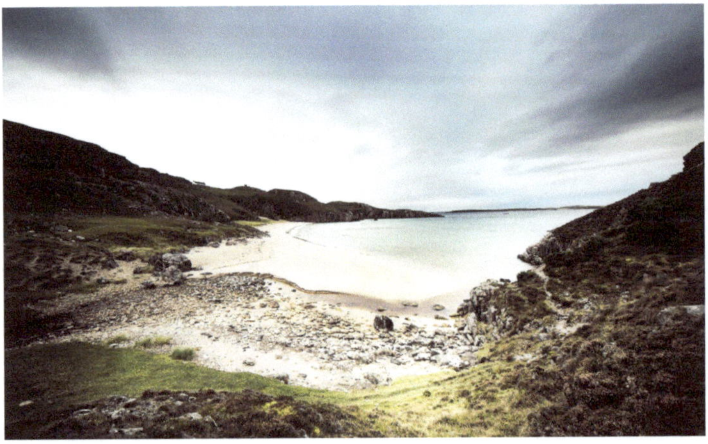

Top right:
Ceannabeinne Beach: a fairly dreary shot, taken at sea level.
6D, 11-24mm at 15mm, ISO100, f9, 1/80th.
Bottom right:
Ceannabeinne Beach: a more engaging shot, taken at around the same time, but from a point half-way up the cliffs.
6D, 11-24mm at 11mm, ISO125, f6.3, 1/80th.

2. Get down low

If you want to shoot at sea level, make sure you have a compelling foreground, and make sure it is sharply in focus.

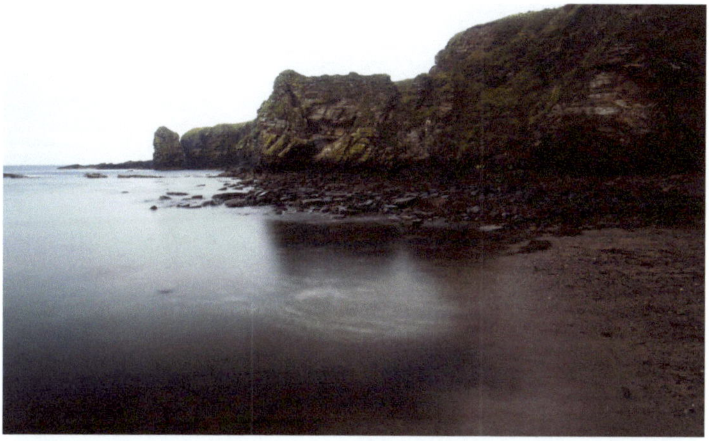

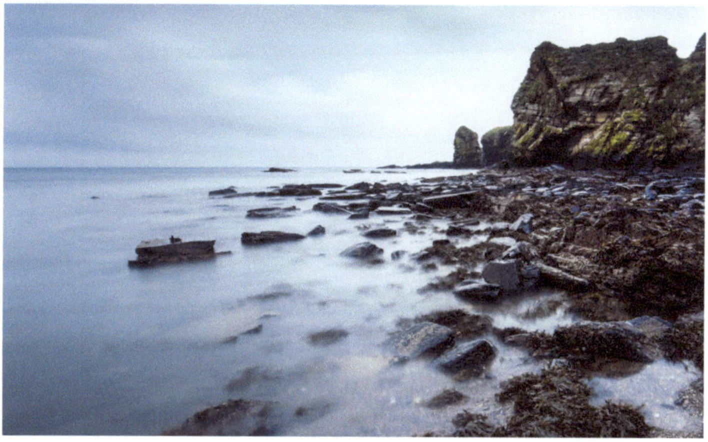

Top left:

Brough Bay: shot at sea level with an utterly uninteresting foreground.
6D, 11-24mm at 24mm, ISO100, f20, 30 seconds.

Bottom left:

Brough Bay: shot at sea level with a much more interesting foreground.
6D, 11-24mm at 16mm, ISO100, f22, 15 seconds.

3. Abstract and intimate shots

If you have time, or if the weather isn't playing ball, search out some alternative shots. You are never more than five minutes away from a great shot.

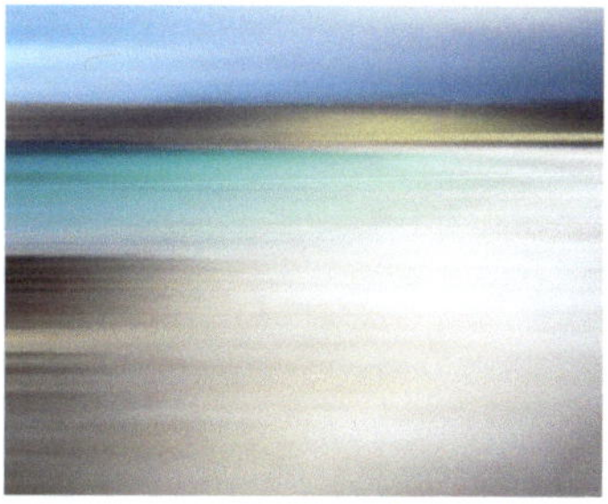

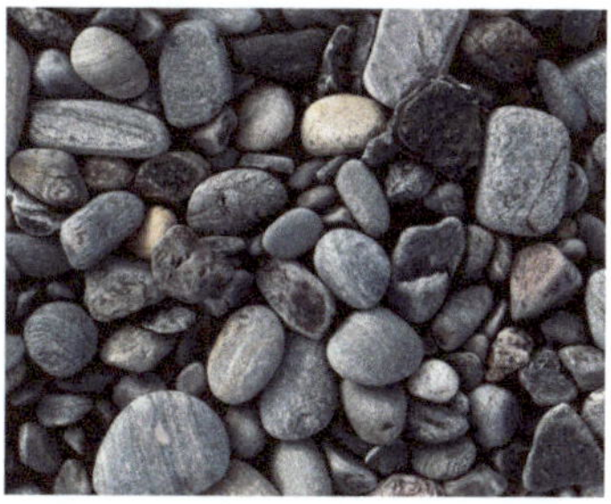

Left:

Achmelvich beach: nice light but composition wasn't happening. Move the camera left to right whilst the shutter is firing to get this effect.
6D, 11-24mm at 24mm, ISO100, f11, 1/2 sec.

Right:

Skerray beach: a very grey day, perfect light for detail shots.
6D, 50mm, ISO100, f5.6, 1/400th.

4. Lens choice
Use a longer lens to compress perspective, and use a wider lens to show a sweeping bay. Remember to think about your foreground whichever lens you use, and how the viewer's eye will travel around the frame.

PRACTICAL TIPS

1. Keep your lens clean
All that salt water spray will collect on your lens (or filter) and gradually build up a residue. Keep a stack of lens wipes handy, and wipe your lens between shots. Keep an eye out for stray grains of sand on your lens – it's easy to scratch the glass.

2. Don't walk across the sand
You will ruin a pristine beach with your footprints. Only ever walk behind the camera.

3. Bad weather is your friend
Stormy skies and crashing waves will make a more epic shot than blue skies and calm seas. But be careful to stay out of reach of the waves (both you and your kit). ***It's too easy to be swept away by a strong tide - people die because of this.***

4. Keep a note of tide times
Do your research before you arrive. ***Never*** set up on a beach without knowing if the tide is coming in or going out, and what the high tide mark will be. As you start to concentrate on your shots you can find yourself cut off by an incoming tide. Sites like Magic Seaweed will give you tide times months in advance.

5. Be aware of high winds
It's no good setting up on a tripod if the wind is so strong that the tripod is buffeted and starts to move during a shot. Keep an eye on your shutter speed, and make sure it's fast enough to cope with the wind conditions. If your tripod has a hook underneath, use it to suspend your camera bag to weight the whole tripod down.

6. Get the salt off your kit
As soon as you are out of the salt spray, wipe or rinse all the salt off your kit.

SETTINGS - COASTAL

1. Shutter speed in windy conditions

Is your camera going to wobble even on a tripod? If so, you'll need a shutter speed faster than if you were hand-holding. Select 1/100th or faster. If your tripod lets you spread the legs wide and drop the height, this will make a sturdier base in high winds.

2. Allowing movement in the shot

If you want to show some movement in the waves you'll need a shutter speed of at least half second and up to multiple whole seconds (see Chapter 19 – Long exposure).

3. Depth of field

You can't always get front-to-back depth of field, especially in windy or darker conditions. Be ready to compromise. Don't forget, a large hole (e.g. f4) gives a small depth of field. If in doubt, make sure the thing closest to the camera is acceptably sharp.

4. Assessing the sky

You might need a graduated neutral density filter to even-out the contrast between a bright sky and the landscape. If you don't have one you can try taking three shots at different exposure values and combining them in an HDR merge (see Chapter 3 – Camera controls).

5. ISO

Keep your ISO as low as you can for as long as you can. But if it's very windy, quite dark, and you want a small aperture, you are going to have to let it creep up.

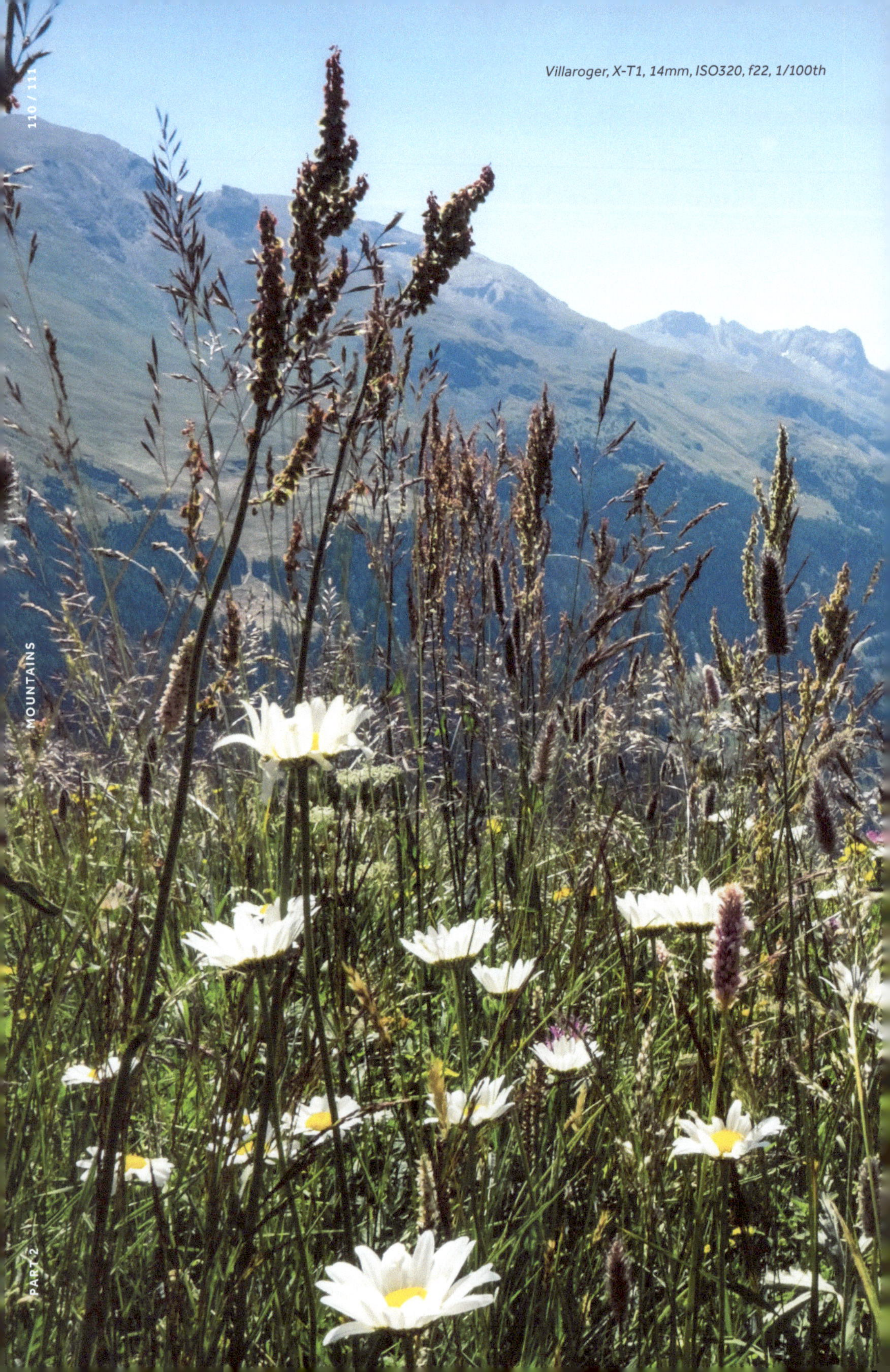

Villaroger, X-T1, 14mm, ISO320, f22, 1/100th

12

MOUNTAINS

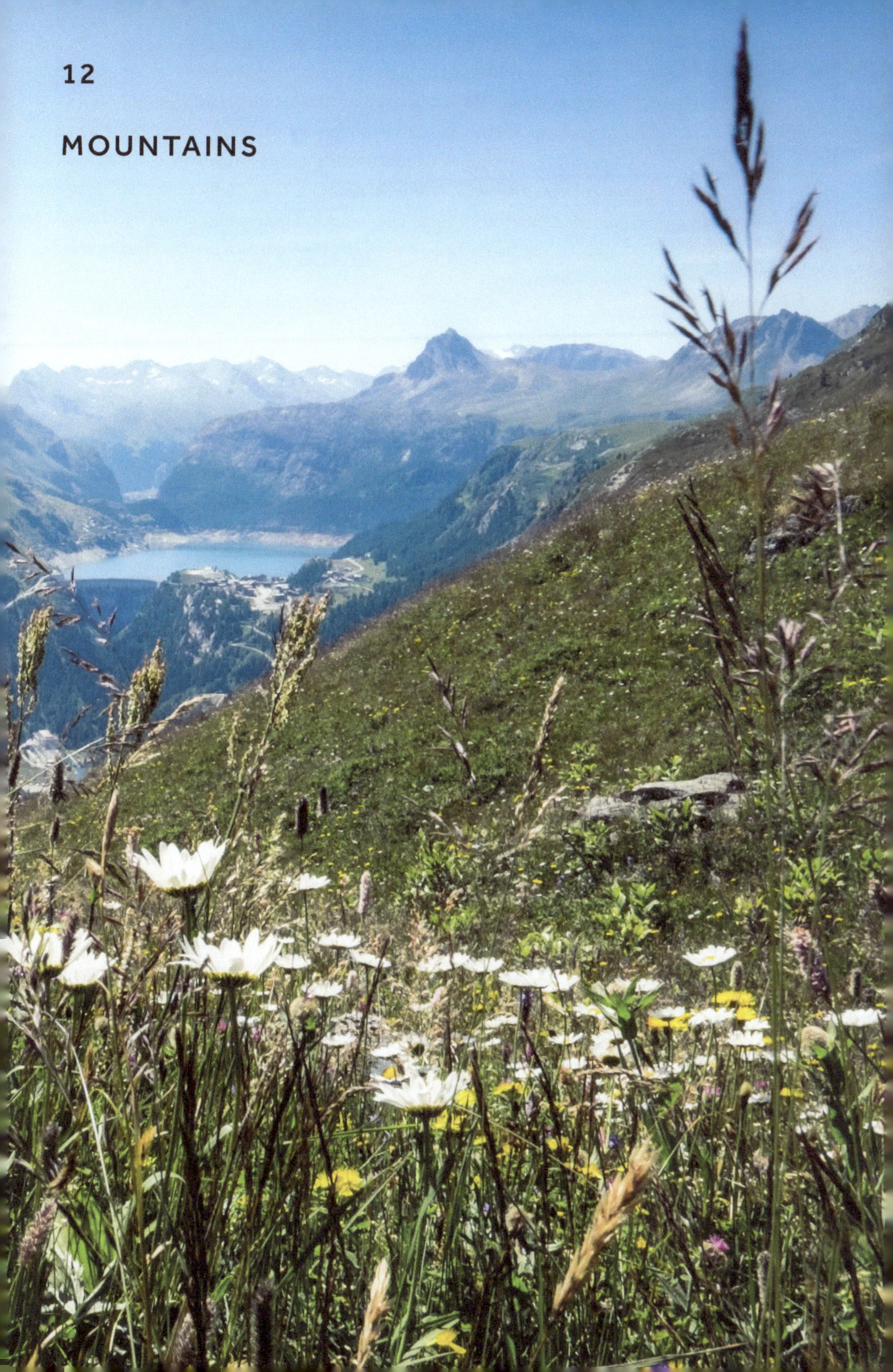

Drama and wilderness are the two words that usually spring to mind when you think of mountain landscape photography. You *can* shoot mountains from the side of the road, but to find the epic locations you usually need to be a long way away from civilisation, and be blessed with dramatic weather. This is why so many landscape photographers will hike and then camp on location, so they can be up before dawn to get the light and the composition they want.

COMPOSITION TIPS

1. Shoot the valley

Instead of pointing your camera only at the peaks, try including the valley to give a sense of scale.

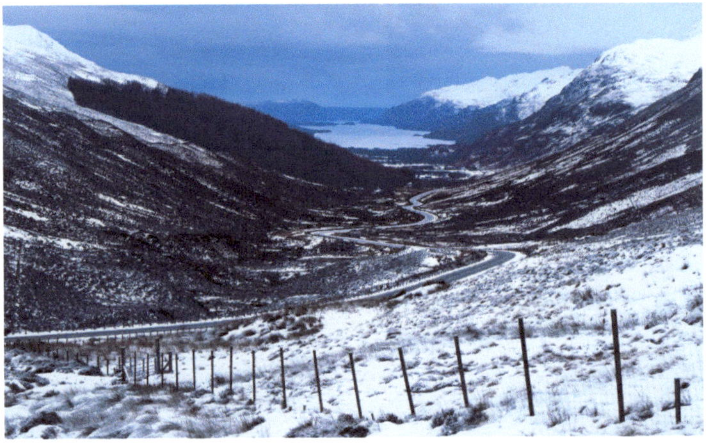

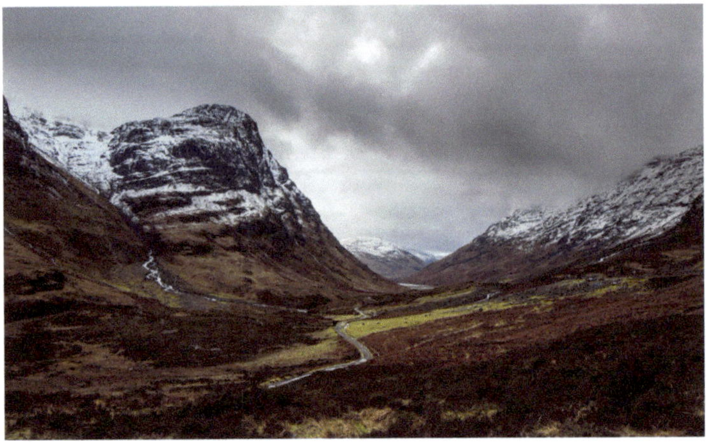

Top right:
Loch Maree from Glen Docherty (shot from a car park).
X-T1, 50-140mm at 54mm, ISO200, f2.8, 1/480th.
Bottom right:
Three Sisters at Glen Coe (shot 5 minutes walk from the A82).
X-T1, 50-140mm at 54mm, ISO200, f2.8, 1/480th.

2. Light will make or break your shot

Don't forget everything from Chapter 4. There is no short cut to this one. Learn how the light shapes the mountains, find out when is the best time of day is for the golden side light for the time of year you are visiting, arrive in good time and be patient. The two shots that follow were taken from the same place only 40 seconds apart, yet the second one is brought alive by the sunlight hitting the side of the fell.

Top:
Brotherswater from the Kirkstone Pass.
5DIV, 50mm, ISO100, f14, 1/50th.
Bottom:
5DIV, 50mm, ISO100, f14, 1/100th.

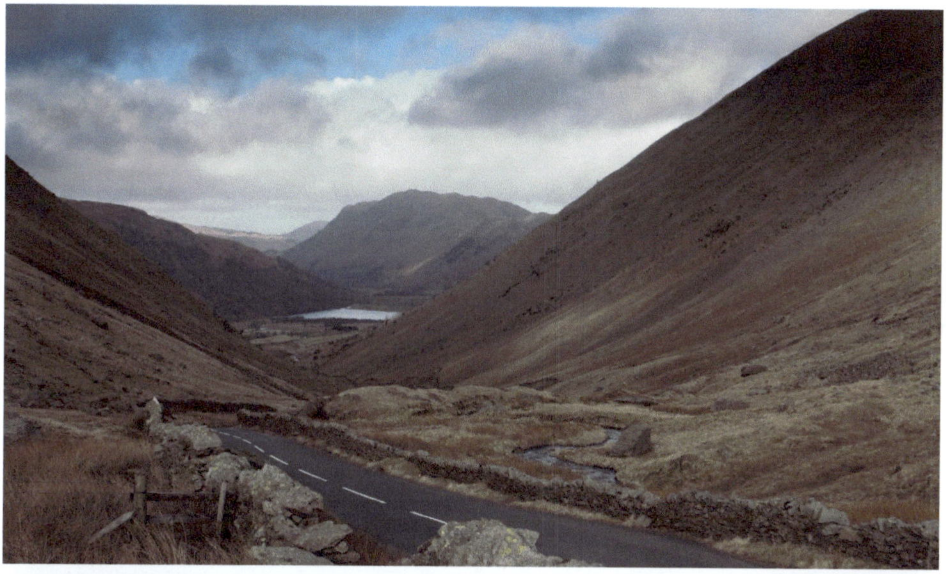

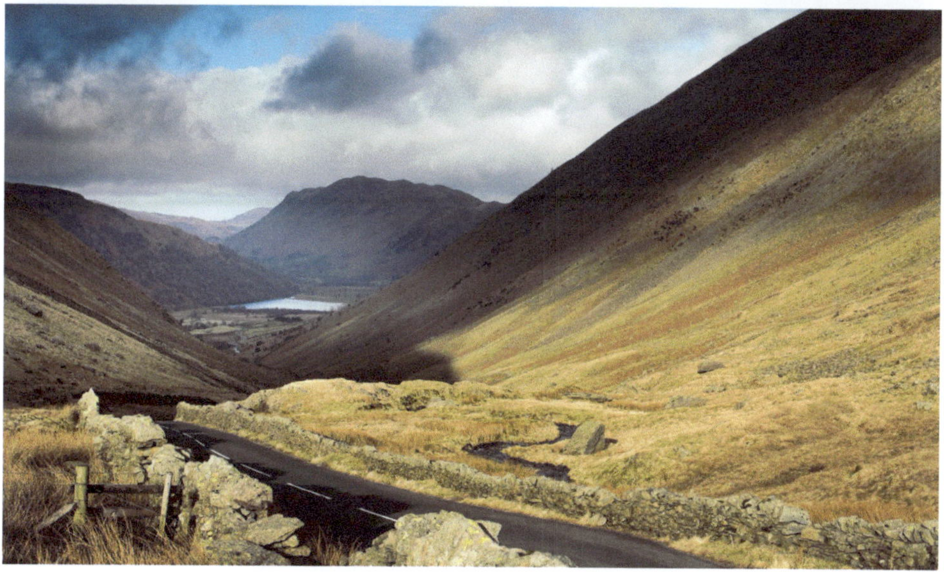

3. Three-dimensional or two-dimensional?

In Chapter 5 – Composition, we looked at creating images with depth versus those that are flat. This decision sets the tone for your mountain photography. Try to imagine how the shot would look if you traced over it. Are you aiming for a static two-dimensional feel, or a more three-dimensional shot with movement and depth? Don't forget – neither is better than the other – they are simply different.

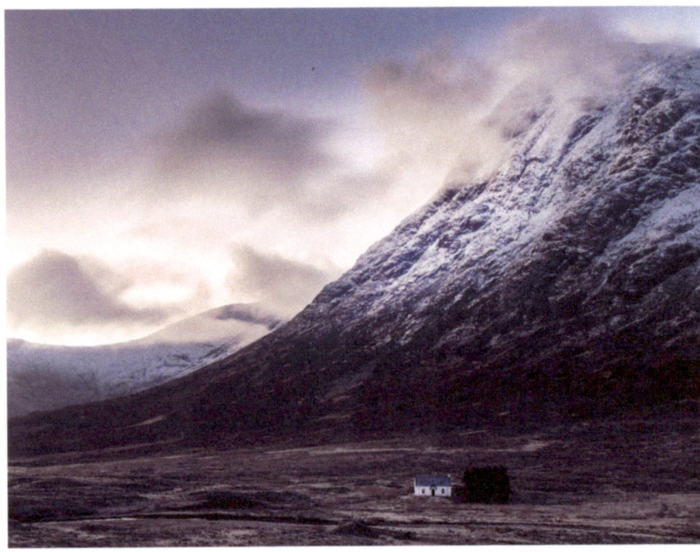

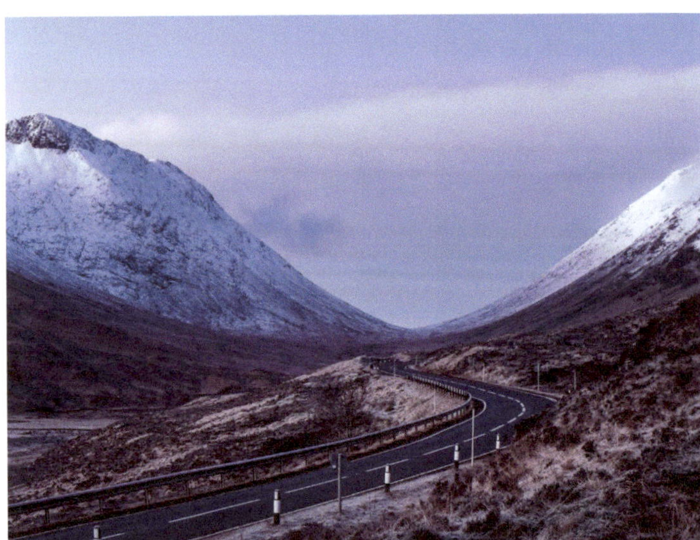

Above right:
Two-dimensional shot of a farm in Glen Coe (shot from the A82).
X-T1, 18-135mm at 30mm, ISO400, f14, 0.6 sec.

Below right:
Three-dimensional shot to the right of the farm, looking back up Glen Coe (shot from the A82).
X-T1, 18-135mm at 45mm, ISO400, f14, 1 second.

SETTINGS - MOUNTAINS

1. Depth of field

Your aperture is probably your first decision with mountain photography because, unlike the sea, this landscape doesn't move. Try to keep your aperture as close to your sweet spot as possible (see Chapter 3 – Camera controls), usually around f8. But if you need to use f16 or higher to keep the foreground in focus, do it. Use hyperfocal distance for your focus point (see Chapter 3 – Camera Controls).

2. Shutter speed and ISO

You will probably be using a tripod with a cable release or self timer, so keep your ISO to its lowest (100 or 200), and let the shutter speed climb to whatever is needed. As your shutter speeds start to be multiple seconds, the clouds will start to lose definition if they are moving.

PRACTICAL TIPS

1. Stay safe

The weather in the mountains can change in an instant. Go prepared for the worst. Know how to read a map or go with a guide. Tell someone where you're going and when you expect to be back. Don't rely on being able to make a call to get you out of trouble – phone reception will be patchy.

2. Take everything with you from the car

You don't want to walk for even just ten minutes and find your battery is about to run out, your memory card is full or your tripod head needs tightening. You won't want to go back, and you'll miss the shot. Bring it all: spare batteries; spare cards; screwdriver; lens wipes; coat; hat; suncream; phone; water.

3. Be patient

Get to know the location. Sit, and be still in it. Your first impressions will be valuable, but respect the place and watch the light as it changes. Take the obvious shot, but also look for alternatives.

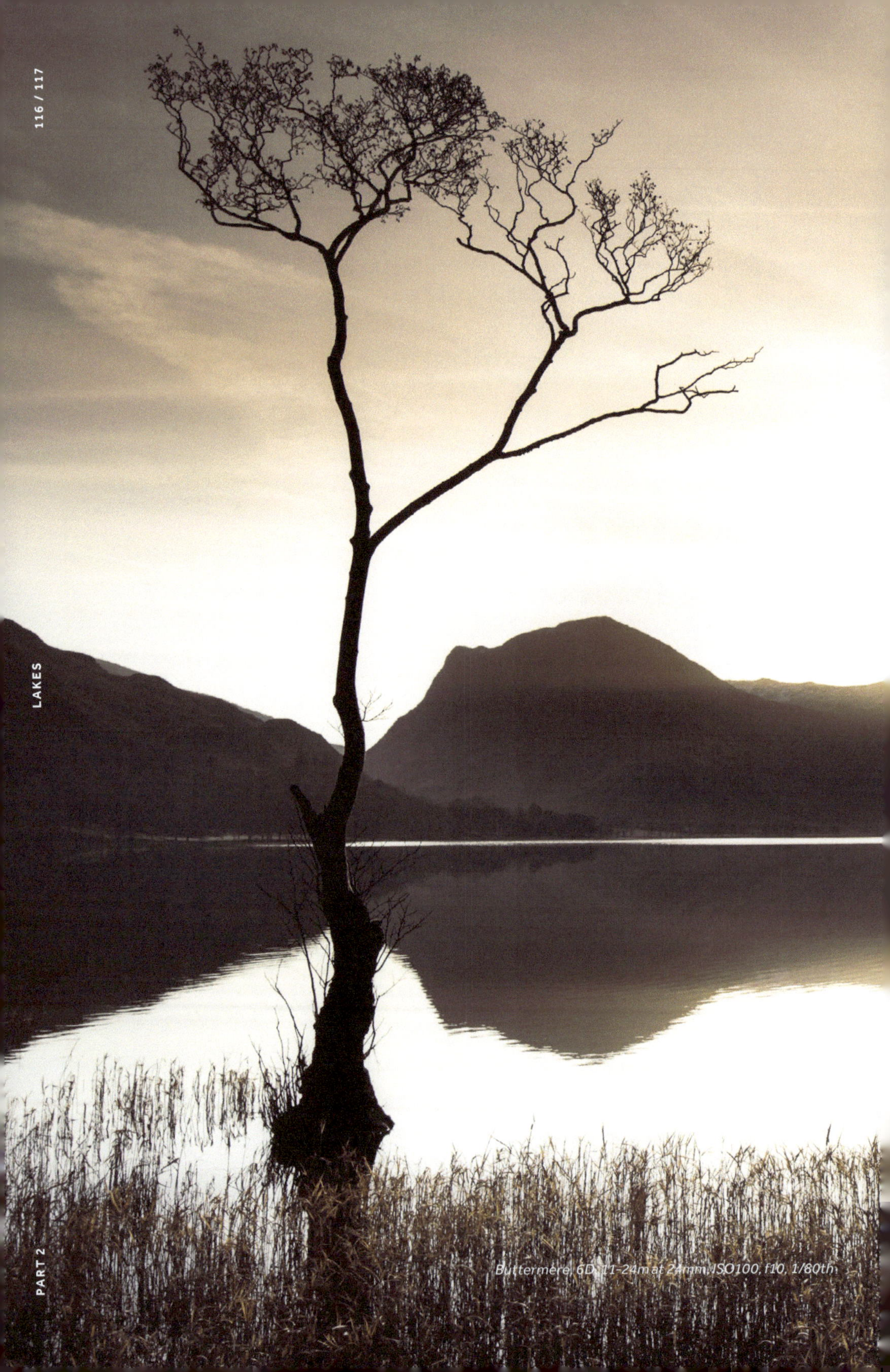

Buttermere, 6D, 11-24mm at 24mm, ISO100, f10, 1/80th

13

LAKES

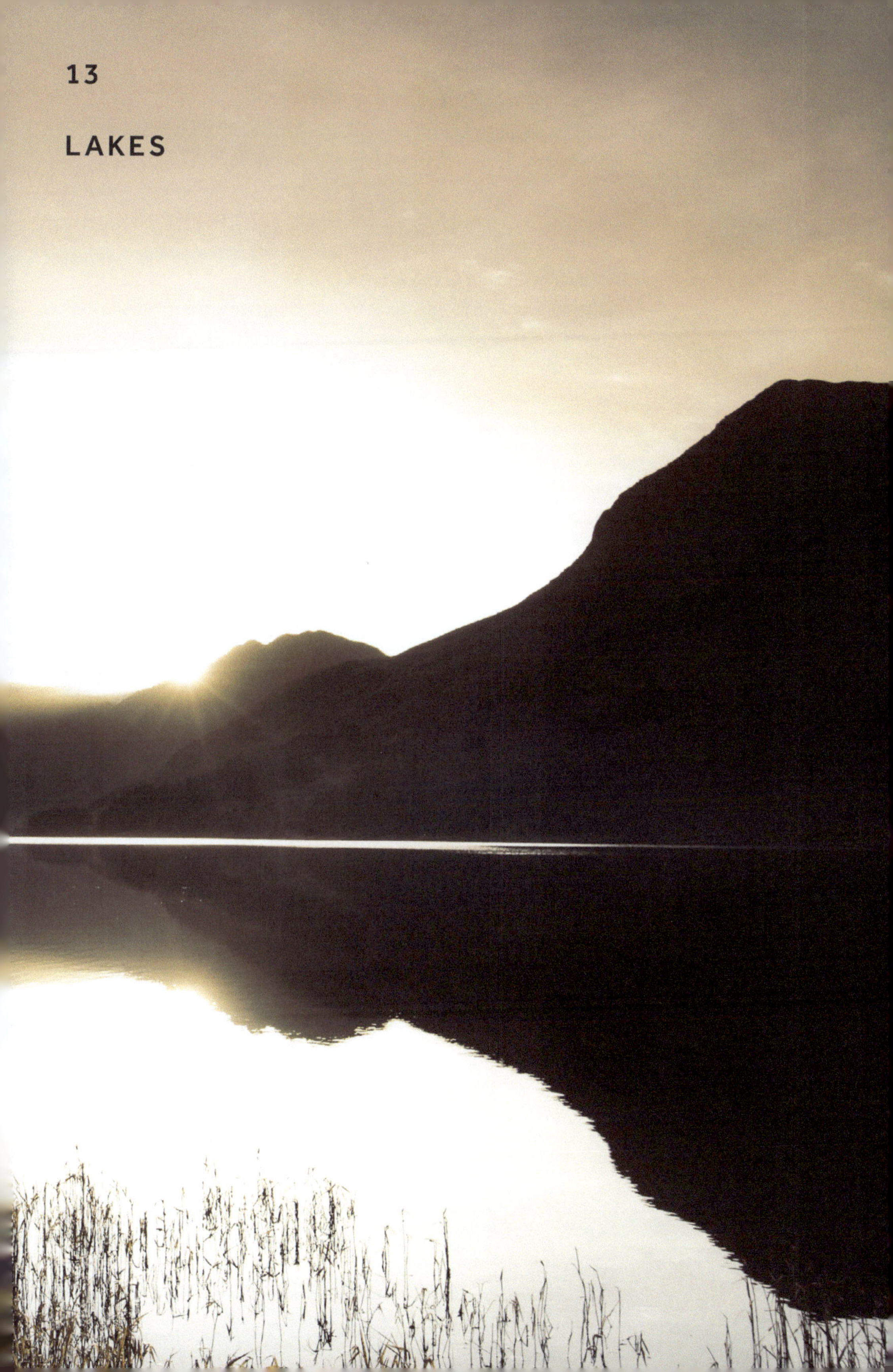

Where seascapes lend themselves to crashing waves and high drama, inland water is usually associated with calmness and serenity. A classic lake shot will feature a perfectly still stretch of water with a beautiful reflection.

COMPOSITION TIPS

1. **Pay attention to the foreground**
Add a bit of depth to your shot by including some foreground interest. A straight shot of the distant reflection can be a little static. If there are trees adjacent to your lake, try shooting through them for a more intriguing composition.
2. **Look for alternative shots**
If your lake shot doesn't lend itself to any foreground interest, consider shooting for a panorama (more details on this in Chapter 21). Or if the weather is stopping any reflections, get creative and look for detail shots.

Below left and right:
Compare these two almost identical shots of the Lac du Chevril, one with no foreground interest and the other with a little detail.
iPhone 6S.

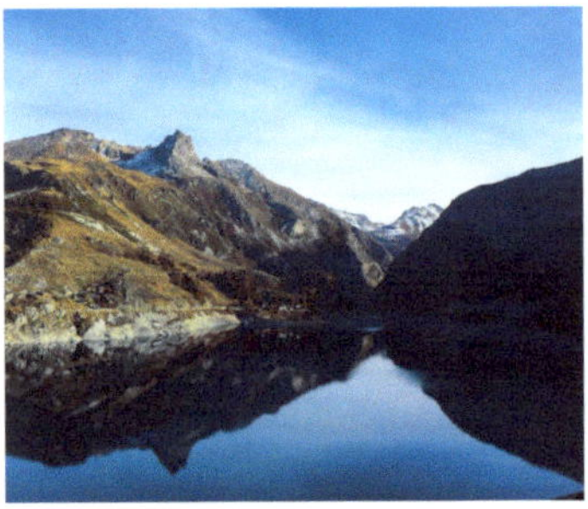

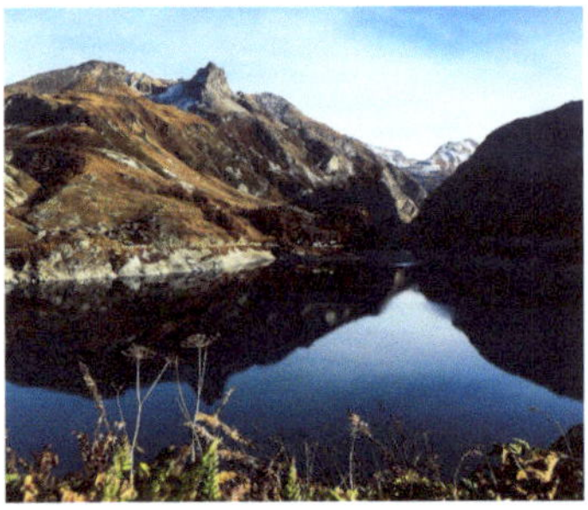

Right:
A more intimate landscape composition shot in a situation with little foreground interest at Loch Droma.
X-T1, 50-140mm at 140mm, ISO200, f2.8, 1/250th.

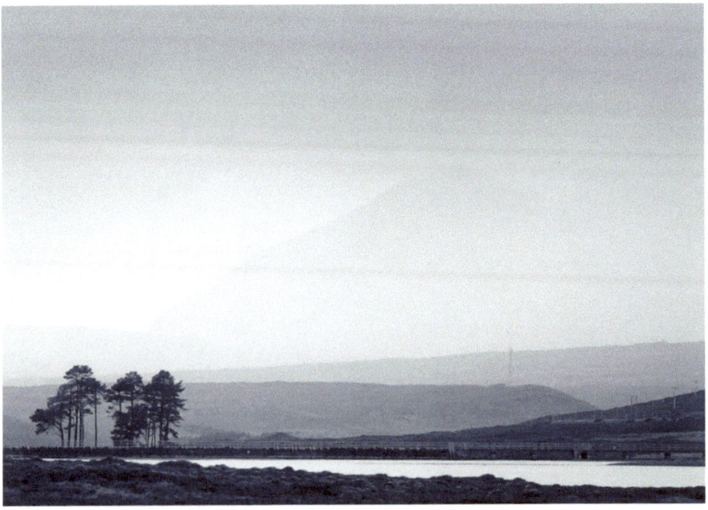

PRACTICAL TIPS

1. **Keep an eye on the wind forecast**

It's important to be aware of the wind forecast if you want perfectly still water. Get to know local factors that will affect the wind on the water such as the position of mountains around the water. It also helps to research how the land warms and cools throughout the year. Use a wind forecasting site (like Windfinder) to predict best times to shoot.

2. **Pick the right time of day**

Often early mornings or later evenings are the stillest times of day, but you will need to get to know a location for the best results. It can be useful to ask a local for help.

3. **Choose the right lens**

Don't automatically reach for your widest lens. Wide angle lenses can make the distant mountains seem very small in the shot.

SETTINGS - LAKES

1. Depth of field

If you are shooting just the distant mountains and reflections, you won't need a small aperture. Try f5.6 or f8. But as you begin to add foreground interest you will need to do some depth of field calculations. Use the hyperfocal distance focus technique (see Chapter 3 – Camera Controls), and decide what your acceptable sharpness is.

2. Shutter speed and ISO

You should be using a tripod, so shutter speed isn't important on a still day. Keep your ISO low (100 or 200). If you have a windy day, consider using a very long shutter speed (15-30 seconds) with a ND filter to blur the surface of the water smooth (more details on this in Chapter 19 – Long exposure).

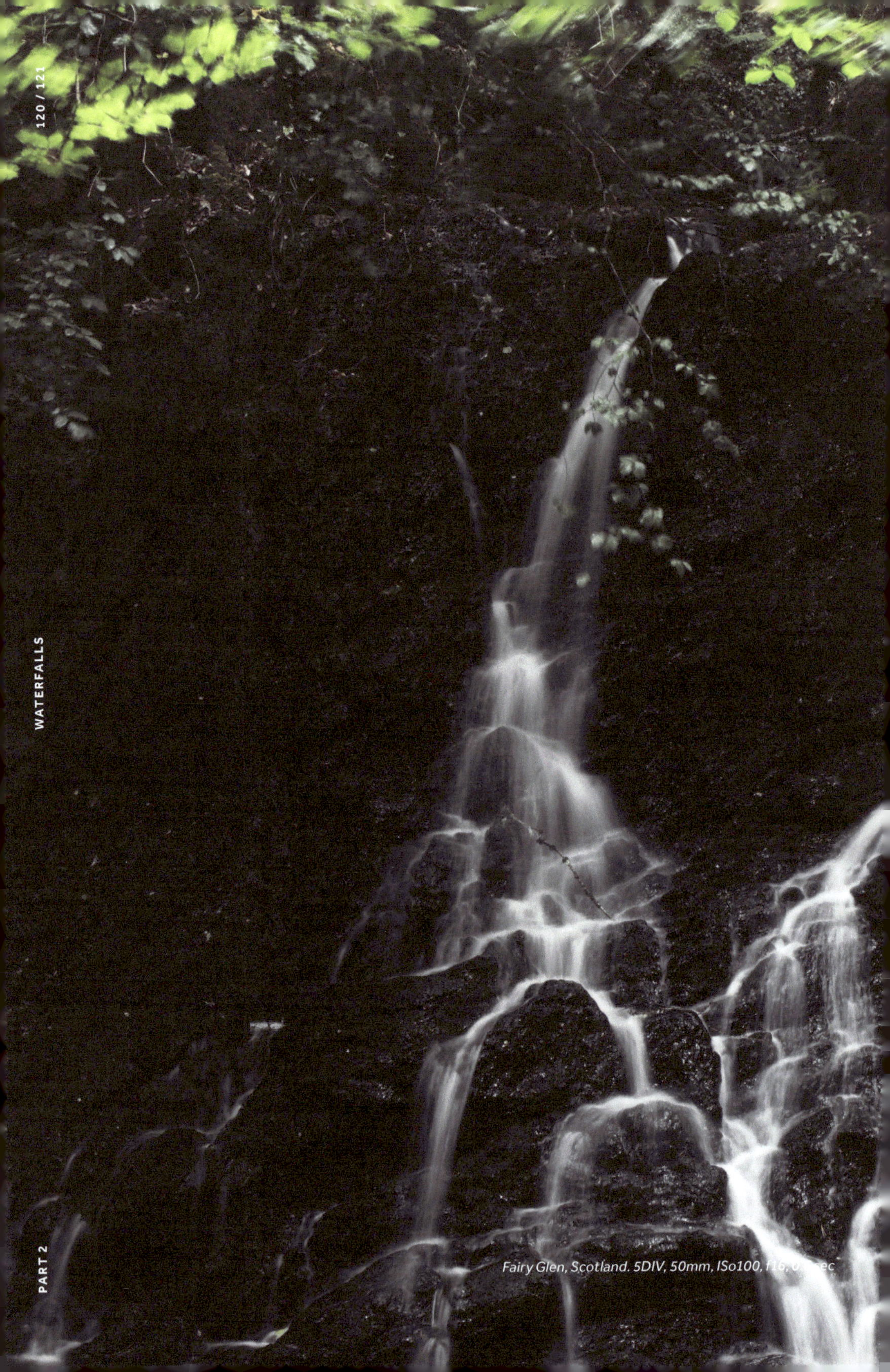

Fairy Glen, Scotland. 5DIV, 50mm, ISo100, f16, 0.[illegible]sec

14

WATERFALLS

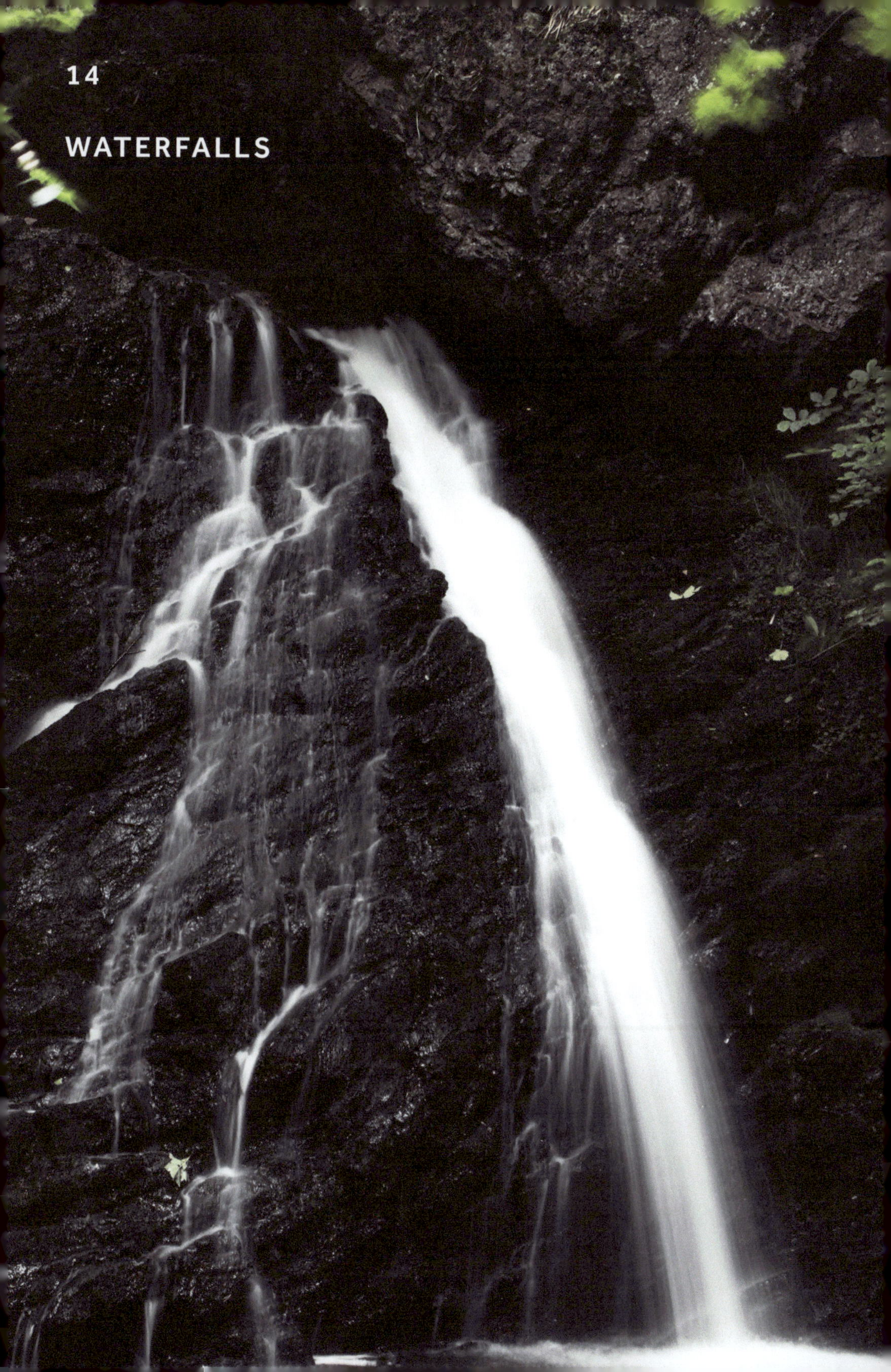

Waterfalls make stunning images, especially if you can use your shutter speed to blur the water attractively.

COMPOSITION TIPS

1. Look all around the frame

It is tempting to focus all your attention on the waterfall, and forget about what else is going on in the frame. But once your crashing water is frozen in time, all the boring rocks and distracting foliage around the edge of the frame will start to reduce the impact of the shot. Look once to decide on your shutter speed. Then look again to create an engaging shot.

2. Avoid a static shot

In Chapter 5 – Composition, you learnt about static vs. dynamic shots. Static shots have predominantly vertical and horizontal lines running through the frame, and it is easy to end up with a very static shot of a waterfall. If you just turn up and shoot the waterfall in the middle of the frame, you will have an uninteresting shot that does not do justice to the force of nature in front of you. Keep moving (safely – don't fall in), and try different angles and viewpoints.

Below left:
The shot on the left at Fairy Glen in Scotland has a very static, central composition with an uninteresting foreground and foliage that doesn't really add anything to the image.
5DIV, 50mm, ISO100, f16, 1/6th.

Below right:
The shot on the right (Glen Coe) has a more dynamic composition, with plenty of movement through the frame from top to bottom.
6D, 11-24mm at 24mm, ISO200, f22, 1/15th.

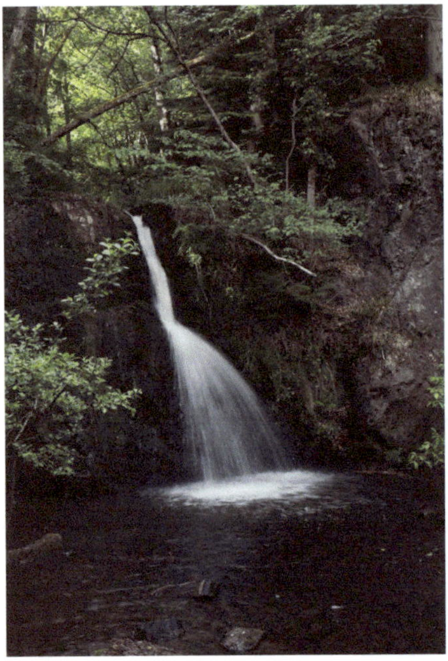

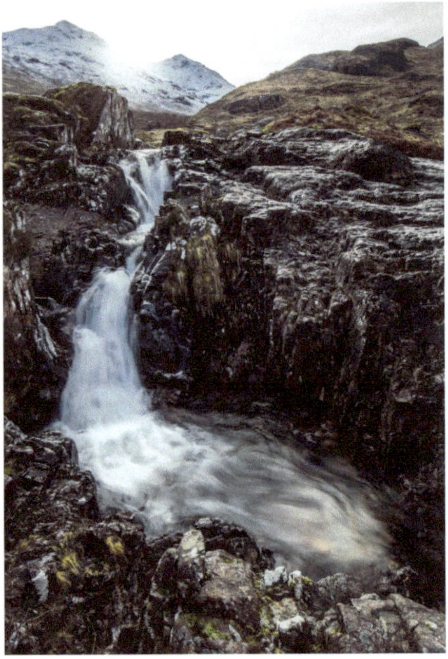

PRACTICAL TIPS

1. Keep your lens clean of water splashes

No matter how far away you are from the water, you always seem to end up with a few splashes on your lens. Keep an eye on the front of your camera, and have some wipes ready. This is what a lens full of water splashes looks like – there's no way of rescuing this with a bit of cloning in editing:

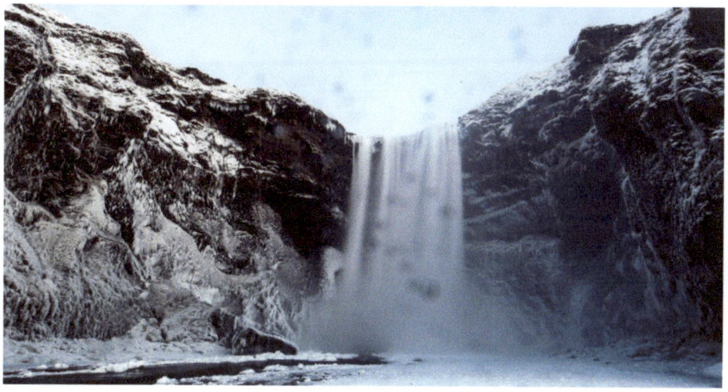

Left:
Skógafoss.
6D, 11-24mm at 20mm, ISO100, f22, 5 secs.

2. Waterfalls work well on cloudy days

Waterfalls are perfect for those overcast, grey days. You don't want a high contrast shot, otherwise all the white highlights will blow out, so waterfalls are the perfect project for a cloudy day.

3. Get rid of the yellow

You'll often get a yellow shadow in waterfalls, especially if it is near peaty soil. You can use a simple desaturate edit in most software to get rid of this if you want to. Just desaturate the yellows/ oranges. The shot on the left is unedited, but the shot on the right has had the oranges desaturated:

Below:
Waterfall off the A832 near Dundonnell.
6D, 11-24mm at 15mm, ISO100, f4, 0.6 sec.

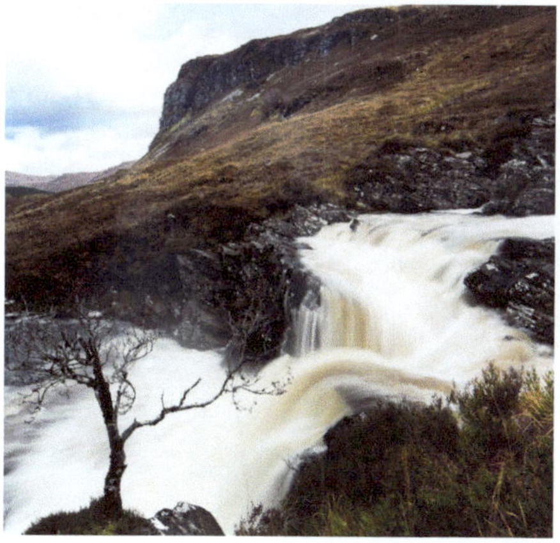

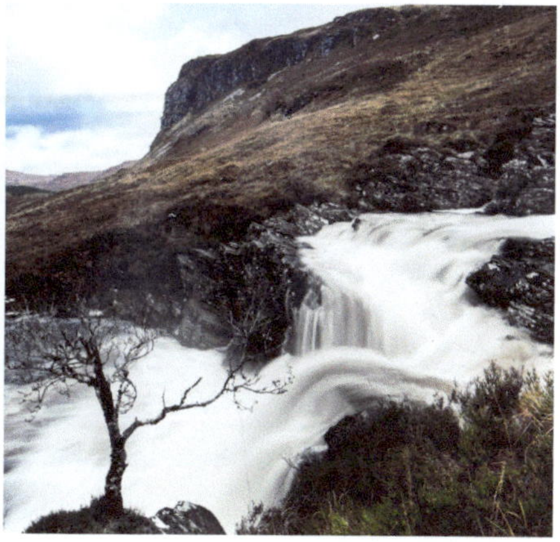

4. To freeze or to blur?

Do you want to freeze the spray or try to get a silky, blurred waterfall? You will need to do a bit of trial-and-error to work out exactly which shutter speed is best for the effect you want, the lens you are using and the distance you are from the waterfall. I recommend bracketing shutter speeds; take 4 or 5 shots at different speeds to make sure at least one of them is right. Half a second is usually a good start for a blurred effect that still keeps enough detail.

Below:
Rogie Falls.
X-T1, 50-140mm at 87mm, ISO200, f2.8. Top left 1/8th, top right 1/30th, bottom left 1/125th, bottom right 1/500th.

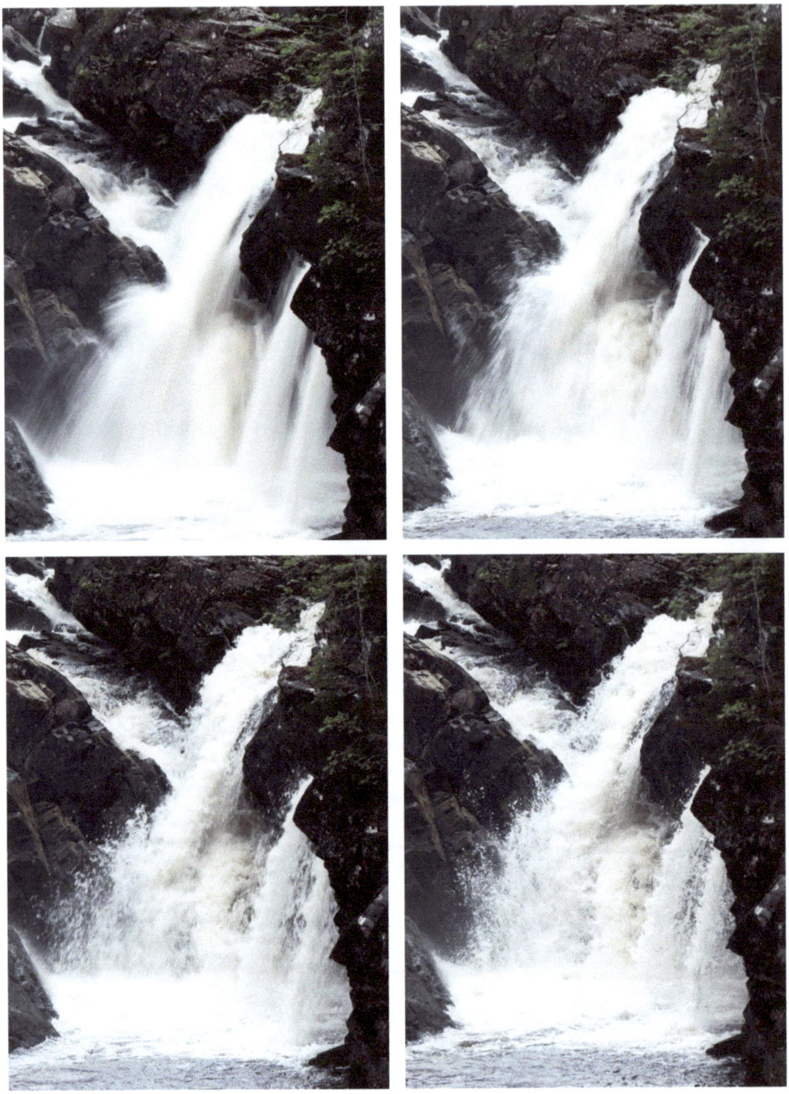

5. Exposure value

It's easy to blow your highlights with waterfall shots, and lose all the detail in the flowing water. Keep an eye on your histogram, and make sure it's not climbing the wall on the right hand side. The shot on the left below is correctly exposed for the rocks, but the waterfall is overexposed and the whites have blown out. You can see this clearly on the histogram – on the right hand side it has climbed all the way to the top. The shot on the right is correctly exposed for the waterfall. You can see the rocks have been thrown into deep shadow, but the histogram no longer touches on the right hand side.

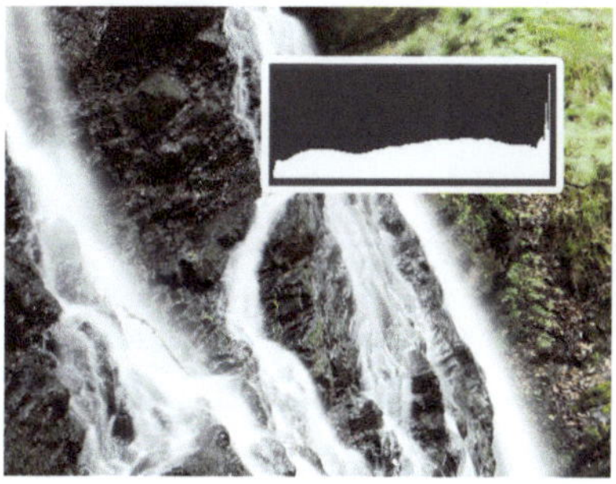

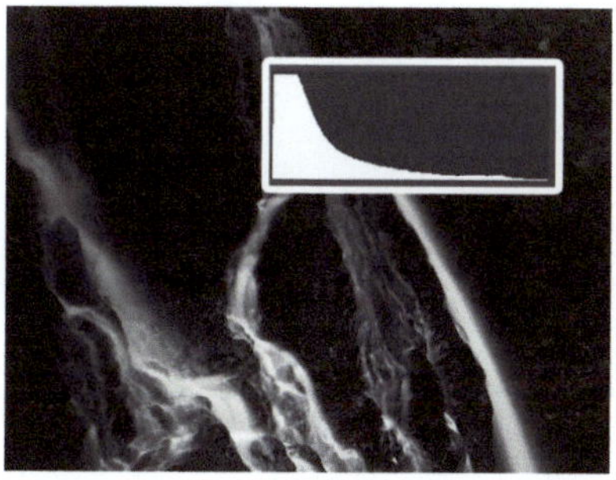

SETTINGS - WATERFALLS

1. Shutter speed

For wispy threads of water start with a shutter speed of about half a second. To freeze the water use at least 1/500th, preferably 1/2000th. Exact settings will depend on how close you are to the water.

2. Aperture and ISO

As shutter speed is the critical creative decision, use both aperture and ISO to achieve the correct exposure, always keeping ISO as low as you can. It's probably best to shoot on manual mode rather than shutter priority, so you can manipulate all three controls separately. Make sure you focus carefully, especially if you are using a wider aperture.

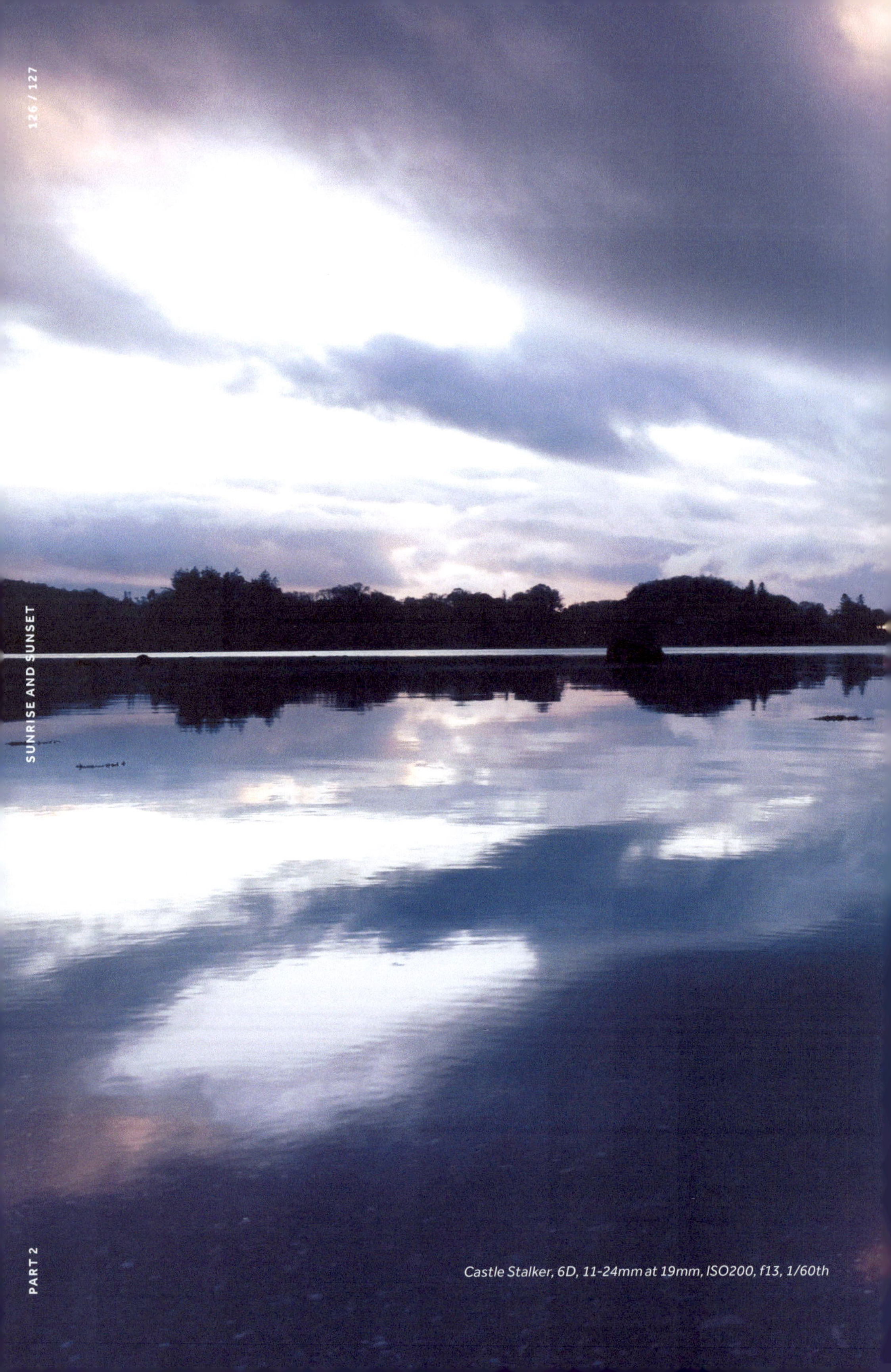

Castle Stalker, 6D, 11-24mm at 19mm, ISO200, f13, 1/60th

15

SUNRISE AND SUNSET

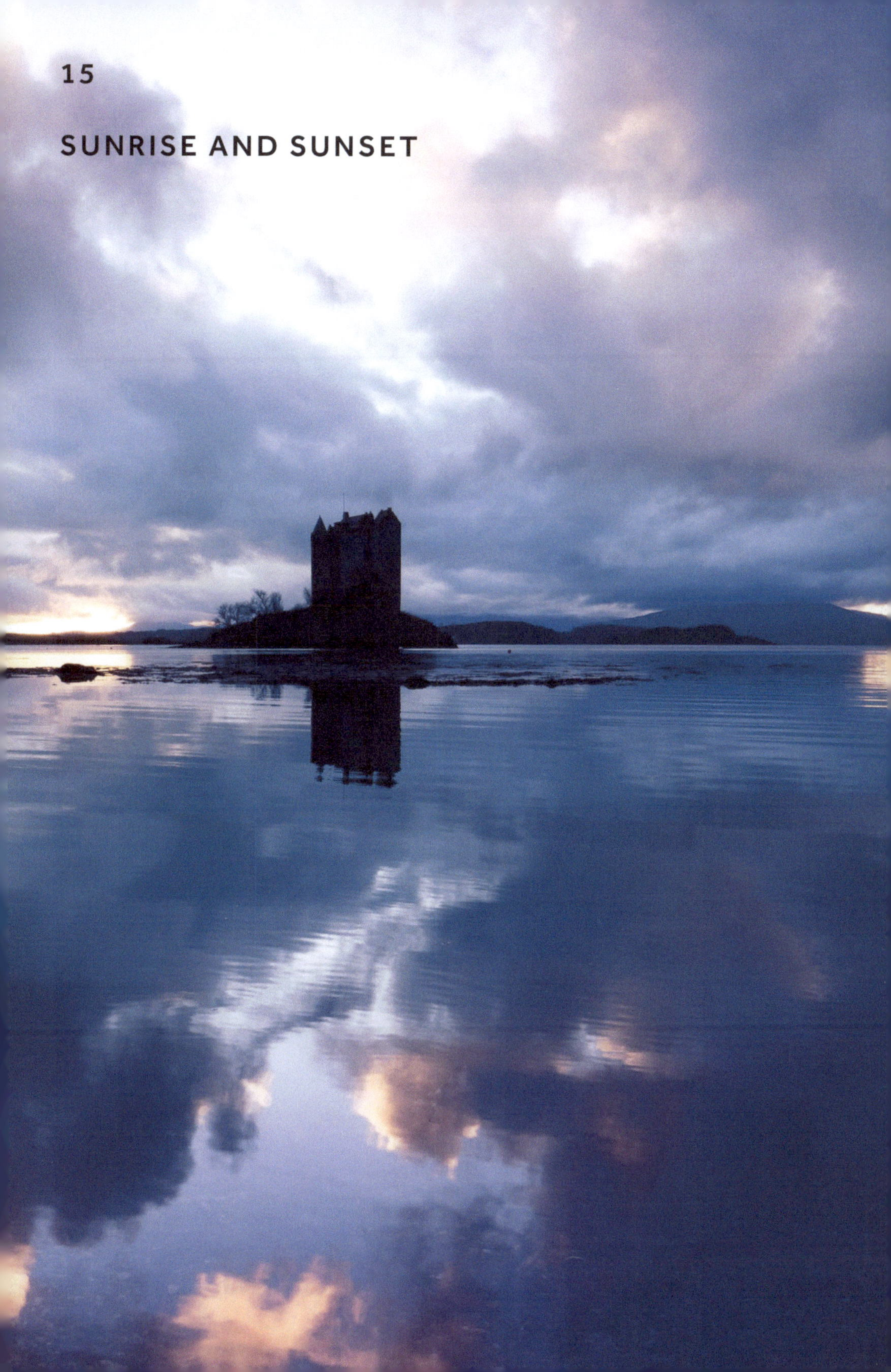

At each end of the day, the light is at its most deceptive. In the blue and golden hours your eye and brain conspire together to make you think you are looking at a majestic display. When you get home and look at your images you find that the camera saw things differently:

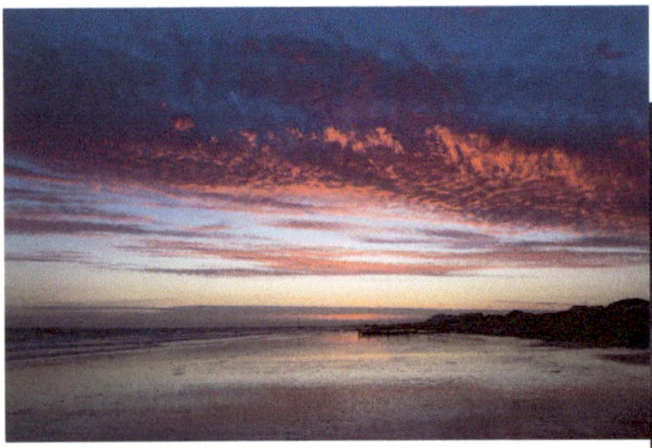

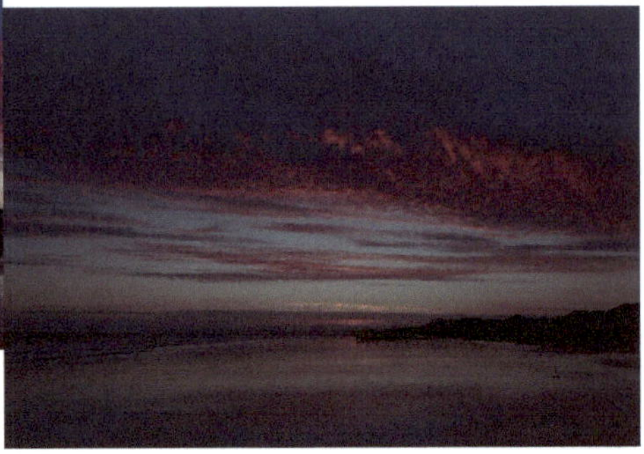

Above left:
What you think you saw.
Above right:
What the camera actually saw.
6D, 11-24mm at 24mm, ISO400, f8, 1/100th.

This happens because of the high contrast between the sky and the landscape, and because of your metering mode. The camera meters from the whole scene (unless you've switched to spot metering) and the contrast between the brights and darks evens out to be usually a lot darker than you remember. You need to choose which part of the sky you want to be correctly exposed *and then ignore the rest*.

PRACTICAL TIPS

1. Shoot RAW

Always shoot RAW images to give yourself the most flexibility when you get home. A RAW file holds all the information that was there when you pressed the shutter and you just need to coax it out of the shadows.

2. Watch your histogram

Be objective about the range of tones. Critically assess what the brightest point in the shot is (usually the sun, if it is in shot), and the darkest (some point on the landscape in shadow). Your eye will be able to see the detail in both, but your camera will not (see dynamic range, in Chapter 3). As you get to know your camera you will become familiar with its dynamic range capabilities. Consider exposure bracketing and an HDR merge in editing.

3. Watch your metering mode

Be aware of where your camera is metering from in the frame and either change it to something that gives a more accurate exposure, or just use manual mode.

4. Expose for the sky

If in doubt, expose for the sky and let the landscape drop to a silhouette.

5. What time does the action happen?

You can get exact sunrise/sunset times months ahead of time. Use apps like The Photographer's Ephemeris, or just a weather forecasting site.

Your latitude affects the seasonal shift in timing. The closer you are to the poles, the more extreme the seasonal change in sunrise/sunset times. In the UK, a sunrise shot in June might be at 5am, but in December it will be at 8am. If you are close to the equator, then sunrise won't change much from 6am year-round.

The sky starts to change colour up to an hour before the sun actually rises, so for a sunrise shot aim to arrive before it starts to get light. Check out your route the day before if you will be arriving in the dark (and bring a torch). Pre-dawn can be cold, so come prepared. Once the sun approaches the horizon the light changes rapidly, so have your settings ready prepared, and adjust them as it gets brighter.

6. Hang around

If you're shooting a sunset, don't rush off the minute the sun goes down. The light can keep changing as the sun moves away.

7. Cloud height

Colourful sunrises/sunsets happen when the angle of the sun's light catches the underside of the clouds. Clear skies may briefly turn orange or red, but for a classic shot you will want some cloud cover to catch the colour.

Broadly speaking, higher clouds produce more colourful sunsets, because there is less atmospheric pollution for the sun's rays to fight through. In the Annex, there is a link to a paper from the US National Weather Service which explains this in much more detail.

Don't forget to turn around and look at the sky opposite the sun – the action may all be happening behind you.

6. Use your graduated filter

If you have one, now is the time to use your graduated neutral density filter. Line it up carefully with the horizon, and it will even-out the contrast between the sky and the landscape.

7. Silhouettes

To force foreground details into a silhouette, make sure you expose for the sky. With auto exposure metering your camera may take the foreground into account, and your whole shot will be over exposed – you'll lose the detail in the sky and the foreground becomes correctly exposed. Either spot meter off the sky, or dial in minus 2 or 3 stops of exposure compensation.

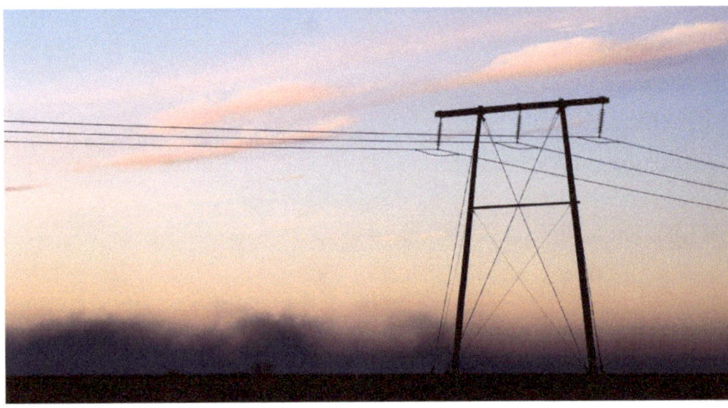

Right:
Electricity pylon in Iceland silhouetted against the sunset.
X-T1, 50-140mm at 75mm, ISO320, f8, 1/160th.

COMPOSITION TIPS

1. Use the rule of thirds

If you have a sky on fire, this is going to be the main interest in your image. So you would usually place the horizon on the bottom "rule of thirds" line, rather than either centrally or in the top half of the shot.

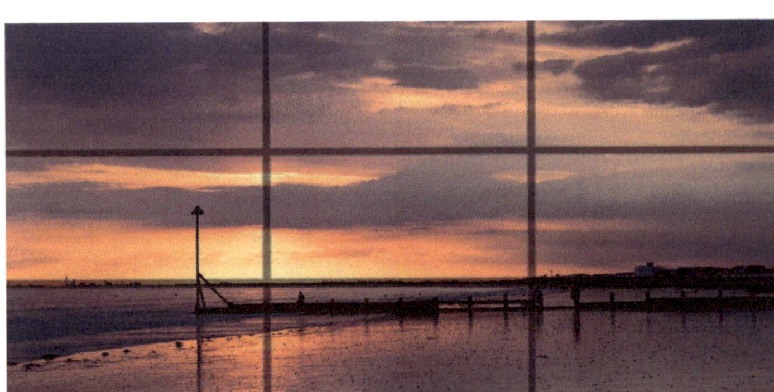

2. Break the rules

If you have a sunset where a strong symmetrical composition is needed, then place the horizon in the middle. And if you have a stronger foreground than sky, place the horizon on the upper thirds line. The only rule I don't think you can break is having a straight horizon – so make sure it is level, and straighten it in editing if necessary

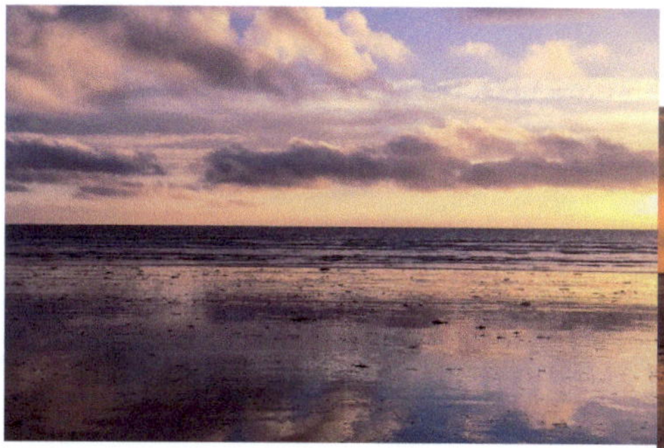

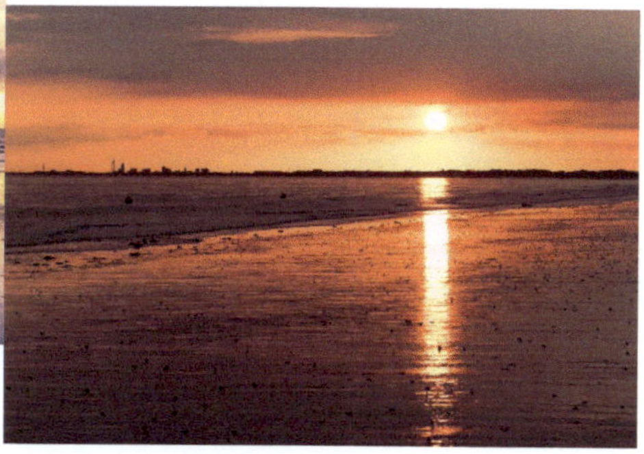

Above left:
Bracklesham Bay, horizon centrally composed.
iPhone 5S.

Above right:
Bracklesham Bay, composed according to the rule of thirds.
X-T1, 50-140mm at 50mm, ISO200, f4, 1/170th.

SETTINGS - SUNRISE/SUNSET

1. Depth of field

You will usually be shooting the sky and the horizon, so you can get away with very wide apertures if needed (f2.8, f4). If you want to include foreground, calculate your hyperfocal distance to ensure it stays sharp, and increase the aperture as required.

2. Shutter speed and ISO

Unless you are using a very long shutter speed to blur the clouds (see Chapter 19 – Long Exposure), the shutter speed usually isn't important if you have a tripod, so let it extend to whatever is needed. You may find shooting on manual mode gives you more control over the exposure as the light changes. Keep your aperture fixed, and use shutter speed/ISO to manipulate the exposure as required.

3. White balance

If you leave your white balance on "auto" you may find odd colour casts as the light changes. Shoot RAW so you can correct any mistakes, and set your white balance to "cloudy" or "sunny" to force a warmer white balance.

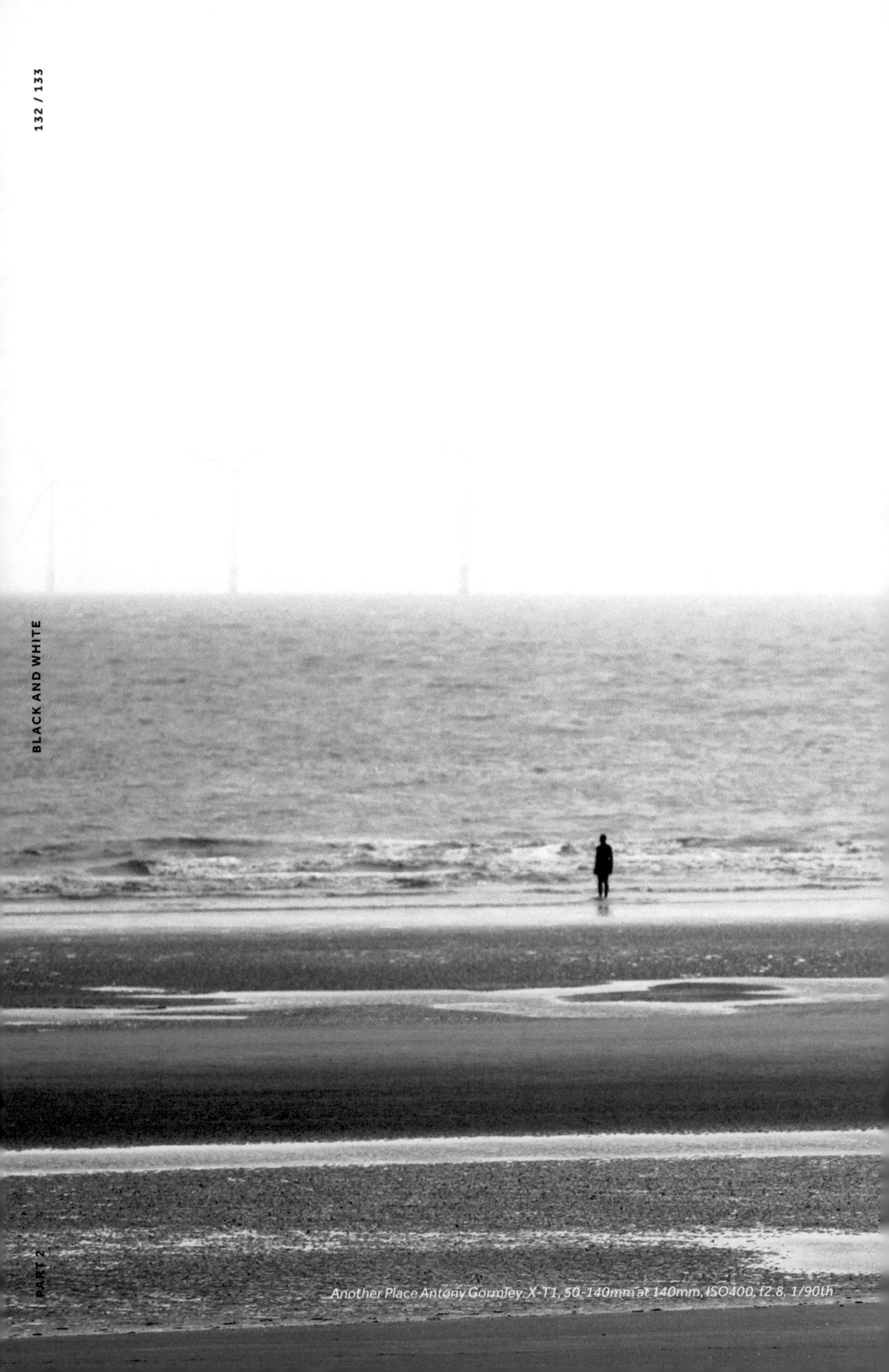

Another Place Antony Gormley. X-T1, 50-140mm at 140mm, ISO400, f2.8, 1/90th

16

BLACK AND WHITE

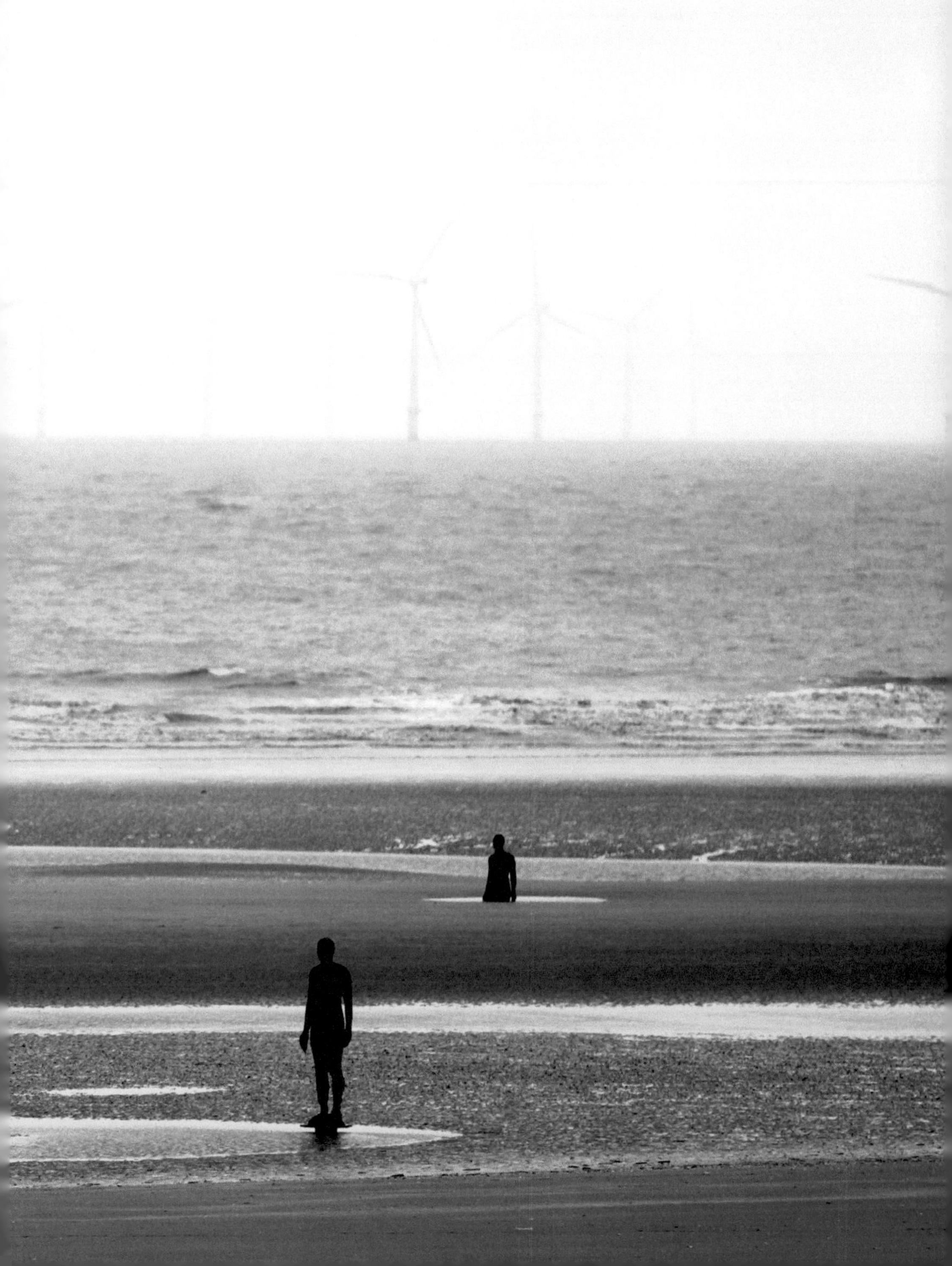

There are some shots that lend themselves to black and white, especially when the subject is so strong that any colour would be a distraction. In particular, texture, shape and tonal contrast work well in black and white.

1. Texture

Right:
The texture in the sand at Mellon Udrigle beach is more striking when shown in black and white.
6D, 11-24mm at 21mm, ISO100, f22, 13 seconds.

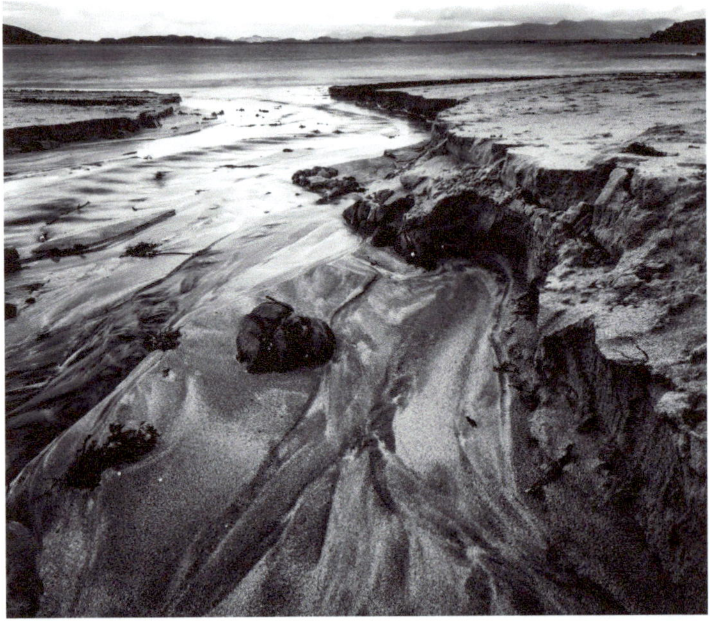

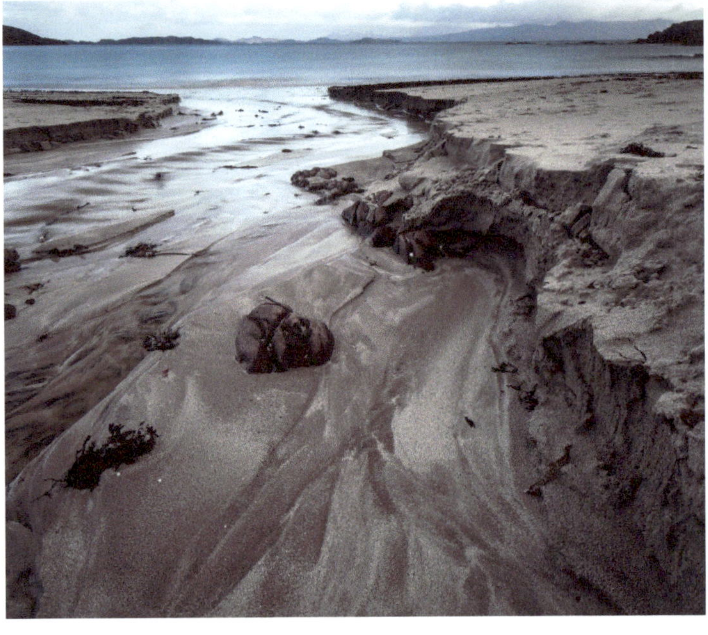

2. Shape

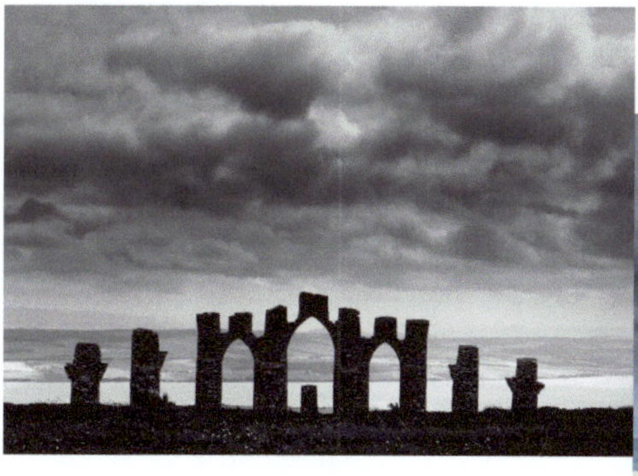

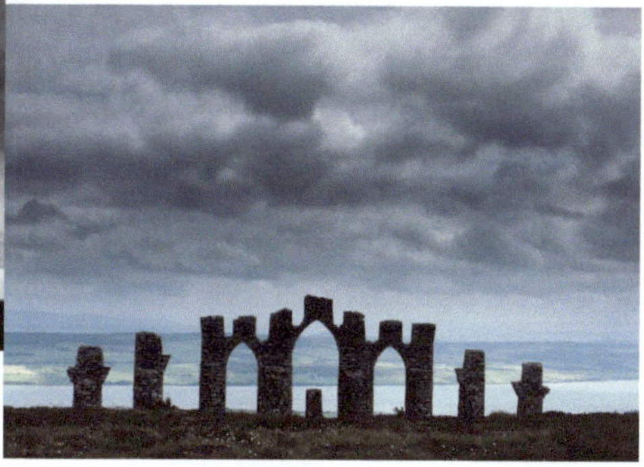

3. Tonal contrast

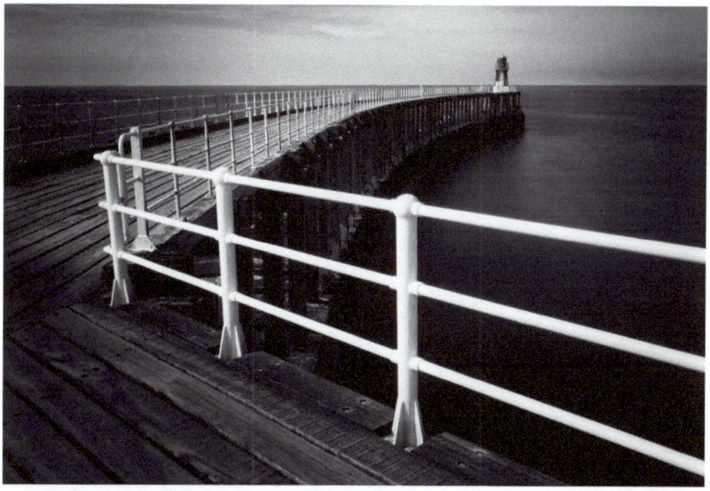

Above:
Cnoc Fyrish - black and white allows the shape of the monument to dominate, without being distracted by the blues and greens beyond.
5DIV, 50mm, ISO100, f5.6, 1/2000th.

Left:
The contrast between the dark and light tones on Whitby Pier is enhanced by the monotone treatment.
5DIV, 11-24mm at 24mm, ISO100, f22, 55 seconds.

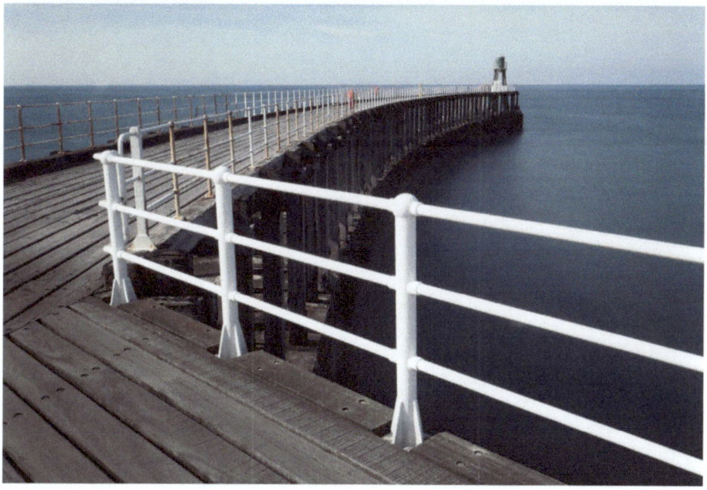

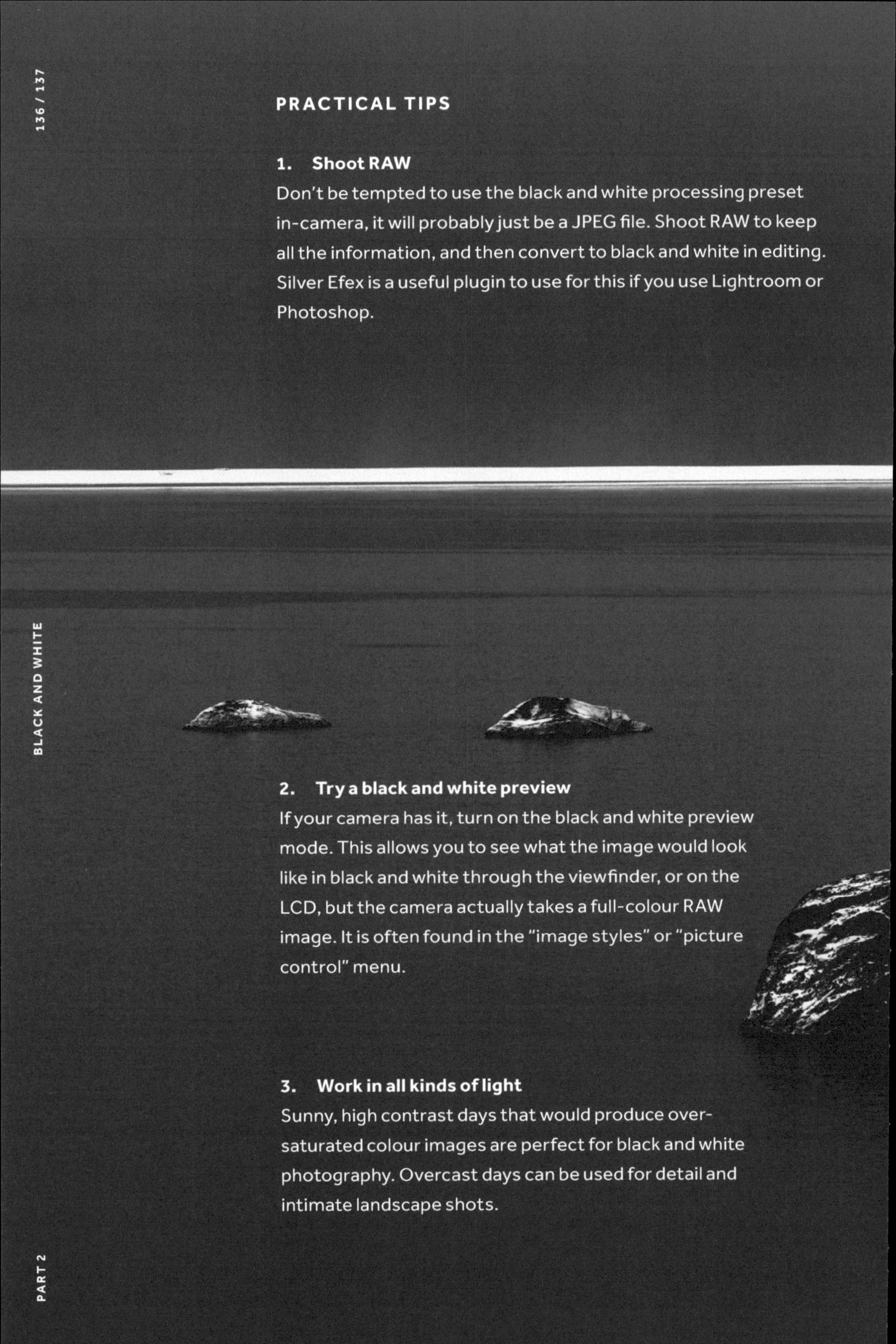

PRACTICAL TIPS

1. Shoot RAW

Don't be tempted to use the black and white processing preset in-camera, it will probably just be a JPEG file. Shoot RAW to keep all the information, and then convert to black and white in editing. Silver Efex is a useful plugin to use for this if you use Lightroom or Photoshop.

2. Try a black and white preview

If your camera has it, turn on the black and white preview mode. This allows you to see what the image would look like in black and white through the viewfinder, or on the LCD, but the camera actually takes a full-colour RAW image. It is often found in the "image styles" or "picture control" menu.

3. Work in all kinds of light

Sunny, high contrast days that would produce over-saturated colour images are perfect for black and white photography. Overcast days can be used for detail and intimate landscape shots.

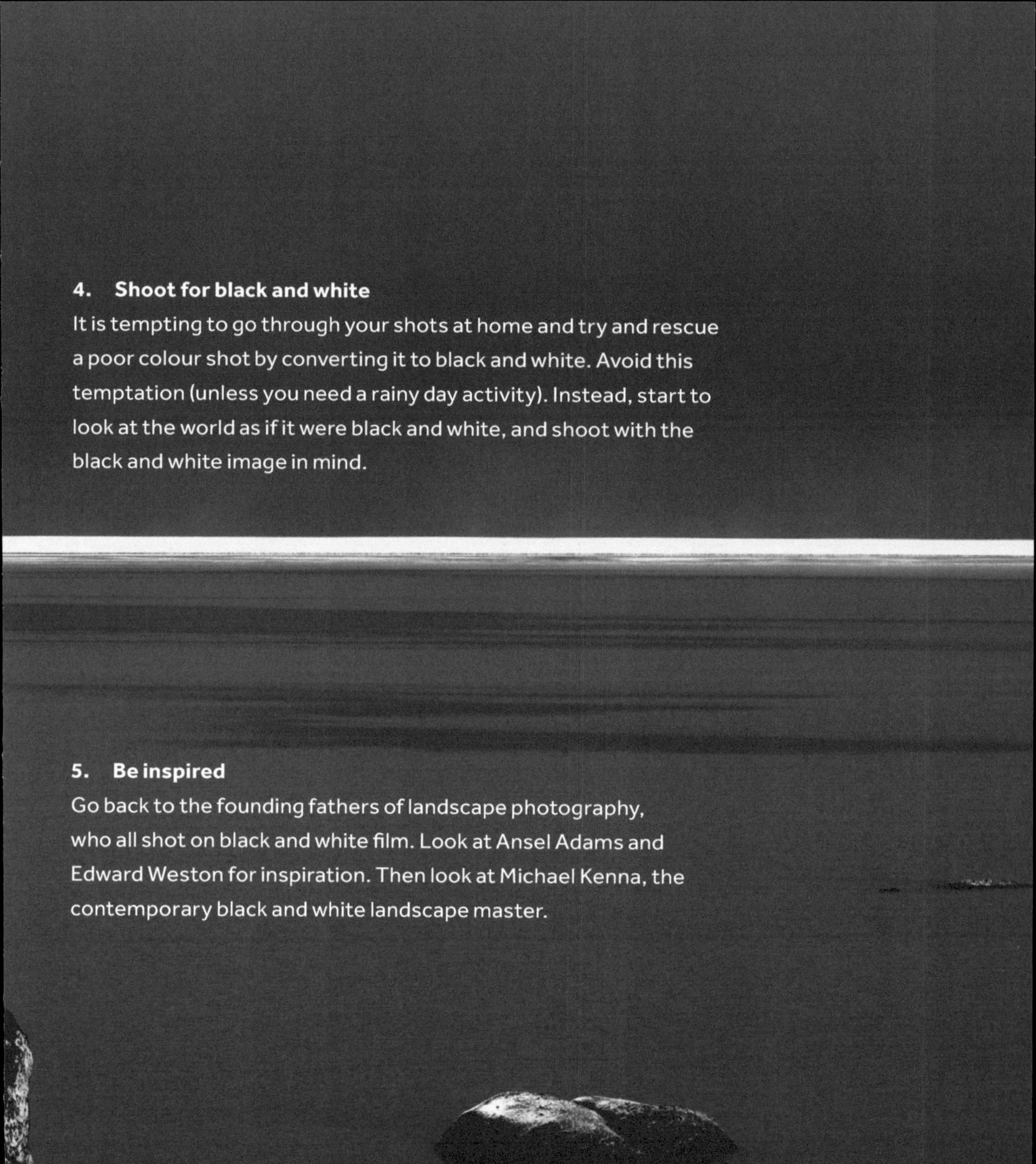

4. Shoot for black and white

It is tempting to go through your shots at home and try and rescue a poor colour shot by converting it to black and white. Avoid this temptation (unless you need a rainy day activity). Instead, start to look at the world as if it were black and white, and shoot with the black and white image in mind.

5. Be inspired

Go back to the founding fathers of landscape photography, who all shot on black and white film. Look at Ansel Adams and Edward Weston for inspiration. Then look at Michael Kenna, the contemporary black and white landscape master.

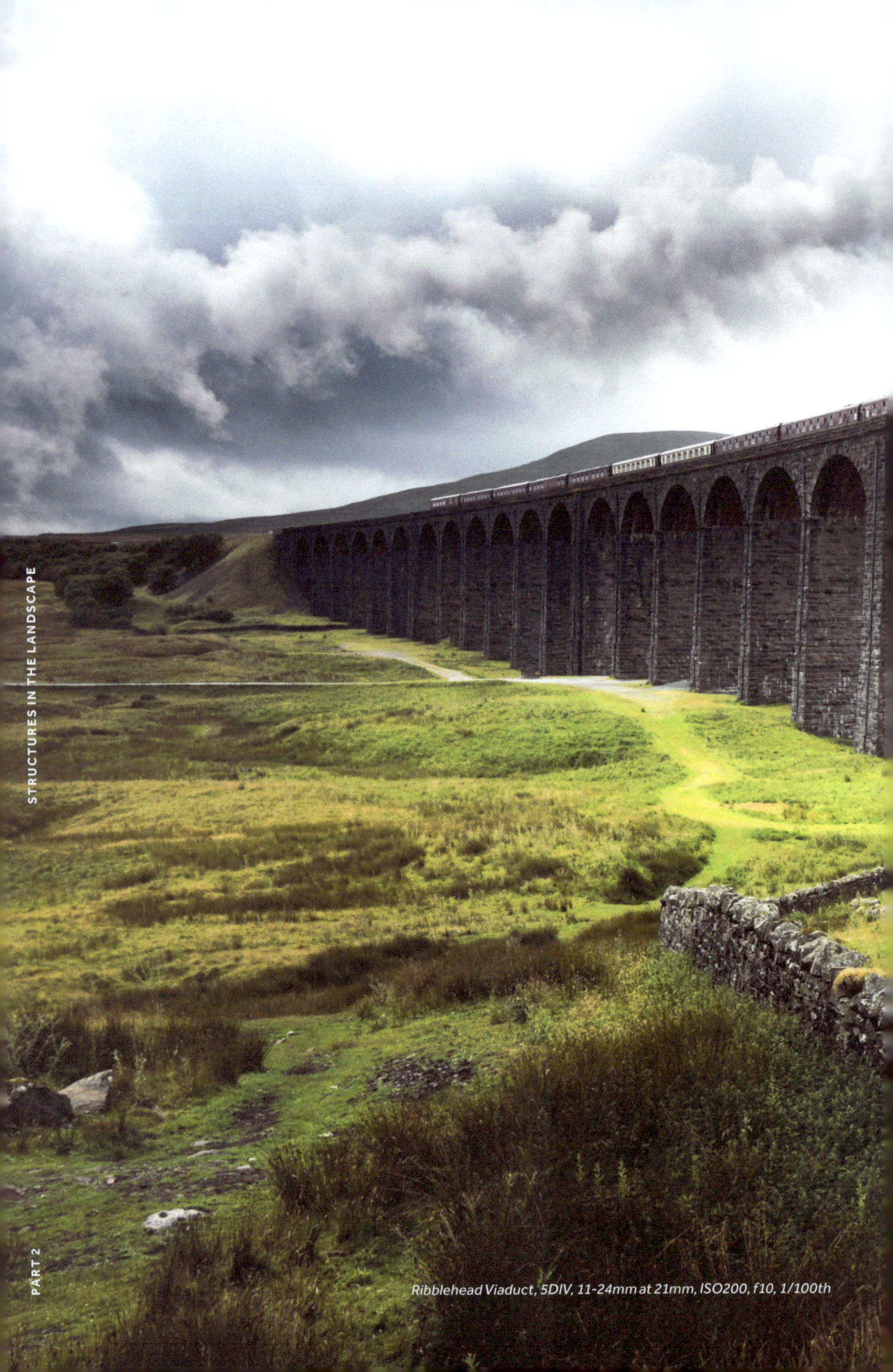

Ribblehead Viaduct, 5DIV, 11-24mm at 21mm, ISO200, f10, 1/100th

17

STRUCTURES IN THE LANDSCAPE

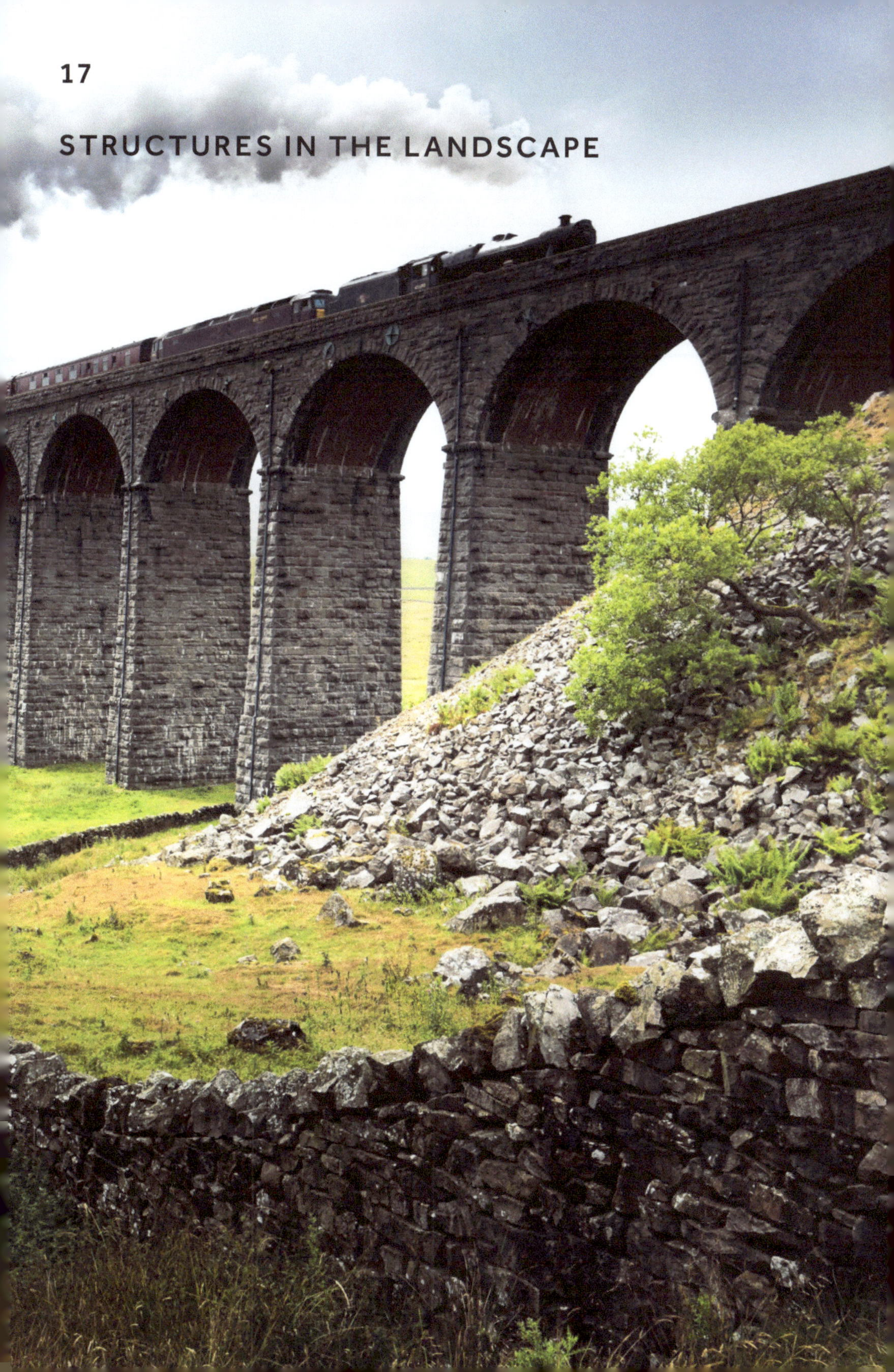

Anything built by humans can become part of a landscape shot. A classic lighthouse on a peninsula adds context and purpose to an otherwise unremarkable seascape. The ruins of a castle in the hills remind us that many have come before us and many will come after.

Be careful not to tip over into architectural photography. Buildings in the landscape should be just that: a structure that adds to the story of the landscape shot you are composing, not a portrait of a building that could be anywhere.

The shot below left of the church at Burnsall shows the building set against the landscape of the Yorkshire Dales. The shot below right is becoming less a landscape shot and more a straightforward architectural portrait.

Below left:
X-T1, 50-140mm at 50mm, ISO200, f4, 1/800th handheld.
Below right:
X-T1, 50-140mm at 80mm, ISO400, f8, 1/680th handheld.

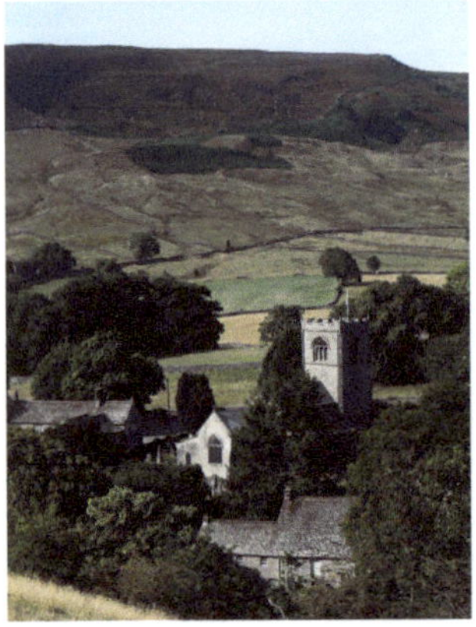

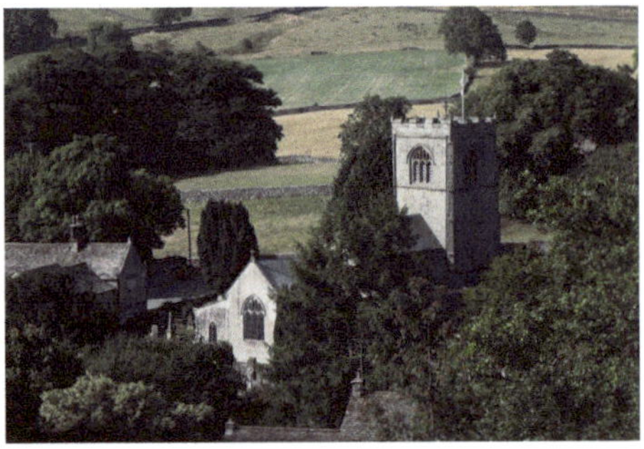

COMPOSITION TIPS

1. Consider your focal point

A built object in the environment will always draw the eye, so usually you will deliberately place it in the frame to form your focal point. Be careful if you don't want it to be your focal point - it will probably compete for attention anyway.

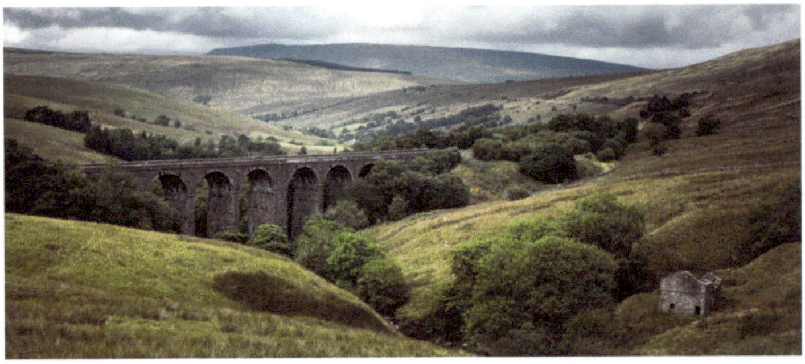

Right:
Dent Head Viaduct as the focal point, with the old barn as a counterpoint. Notice how your eye doesn't really settle anywhere else in the image apart from these two points. *6D, 50mm, ISO100, f9, 1/250th handheld.*

2. Be aware of where your structure is within your frame

Your main decision will be how much of the frame the structure will occupy: is it a distant point drawing the eye through the frame, is it front-and-centre in the foreground, or does it lurk peacefully in the middle-distance?

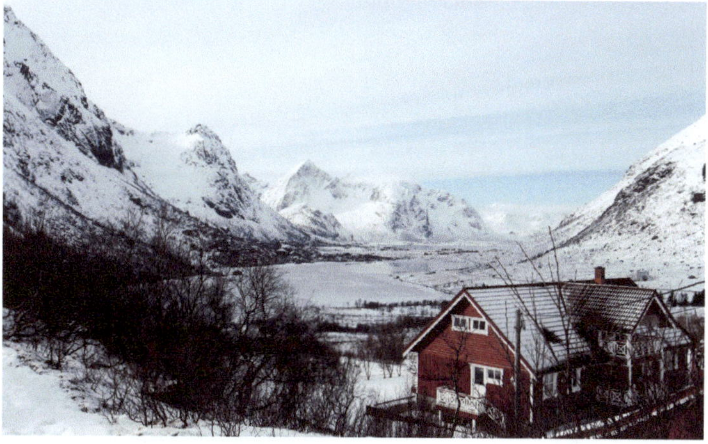

Left:

The traditional Norwegian building in the foreground acts as a stepping-in point to the shot, before the eye travels to the landscape beyond.

X-T1, 50-140mm at 50mm, ISO200, f4, 1/800th handheld.

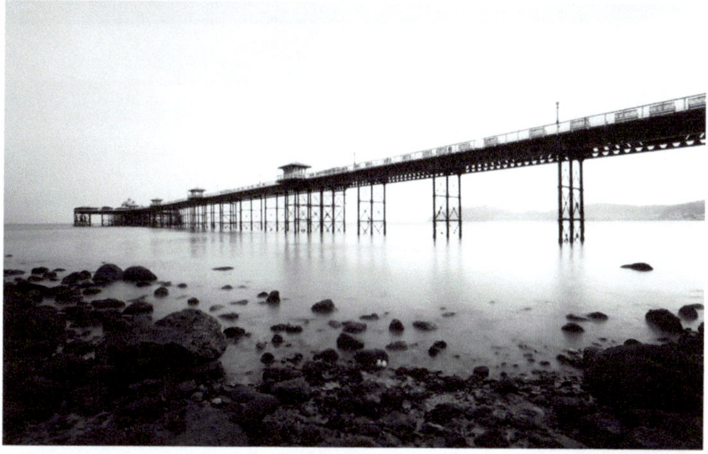

Left:

The pier at Llandudno stays in the mid-ground of the image, with the stones as the foreground and the hills beyond as the background.

6D, 11-24mm at 18mm, ISO100, f22, 4 seconds.

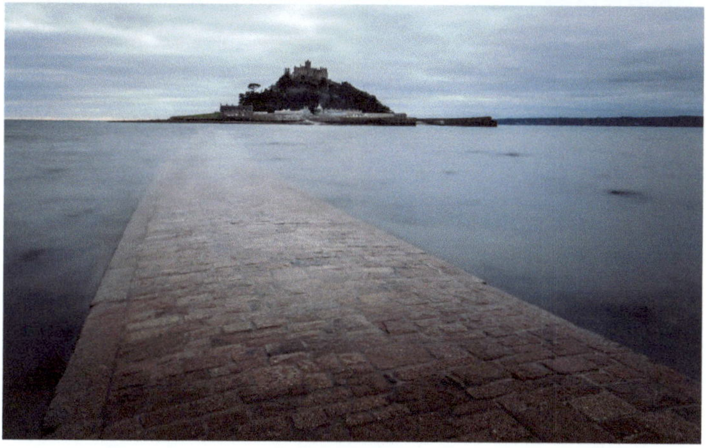

Left:

St Michael's Mount in the far distance of the image with the causeway leading the eye through the shot.

5DIV, 11-24mm at 24mm, ISO100, f22, 5 seconds, 6-stop ND filter.

3. Consider the age of the structure

Somehow castle ruins or a weathered bridge seem to be a more integral part of the landscape than a more contemporary structure. There's no reason not to shoot modern buildings in the landscape, but just be aware that they will often interrupt the viewer more than an ancient building.

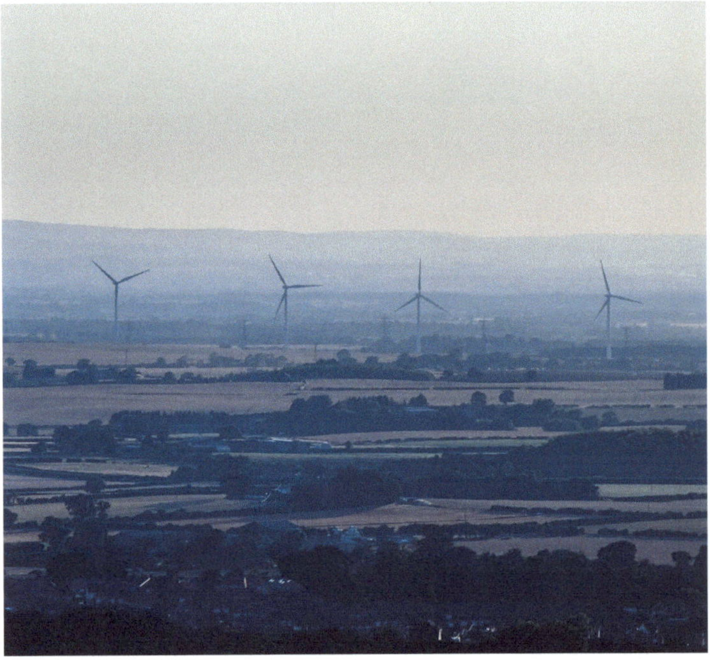

Right:
The view from Roseberry Topping.
X-T1, 50-140mm at 140mm, ISO200, f4, 1/2500th handheld.

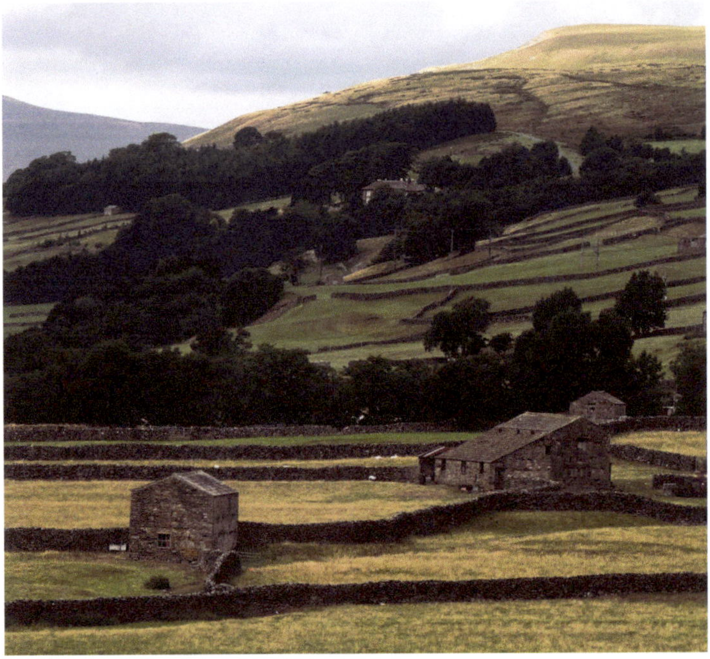

Right:
A more traditional view of the Yorkshire built landscape: Swaledale.
X-T1, 50-140mm at 140mm, ISO200, f8, 1/240th handheld.

PRACTICAL TIP: DEALING WITH PEOPLE IN THE SHOT

Popular built structures are often crowded with other people. You have 4 choices:

1. Arrive early, before the crowds.
2. Choose a viewpoint that hides them.
3. Clone them out in editing (which may not be an option if your shot is for a competition).
4. If they are moving, you can use a very, very long exposure so that they don't record on the final shot:

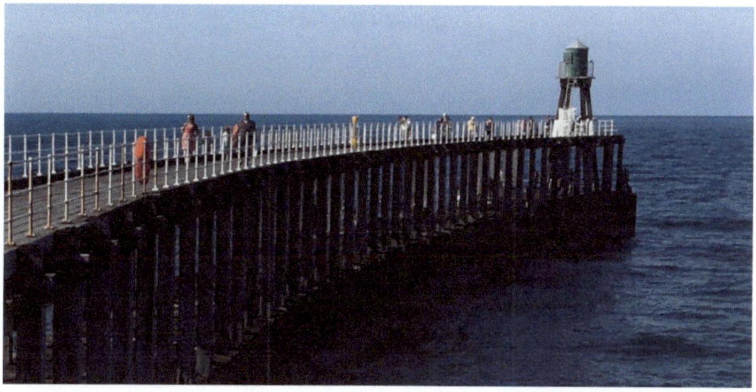

Left:
iPhone shot showing the people on the pier at Whitby.

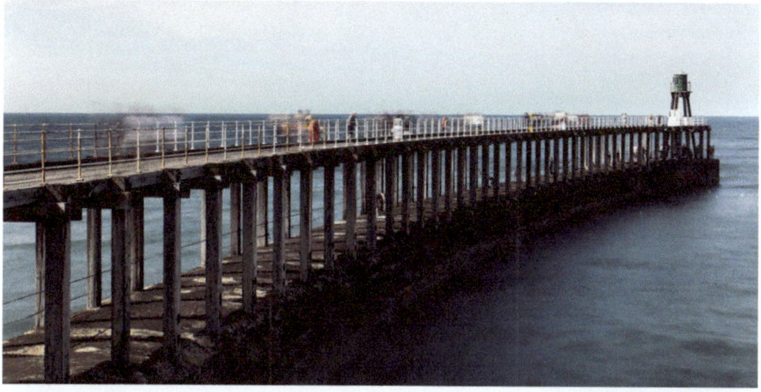

Left:
At 3 seconds, the people have started to blur out.

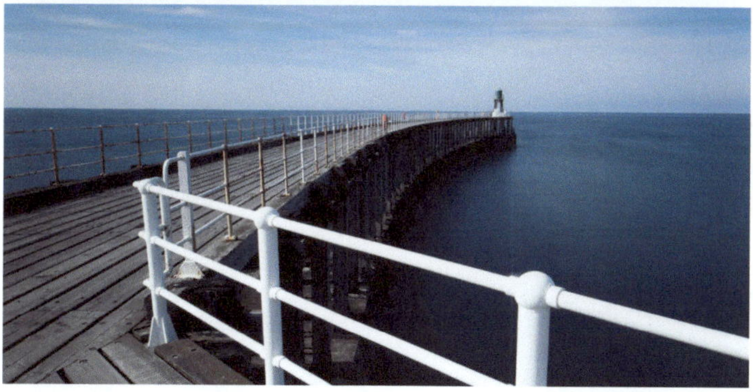

Left:
At 47 seconds, the people have vanished. Only the lifebelt remains. The pier was still full of people, but they didn't stay in one place long enough to register on the final shot. *5DIV, 11-24mm at 24mm, ISO100, f22, 47 seconds, 10-stop ND filter.*

Kielder Forest, 6D, 11-24mm at 11mm, ISO3200, f5, 30 secs

18

NIGHT

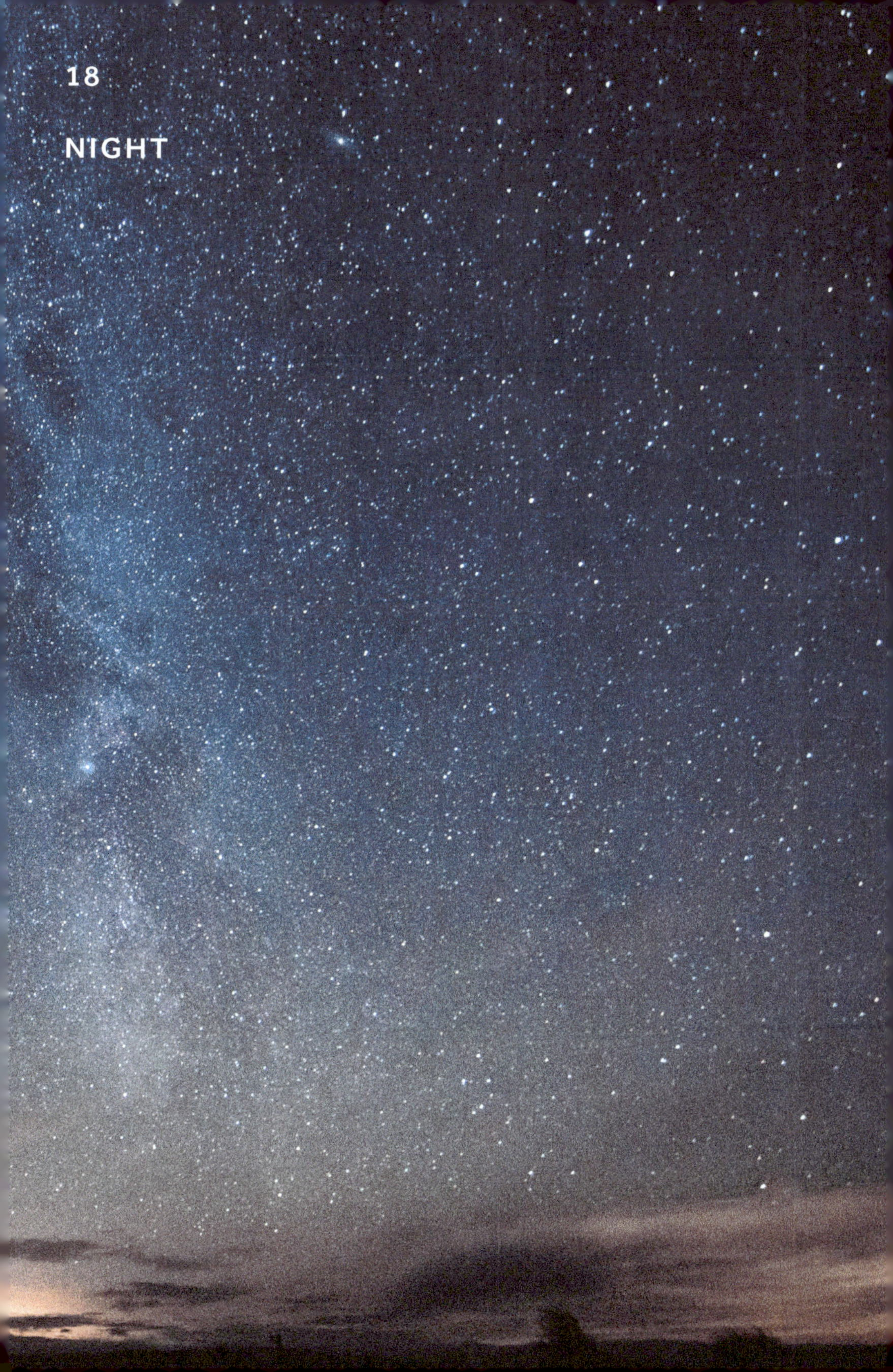

Night photography opens up a whole new set of opportunities and challenges. You will need to work with longer exposures, but the camera is able to see a new world that is hidden from the naked eye. Stay warm, stay safe, and have fun.

PRACTICAL TIPS

1. Stay safe

Scout your location during the day so you know the lie of the land. Tell people where you are going, and what time you expect to be back. Go with a group if you can.

Check the weather forecast and remember it usually feels colder when you are standing still for long stretches of time. Take food and drink.

2. Research the weather

We are spoilt for choice now, with online forecasting information. You can look up sunset and moonrise times months in advance. You can pinpoint where the moon will be in the sky on any day and at any time. You can even get a good idea about prospective cloud cover a week ahead of your shoot.

Nighttime landscape photography is mostly sky-at-night photography, but with a portion of the actual landscape included for scale and counterpoint. You need to learn how to imagine what the night sky will look like above a particular landscape, then plan ahead to work out when the moon or the stars will be in the most attractive formation relative to the ground.

Some apps, such as PhotoPills, have an augmented reality function, where you can overlay the night sky with the place you are standing, to work out which way you need to be facing on any given night. Links to PhotoPills and other research resources are included in the Annex.

The Milky Way core is visible in the northern hemisphere in the southern skies towards the southeast in the Spring, towards the south in the Summer, and towards the southwest in the Autumn. In the southern hemisphere, it starts in the southern skies towards the southwest in the Spring, and moves to the southeast as the year goes on. When planning your Milky Way shot, aim for a night with no moon.

3. Last minute research

On the day (night) it is cloud cover that will make or break your shot. You can't shoot interesting night skies when they are covered in a bank of impenetrable cloud. Patchy cloud can look attractive, and may not register on your final image if it is moving and your exposure is long enough.

Nothing beats looking up into the sky to see what's happening, but you can also find live cloud cover radar tracking services online (links in the Annex).

4. Shoot RAW

Shoot RAW to give yourself the most options when you get home. You will be able to recover details that the camera throws away if you shoot JPEGs.

Preserve your night vision as much as possible. Ideally use a red night-vision torch. Try not to keep checking your phone – the bright light will make you temporarily less able to see the detail in the sky. If it's essential, turn on night mode and turn the brightness right down.

Be considerate of other photographers. Don't leave a torch on while people behind you are trying to shoot, and cover your LCD if you are in front of them so it doesn't spoil their shots.

5. Focussing

It can be very tricky to get your focus correct in the dark. Some people advise focusing on the horizon during the day, and then taping your lens in place. I've found that when I do this the lens gets jogged out of place and I have to start from scratch anyway. I prefer to turn Live View on and zoom in until I can see a single bright star on the LCD. I then use manual focus to get that star sharp, and work from there. You might be tempted simply to use your lens's "infinity" setting – but often that isn't calibrated correctly and you will end up with a soft image.

6. Stay warm

Until you've shot in minus ten degrees at three in the morning, you don't really appreciate just how cold you can get. Take gloves, hat, handwarmers, boots that don't let the cold seep up into your feet, something to sit on, a hot drink and, if all else fails, shoot from inside your car with the window down a crack to fire the shutter.

7. Using your editing software

If you shot RAW you can rescue all that detail in the file that is not visible on the LCD. Open up your editing software and start by taking your white point all the way over to the right, and the black point all the way over to the left, so the histogram stretches the full distance. You should see stars pop out all over the place, and muddy shadows take on a bit of depth. You might not leave the histogram this stretched, but it's a good place to start so you can see what information you have in the file.

Manage your expectations – be aware that many impressive images you see online were actually impossible to produce without heavy editing. The photographer may have taken two images at different times and in different places, and simply stitched them together in Adobe Photoshop. Or they may have taken two or more shots of the same scene at different ISOs and blended the images to reduce the noise in the finished image.

If you have Adobe Lightroom, learn to use the Noise Reduction function if you shoot at higher ISOs. It's in the Develop module and you can see the effect the different sliders have if you view the image at 100% whilst you drag them left and right.

SETTINGS

1. The moon

Most people start with a simple moon shot – it's something you can try from the comfort of your own home. Look up online when the next full moon is, and hope for no cloud cover.

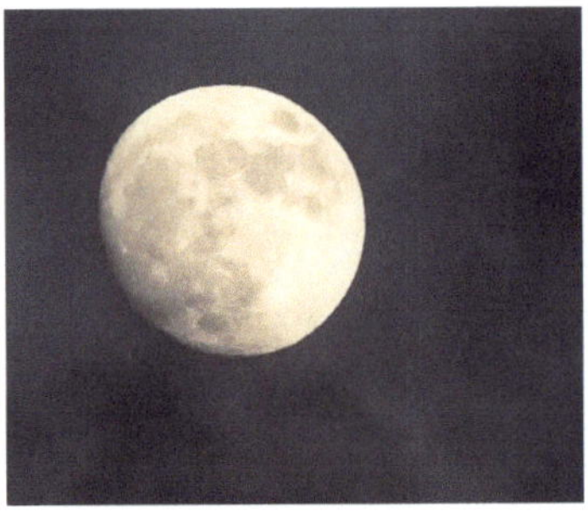

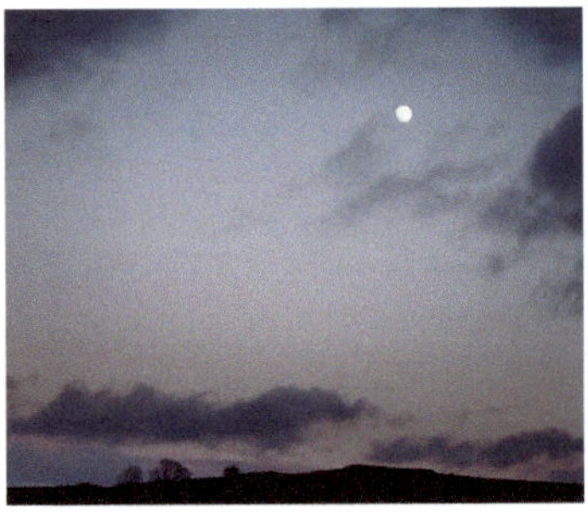

Below left:
The moon is so far away that you don't need a small aperture for depth of field reasons, as long as you focus on the moon itself.
X-T1, 50-140mm at 140mm, ISO200, f2.8, 1/450th.

Below right:
Once you have your settings set to correctly expose the moon, you can start to try alternative compositions. Including some cloud cover always looks attractive, if the weather is on your side. Try including some landscape for scale. This is easier when the moon is lower in the sky. You can predict when this will happen by looking up moon-rise times.
X-T1, 50-140mm at 50mm, ISO200, f2.8, 1/480th.

The issue with shooting the moon is that, on auto exposure, the camera takes the whole sky into account and overexposes the moon itself. You want *the moon* to be correctly exposed, and you may be surprised at how much you need to underexpose. Shoot on manual mode, and use settings you would opt for during daylight. Start with: ISO200, f5.6, 1/125th and adapt them as needed – but only look at the moon to check the exposure, not the surrounding sky.

2. Single stars and Milky Way

For sharp enough stars, the rule of thumb is that you divide 500 by your focal length to get your shutter speed. For example, with a 24mm lens, 500 divided by 24 gives a speed of about 20 seconds. Use the full-frame equivalent if you are using a cropped sensor camera. Use your widest aperture, focus carefully and let your ISO climb to whatever it needs to.

Review your image on the LCD at 100 percent zoom, and check whether the stars have smears (it will depend on the focal length of your lens to some extent – wider lenses take longer to show smears). No smears? Then tweak your exposure as needed using the ISO. If you have smears, drop the shutter speed to 20 seconds, and increase the ISO to compensate.

Don't forget your LCD image won't look anything like your final image. Shown below is the straight-out-of-camera RAW file from the Milky Way shot that starts this section. All the brighter detail was revealed in Adobe Lightroom.

Left:
The straight-out-of-camera shot that heads up this chapter.
6D, 11-24mm at 11mm, ISO3200, f5, 30 seconds.

3. Star trails

The best method to shoot star trails is to use stacking software. This technique allows you to take a series of shots over an hour or more and blend them together when you get home to create the finished image. I use StarStax which is free, with an optional

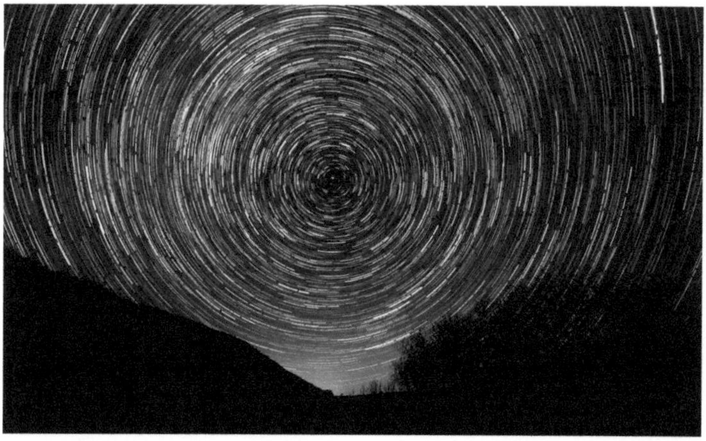

Left:
A blend of 72 individual shots using StarStax. The gaps are caused because I had to delete 3 or 4 shots in the sequence because a car passed and lit up the foreground.
Each individual shot: 5DIV, 11-24mm at 11mm, ISO2500, f4, 30 seconds.

donation (please donate). On an Ollie Taylor Photography workshop in Iceland I learnt that the best settings to use are: your widest aperture, 30 second shots 32 seconds apart (to allow the camera to save the image), with whatever ISO you need.

4. Aurora Borealis

Use the same starting point as for Milky Way photography, and remember that the camera often picks up more colours than the eye can see, so keep shooting. If the lights start to dance, use a much shorter shutter speed to catch the patterns (2-4 seconds, recommended by Ollie Taylor).

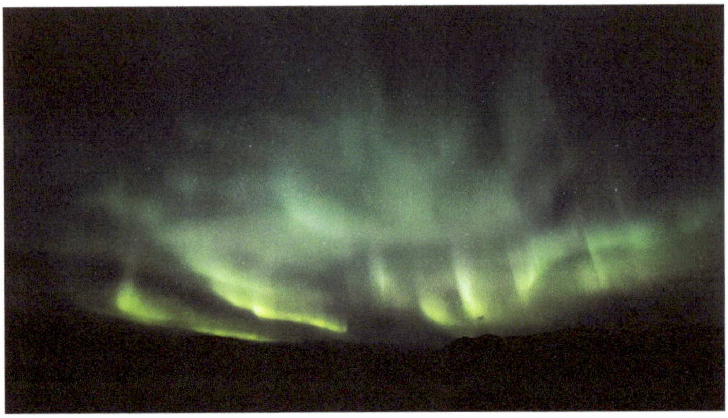

Right:
Aurora Borealis in Iceland shot on an Ollie Taylor Photography workshop.
5DIV, 11-24mm at 11mm, ISO3200, f4, 5 seconds.

5. Mixed light temperatures

Keep an eye on your white balance setting when shooting at night, especially if there are artificial lights in the shot which may make the auto white balance inaccurate. You usually want a cooler temperature to make sure the night shows at the bluer end of the spectrum, so either manually set your temperature to about 3000 Kelvin, or tweak it in editing.

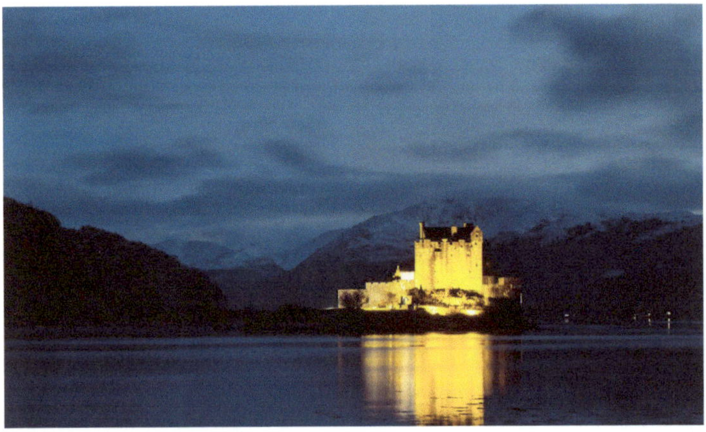

Right:
Eilean Donan castle.
6D, 50mm, ISO100, f11, 25 seconds.

SETTINGS - NIGHT

1. The moon

Shoot on manual mode, and use daylight settings. Start with ISO200, f5.6, 1/125th.

2. Single stars and the Milky Way

Shutter speed: divide 500 by the focal length of your lens.
Aperture: the widest possible for your lens.
ISO: as low as you can.*

3. Star trails

Use software like StarStax to combine images. Take at least 2 hours' worth of shots. Shoot JPEG so you don't fill up your memory card. Try ISO2500, f4, 30 seconds, at 32 seconds apart.* (Do test shots first). If you have an intervalometer you can automate the whole sequence (check whether your camera has one built-in).

4. Aurora borealis

If the Aurora is dancing, keep your shutter speed to 2-4 seconds. Let the ISO climb to what it needs to. Use the widest aperture on your lens.*

5. Mixed light temperatures

Watch your white balance when shooting at night, especially if you have mixed temperatures. Consider moving off auto white balance and setting it manually.

* These settings are recommended by expert astro and night landscape photographer, Ollie Taylor (www.ollietaylorphotography.com).

This chapter is designed to get you started in night photography. The settings will give you the best chance of coming home with an OK shot. But astrophotography is a complicated business and I recommend seeking specialist help if you want to take it further.

Slea Head, X-T1, 50-140mm at 50mm, ISO200, f22, 0.8 secs

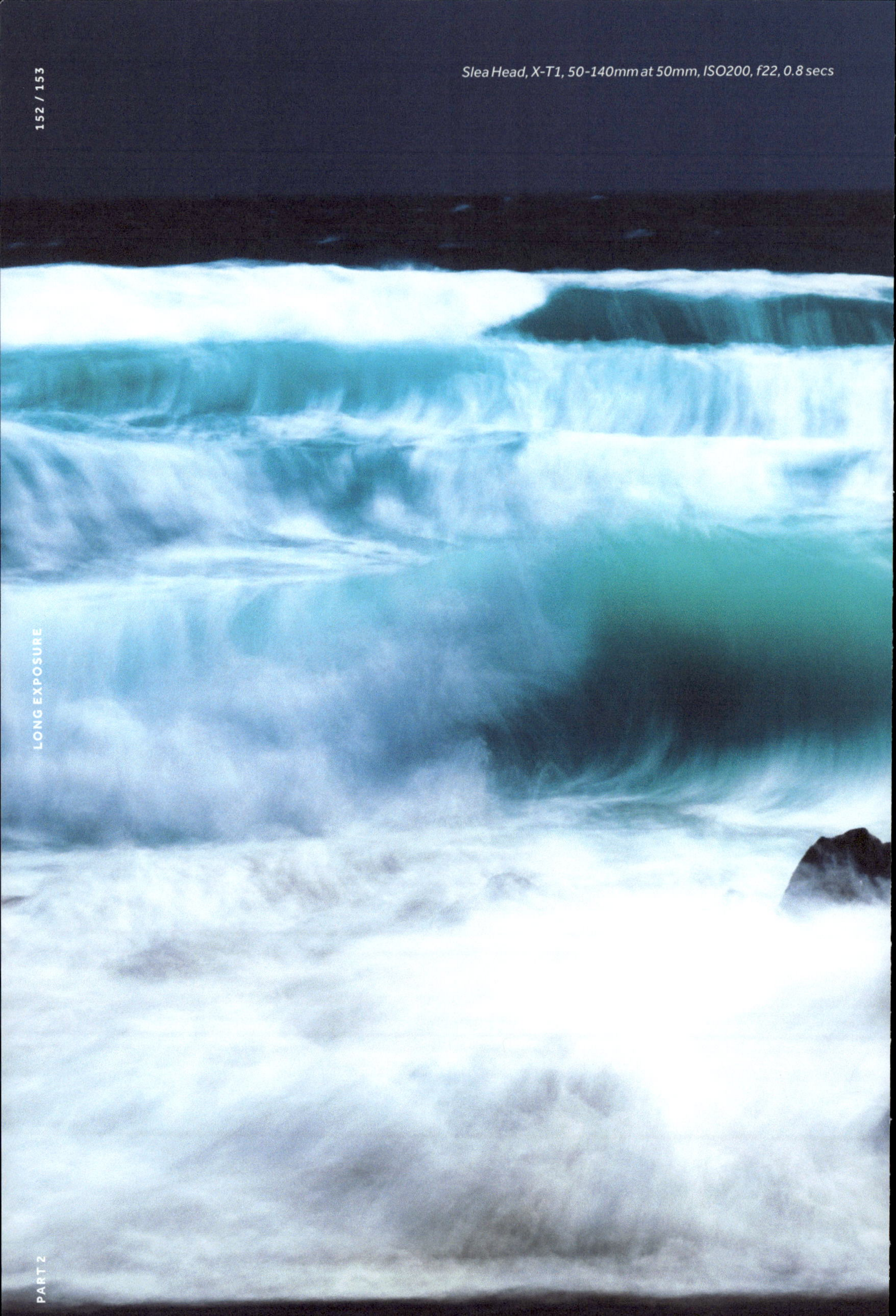

19

LONG EXPOSURE

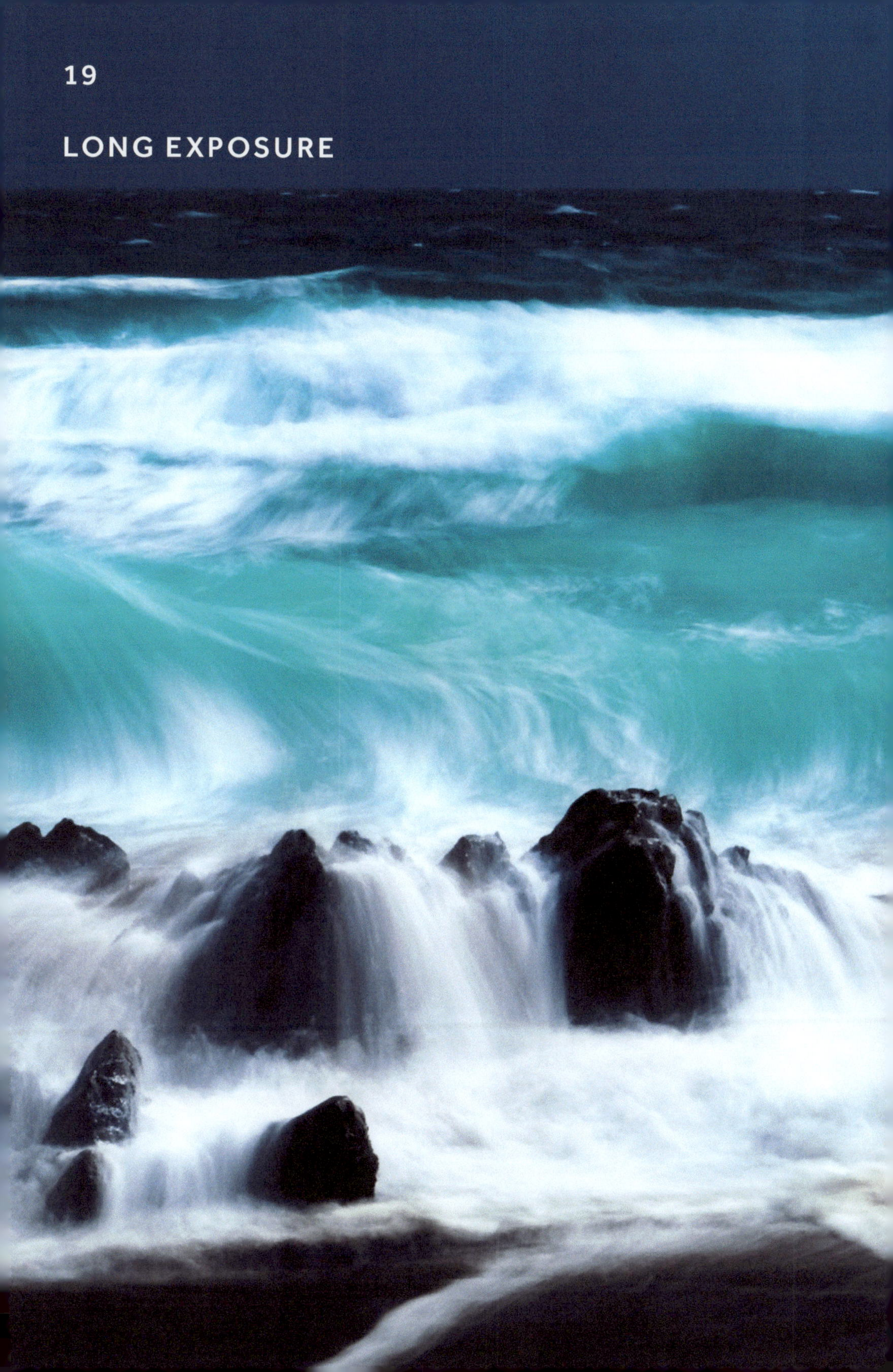

Long exposure photography, like night photography, opens up a whole new world of creative opportunity. The tools of the painter are paint and a canvas. The tools of the photographer are light and time. The time part of the equation is measured in fractions of a second for the most part. But what if you hold your shutter open for full seconds or even minutes? What happens to the landscape?

WHEN TO TRY LONG EXPOSURE

1. To capture the pattern left by movement as time passes

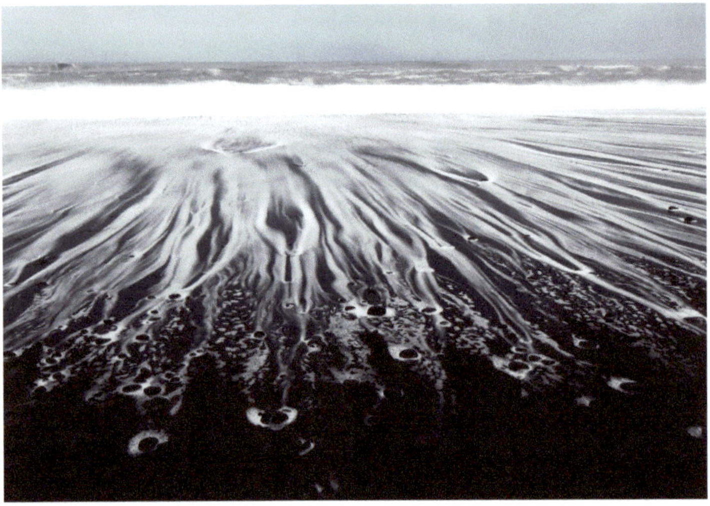

Right:
The receding water at Reynisfjara leaves a pattern not caught by a short shutter speed.
6D, 11-24mm at 24mm, ISO100, f22, 1.6 seconds.

2. To let more light in

Sometimes you simply need more time to let the available light register on the sensor. See Chapter 18 – Night Photography, for more details.

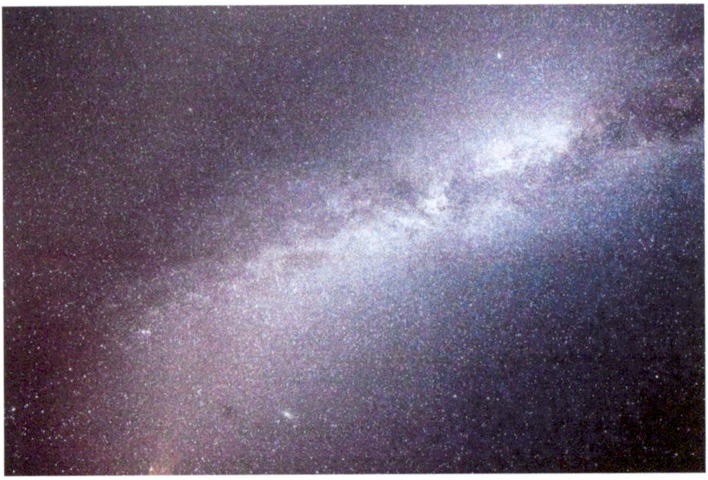

Right:
Milky Way.
5DIV, 11-24mm at 11mm, ISO800, f4, 30 seconds.

3. To even-out a disturbed body of water

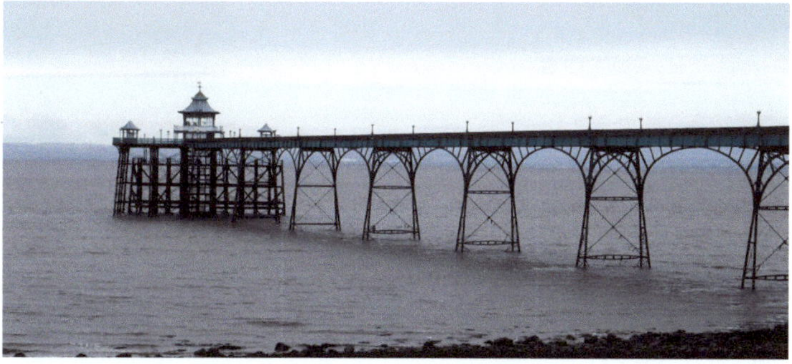

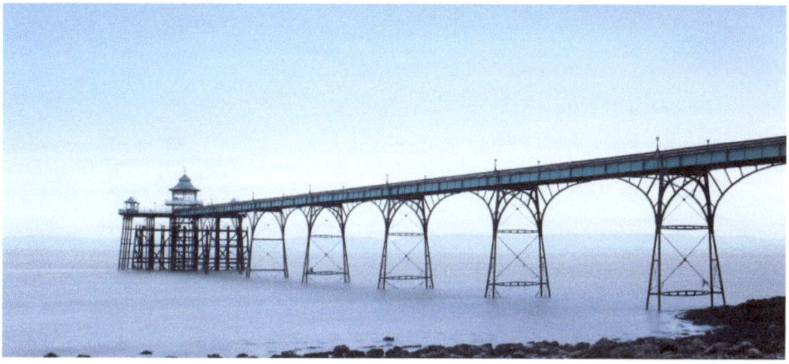

Top left:
A normal exposure at Clevedon Pier results in a grey, nonedescript sea.
X-T1, 50-140mm at 50mm, ISO200, f5.6, 1/250th.

Bottom left:
A long exposure at Clevedon Pier blurs the grey sea into something more attractive.
5DIV, 50mm, ISO100, f16, 20 seconds, 6 stop ND filter.

4. To add interest to a sky

A longer exposure will capture the movement of clouds across the sky:

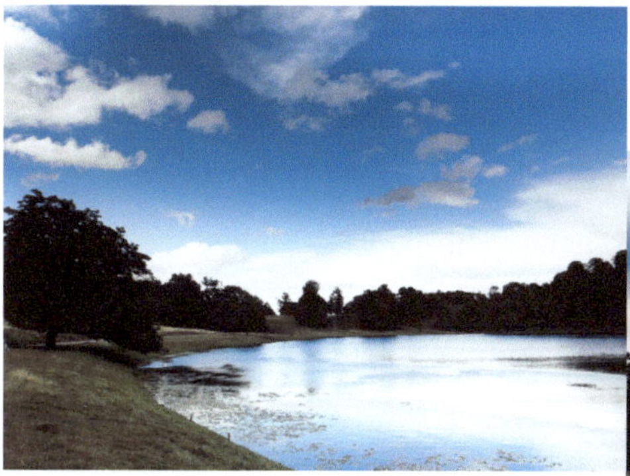

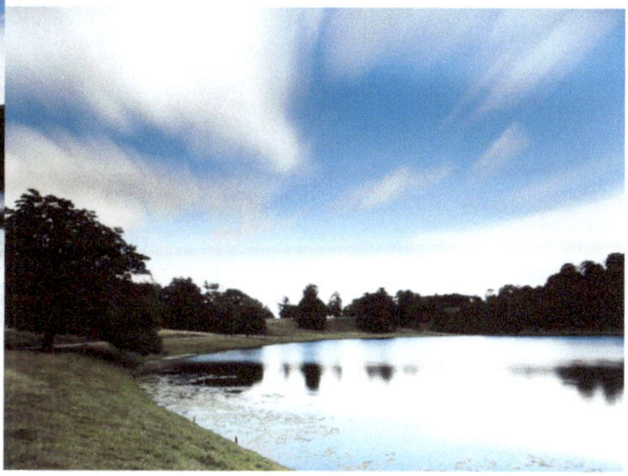

Below left:
5DIV, 11-24mm at 22mm, ISO100, f10, 1/200th.

Bottom left:
5DIV, 11-24mm at 22mm, ISO100, f18, 1 minute, 6-stop ND filter.

5. To remove people

This technique was described in Chapter 17 – Structures in the Landscape.

PRACTICAL TIPS

1. Using filters

Neutral density ("ND") filters permit long exposures during the day when there would otherwise be too much light. They are simply a piece of glass tinted with a neutral grey colour, and are described by how many stops of light they prevent hitting the sensor (think of it as if you are putting sunglasses on your camera). Don't get cheap ND filters. They degrade your image and can add colour tints.

Use an app like the Lee Stopper app to work out the exposure you will need once the filter is in place.

2. Noise reduction

With very long exposures your sensor can get warm and introduce bright spots and a kind of fog around your image. If your camera has a long exposure noise reduction function, it can be used to eliminate this. With it turned on, the camera takes a second image immediately after the first. This second image is called a dark frame. It is shot as if the lens cap were in place. The camera then compares the two shots, and subtracts any noise found in the dark frame from the first image. The only downside is that that it doubles your exposure time.

3. Cover your viewfinder

To prevent light leaking in from the back, cover your viewfinder. You can use the piece of plastic that came with the camera for this reason, or your hat, or some black tape.

4. Avoid any camera shake at all

Turn off stabilisation. Use a cable release or self timer. Use mirror lockup (unless you have a mirrorless camera or are using Live View). Weight your tripod down if there is a breath of wind. Tighten your tripod plate to avoid lens droop, and if you still find your camera slowly tilts down under its own weight, you'll need to buy an L-bracket instead of a simple tripod plate.

SETTINGS - LONG EXPOSURE

1. ISO

Choose the lowest possible ISO (100 or 200). Noise will be a problem anyway with longer exposures – you don't want to add to it. Consider using the long exposure noise reduction setting on your camera (but bear in mind it will double your exposure time). Learn how to use the noise reduction options in your editing sofware.

2. Aperture

Don't automatically pick f22 or f32 to allow a longer shutter speed. Your smallest apertures will start to introduce diffraction errors and reduce the sharpness of your image. Work as close to f8 or f11 as you can, and shoot closer to sunrise/sunset when there is less light (or use an ND filter).

3. Shutter speed

Check your particular camera to see what the longest built-in shutter speed is. Mine is 30 seconds. After that you have to use "bulb" mode, where the shutter stays open for as long as you hold the shutter button down.

A lockable cable release is invaluable here, because you can lock the shutter open for as long as you need without touching the camera. An intervalometer will allow you to use a timer to do all the work for you, so you don't have to close the shutter at the end of the exposure. Check your manual to find out whether your camera has a built-in intervalometer (I was pleasantly surprised to find that mine has one).

The exact combination of ND filters and shutter speeds will depend on the effect you are trying to achieve. Always start with your preferred ISO, aperture and shutter speed and only add an ND filter when you need to.

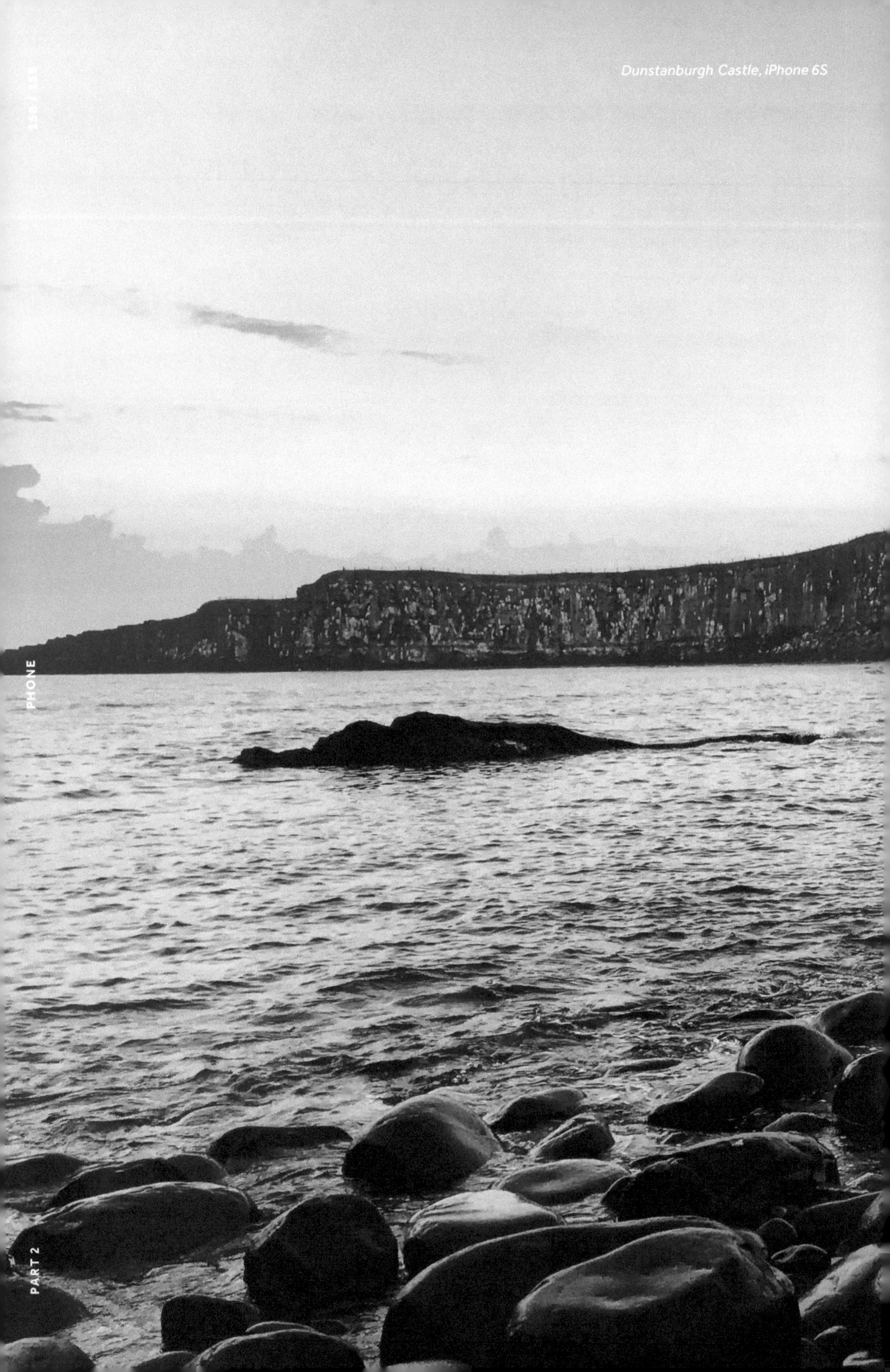

Dunstanburgh Castle, iPhone 6S

20

PHONE PHOTOGRAPHY

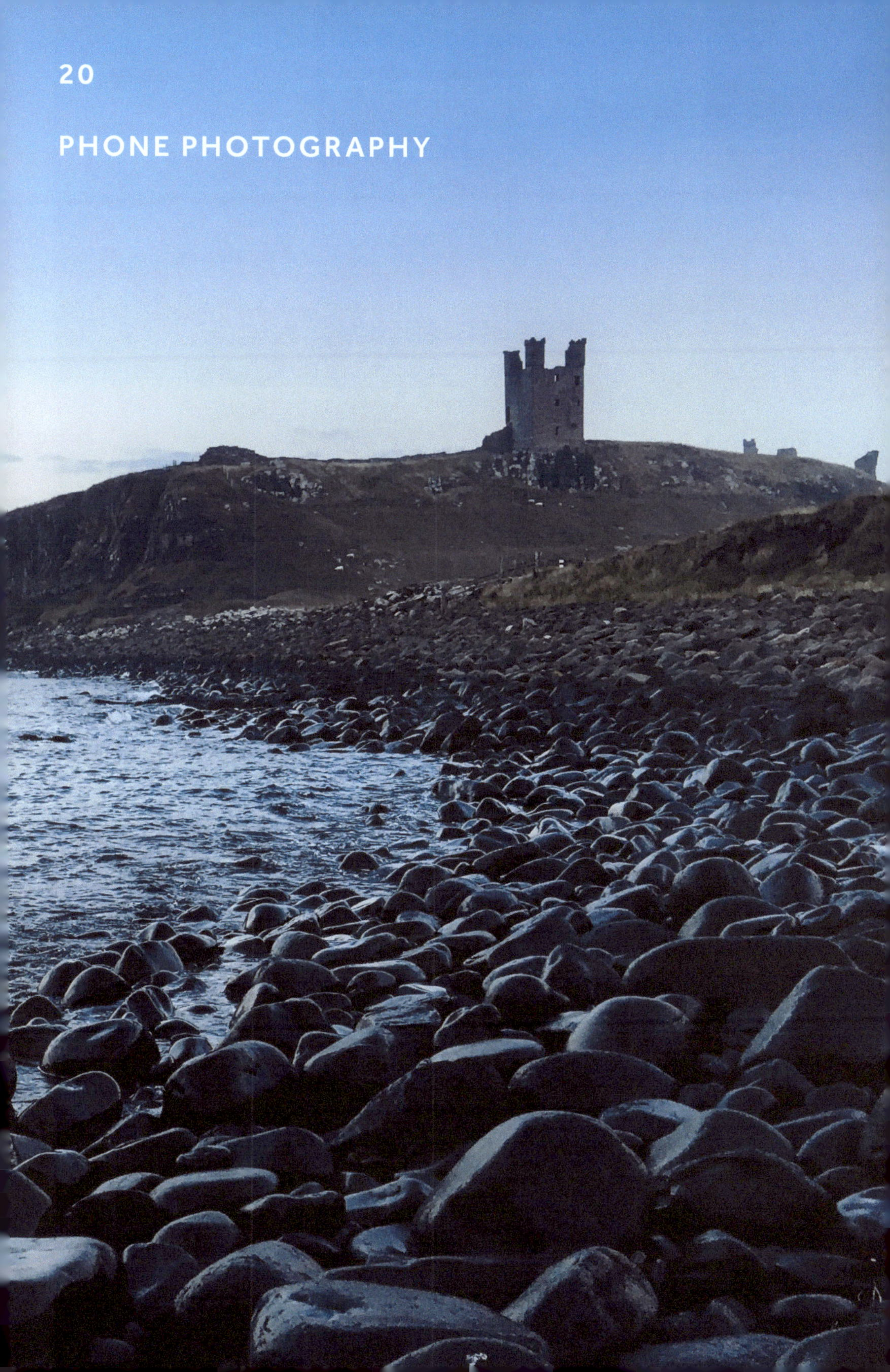

You can take epic landscape shots with your phone, as long as you work within its limitations.

1. Small sensor

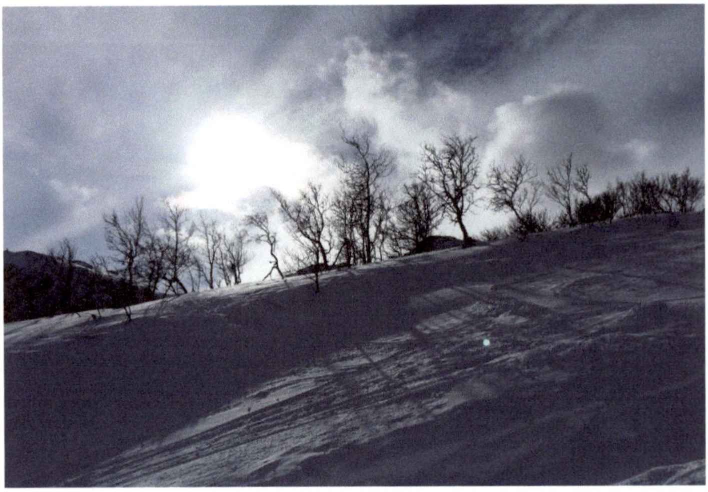

That tiny sensor cannot compete with the sensor on a full-frame DSLR in terms of image quality and dynamic range. Avoid high contrast shots like the one above – you can see that the sun has blown out completely, and not in the subtle way you would get with a DSLR shot. (That circular speck in the bottom right hand quarter of the shot is sunflare – a reflection of the sun on the lens.)

2. Small file size

Phone shots are perfect for sharing online, but you won't be able to enlarge them and print them as big as you can shots from your camera.

3. Small lens

That tiny, tiny scrap of a lens has to do all the work, usually fighting with thumbprints and dust from your pocket. Keep it clean, and don't expect it to work miracles.

4. JPEG files

Most phones still shoot JPEGs, not RAW files, so you can't process images in the same way that you can a RAW file from a DSLR. And every time you run it through an Instagram filter or a Snapseed preset you will be degrading the image still further.

5. Have fun

The best camera is the one you have with you and you always have your phone, so start to use it. It is perfect for strong, graphic compositions. All the images that follow were shot on my iPhone 5S or iPhone 6S.

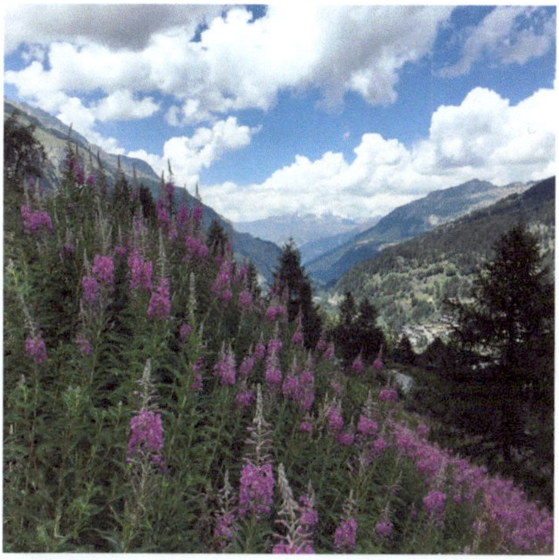
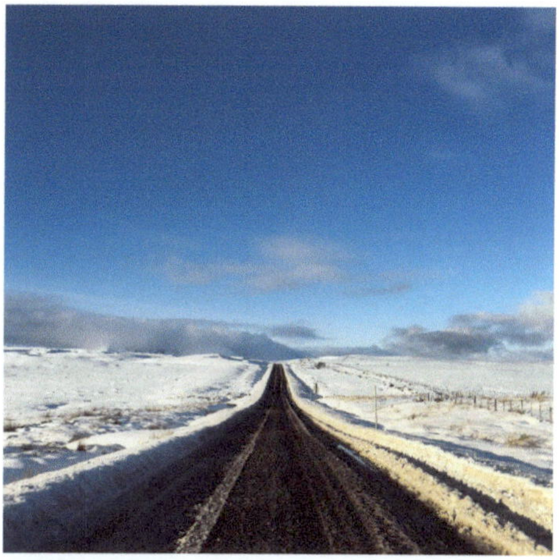
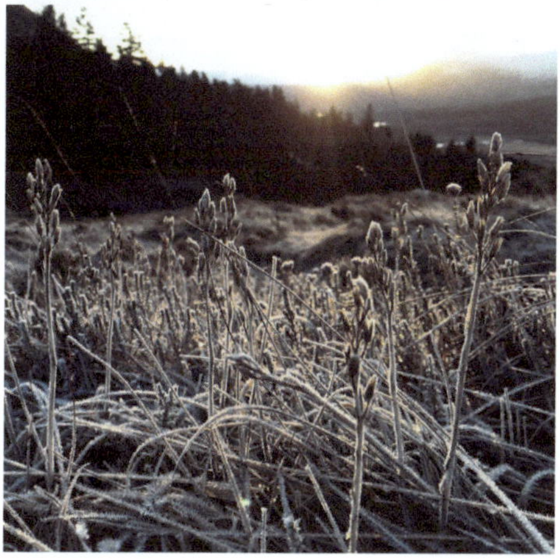
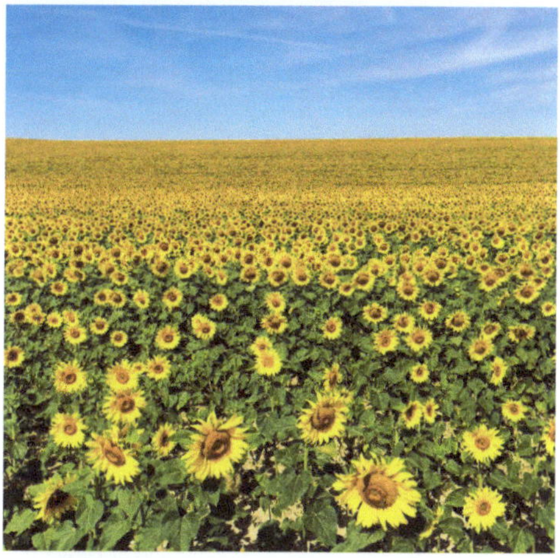
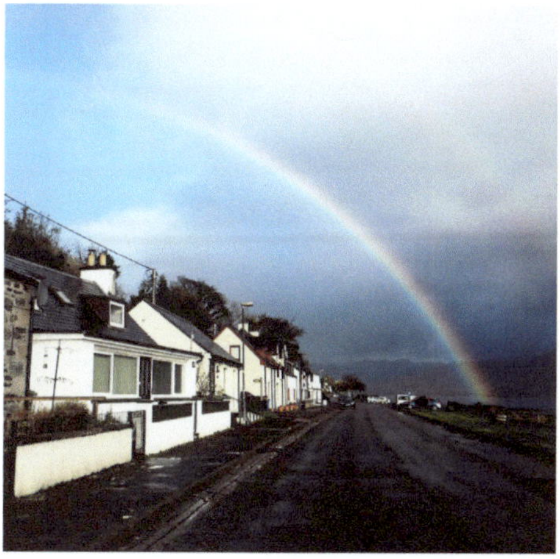
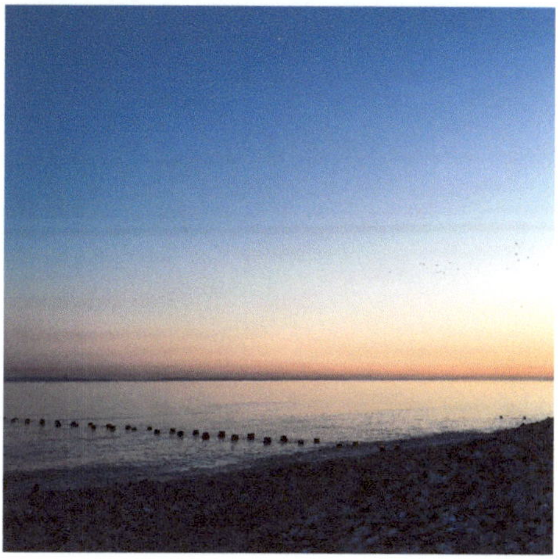

Tignes, iPhone 6S

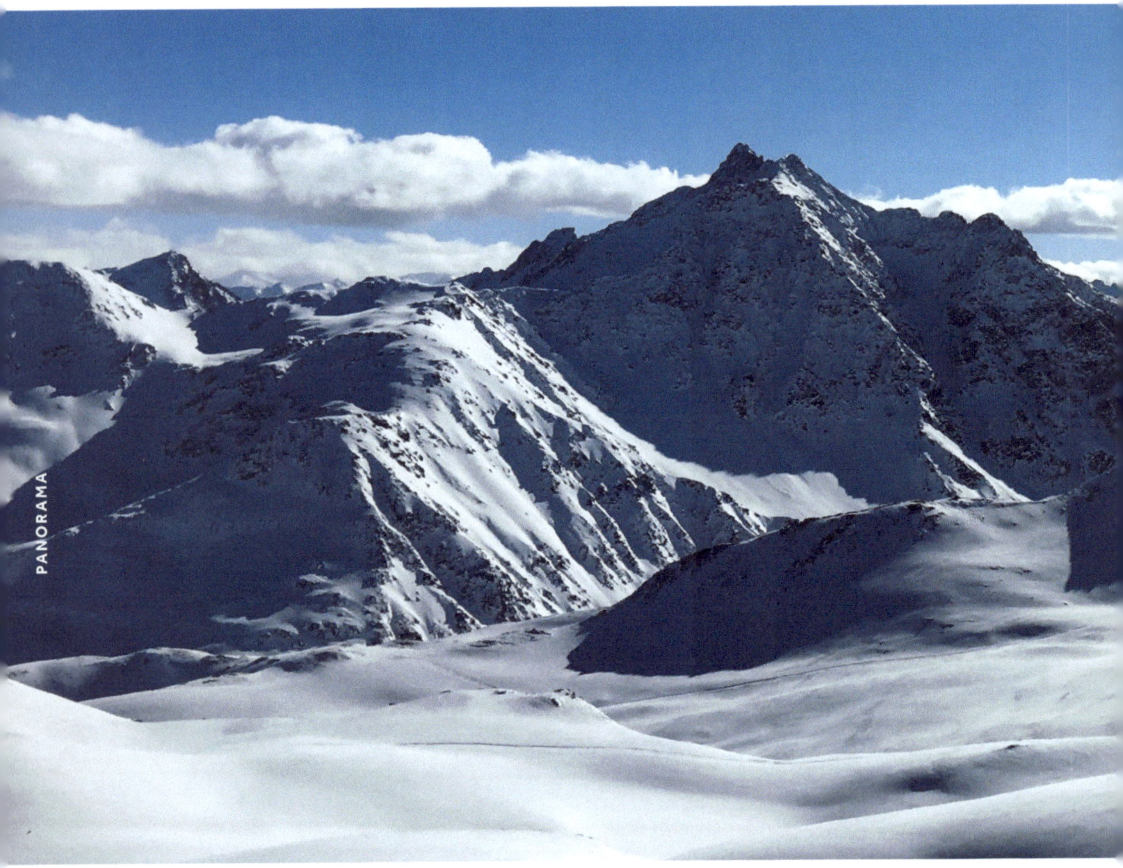

21

PANORAMA

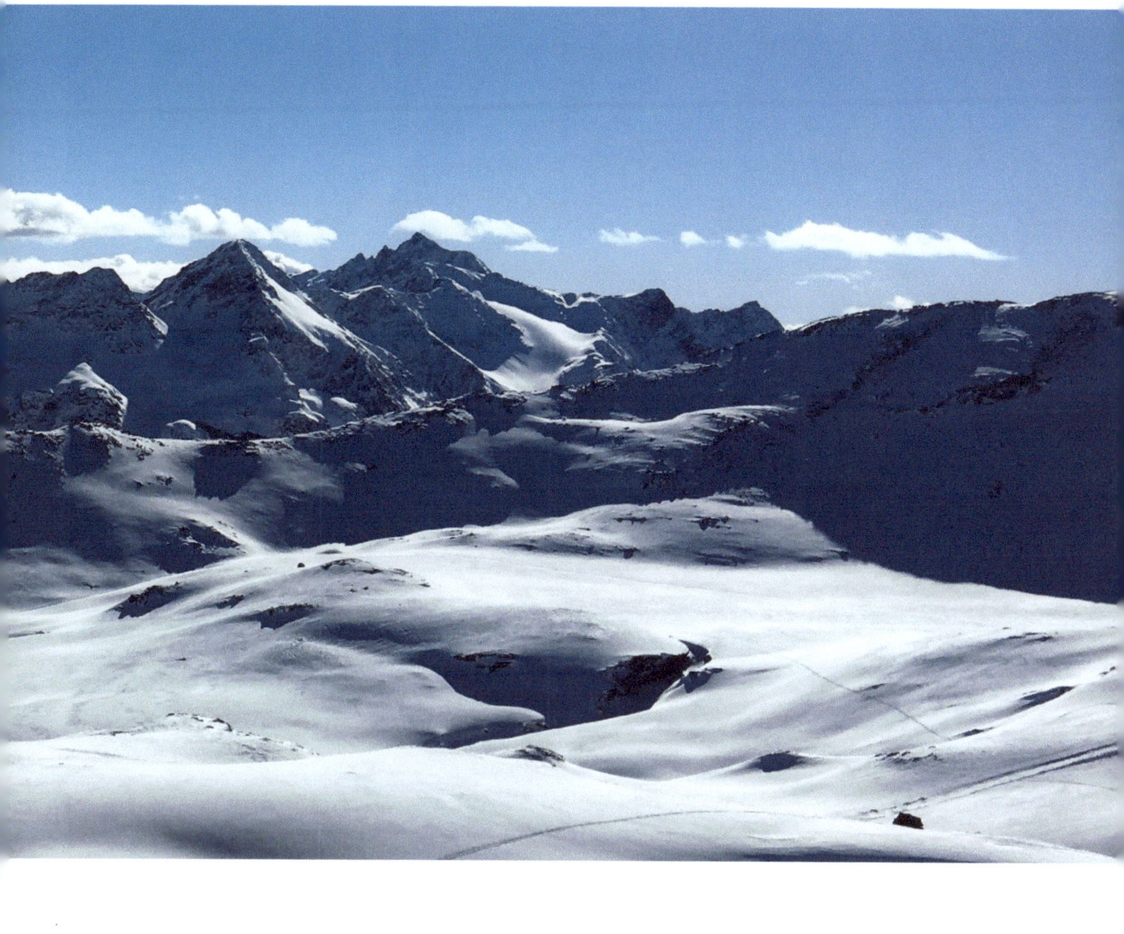

A panorama is simply an alternative format. Traditional photography formats are portrait (like the page of a book) or landscape (like a TV screen). They are simply a reflection of the shape of your sensor, and which way round you held your camera when you took the shot. Landscape photographs, unsurprisingly, are usually shot in landscape format, but occasionally you'll want to try a portrait landscape (for example, if you need a cover shot for a magazine).

A panorama is an extreme landscape format shot. The super-wide angle that you can achieve creates eyecatching shots. As with black and white photography, the most successful panoramas are those that you plan.

Subjects that work well in this format include any kind of horizon shot – reflections, skylines or mountain ranges. You are able to exclude an uninteresting sky or foreground, and focus the viewer's attention on what would otherwise be just the centre of the frame.

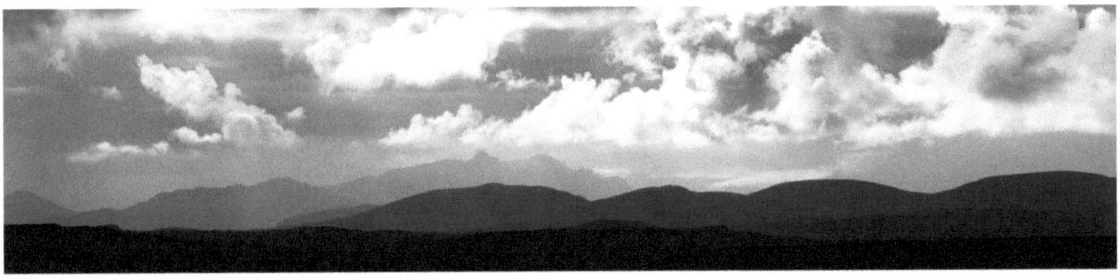

There are a few ways to achieve a panorama, only some of which need new kit.

1. **Crop your shot in editing**

You can take a normal shot, and then simply crop out the uninteresting sky or foreground in the traditional panoramic letterbox shape. But be aware that you are throwing away pixels using this option – and you won't be able to print your final shot as big as with some of the other techniques.

2. **Stitch together a series of shots in editing**

Most software has an option to "stitch" or "merge" a series of shots into a panorama. For the most successful final shot, keep all the individual shots as similar as possible, so the exposure doesn't change as you keep shooting from left to right. That means: manual focus, manual exposure, manual ISO, manual white balance, and no polarising filter (otherwise the sky changes as you move away from the sun). Take your shots in portrait format, include plenty of overlap and try not to drift downwards as you move from left to right, as I did here:

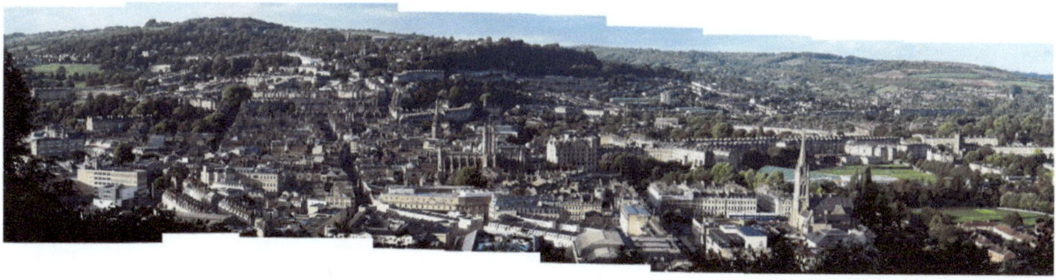

Above:
9 shot panorama of the City of Bath.
X-T1, 50-140mm at 100mm, ISO200, f4, 1/1250th. Handheld.

3. Use your phone's panorama option

This is a surprisingly easy way to get a great panorama. Turn slowly, and keep within the guidelines on the screen, otherwise you risk a wobbly shot with bits missing at the top and bottom as shown below:

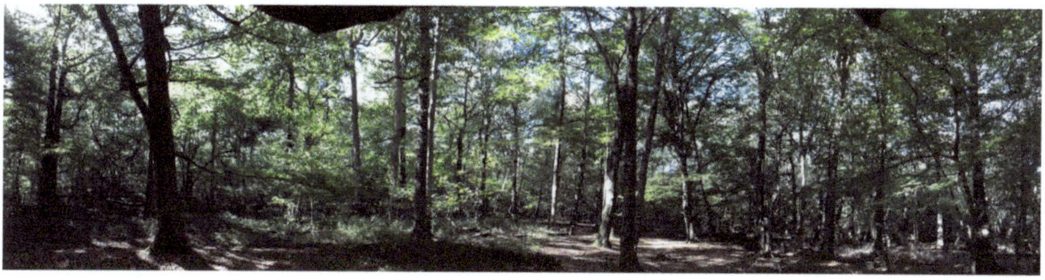

Above:
Wobbly panorama using my phone's built-in panorama mode.
iPhone 6S.

4. Use a tilt-shift lens horizontally

If you have a tilt-shift lens, instead of using the shift option vertically for architectural shots, turn it through 90 degrees and shoot a series of three overlapping images from left to right, using the lens shift to move the field of view instead of turning the camera.

5. Use specialist panoramic kit

To avoid parallax errors in stitched shots (when near and far objects don't align in the overlapping images) you can use a panoramic head on your tripod. This allows the camera to rotate around the optical centre of the lens, instead of further back under the tripod plate.

Or if you want to go old-school, you can buy panoramic cameras that shoot film, and get everything right in-camera.

APPENDIX

For links to more up-to-date resources, visit EmmaDaviesPhotography.com/landscape-links

PhotoPills: https://www.photopills.com/calculators/hyperfocal-table

The Photographer's Ephemeris: https://www.photoephemeris.com/

Landscape Photographer of the Year: https://www.take-a-view.co.uk/

Magic Seaweed: https://magicseaweed.com/

Windfinder: https://www.windfinder.com

Cloudspotter's Guide: https://www.amazon.co.uk/Cloudspotters-Guide-Gavin-Pretor-Pinney/dp/034089590X/

The Colors of Sunset and Twilight, Stephen F. Corfidi, USA National Weather Service: https://www.spc.noaa.gov/publications/corfidi/sunset/

Silver Efex plugin: https://nikcollection.dxo.com/silver-efex-pro/

Ansel Adams: http://anseladams.com/

Edward Weston: http://edward-weston.com/edward-weston/

Michael Kenna: http://michaelkenna.net/imagearchive.php

PhotoPills instructions on how to plan a Milky Way shoot using their augmented reality function: https://www.photopills.com/articles/how-plan-milky-way-using-augmented-reality

Dark skies map: https://darksitefinder.com/map/

Cloud cover radar: https://www.metoffice.gov.uk/public/weather/uk-cloud-cover-forecast

Star Stax: https://www.markus-enzweiler.de/software/software.html

Lee Stopper app: https://itunes.apple.com/gb/app/lee-filters-stopper-exposure/id1105022698

My complete beginner's photography workshop, A Year With My Camera, free by email: https://ayearwithmycamera.com

THANK YOU...

To Nik, Ben & Katie for being my best cheerleaders.

To mum and dad for being the first in a very long line of friends and relations who have stopped the car when asked, so I could take a photo. The poppies in Provence was the first landscape photo I remember taking. I must've been 14 or 15, and I don't think I thanked you at the time (or since) for your patience as I insisted we wait for the sun to drop behind the field.

To Sarah, for not only stopping the car but driving me up hill and down dale in the pursuit of good light. And for bringing the playlists and the second breakfasts.

To everyone who's done A Year With My Camera for giving me a reason to write these books.

To my editor, Caroline Goldsmith, for making me sound better than I actually am.

To my designers, Studo Tangerine, for turning my words and pictures into a book people will want to read.

To photographers Ollie Taylor (who patiently taught me how to do night time landscape photography in very challenging conditions), Glen Campbell (who introduced me to landscape photography in Scotland), and Sandra Bartocha (who gave me the confidence move away from clichéd shots and to have confidence in my own vision).

To all my friends on Instagram for your kind comments, helpful conversations and inspiring images.

Lightning Source UK Ltd.
Milton Keynes UK
UKHW051929170920
370045UK00001B/3

* 9 7 8 0 9 9 5 6 3 2 4 3 1 *